Paper Money Men

PAPER MONEY MEN

Commerce, Manhood, and the Sensational Public Sphere in Antebellum America

DAVID ANTHONY

The Ohio State University Press
Columbus

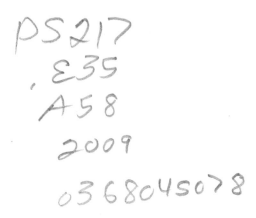

PS217
.E35
A58
2009
0368045078

Library of Congress Cataloging-in-Publication Data
Anthony, David, 1964–
Paper money men : commerce, manhood, and the sensational public sphere in antebellum America / David Anthony.
p. cm.
Includes bibliographical references and index.
ISBN 978-0-8142-1110-6 (cloth : alk. paper)—ISBN 978-0-8142-9207-5 (cd-rom) 1. American literature—19th century—History and criticism. 2. Economics in literature. 3. Masculinity in literature. 4. Money in literature. 5. Wealth in literature. 6. Masculinity—Economic aspects—United States. 7. Sensationalism in literature. I. Title.
PS217.E35A58 2009
810.9'003—dc22
2009023482

This book is available in the following editions:
Cloth (ISBN 978-0-8142-1110-6)
CD-ROM (ISBN 978-0-8142-9207-5)

Cover design by Laurence J. Nozik
Text design by Juliet Williams
Type set in Adobe Minion Pro
Printed by Thomson-Shore, Inc.

9 8 7 6 5 4 3 2 1

As we proceed to develop our investigation, we shall find, in general, that the characters who appear on the economic stage are mere personifications of economic relations; it is as the bearers of these economic relations that they come into contact with each other.

—Karl Marx, Capital, Volume 1 (1867)

I love the paper money, and the paper money men;
My hundred, if they go to pot, I fear would sink to ten . . .

I hold the paper money men say truly, when they say
They ought to pay their promises, with promises to pay;
And he is an unrighteous judge, who says they shall or may,
Be made to keep their promises in any other way.

—Thomas Love Peacock, Paper Money Lyrics (1837)

CONTENTS

I L L U S T R A T I O N S

ACKNOWLEDGMENTS

Much like many of the fictional characters I examine here, I have accrued a considerable number of debts over the course of my professional life. This is especially true of the period in which I have written this book. Fortunately, these are debts of gratitude to the many people and institutions that have helped me with this project, and I would like to acknowledge them here.

For fellowship support I would like to thank the following: the Andrew W. Mellon Foundation for a dissertation fellowship that allowed me to lay the foundation for this project; the American Antiquarian Society for three separate short-term research fellowships that were absolutely essential to the beginning, middle, and end of this project (a Peterson Dissertation Fellowship and two AAS-NEMLA Fellowships); the Library Company of Philadelphia for a short-term Mellon Fellowship; and Southern Illinois University, Carbondale, for a Summer ORDA Fellowship.

A version of chapter 1 of this study appeared in *Early American Literature* 40, no. 1 (March 2005): 111–44; a version of chapter 3 appeared in *American Literature* 76, no. 4 (December 2004): 719–47; a portion of chapter 4 appeared in *American Literature* 69, no. 3 (September 1997): 487–514; and a portion of chapter 5 appeared in *The Yale Journal of Criticism* 12, no. 2 (Fall 1999): 249–68. I would like to express my appreciation to the editorial boards and publishers of these journals for the right to reproduce this material here. I would also like to thank the following for reproduction rights to the various images in this work: the American Antiquarian Society, the New-York Historical Society, The Library Company of Philadelphia, the Library of Congress, and the William L. Clements Library at the University of Michigan.

This book began as a dissertation at the University of Michigan. For mentorship at this stage, I would like to thank Julie Ellison, whose fascination with gender and emotion was infectious; Carroll Smith-Rosenberg, whose enthusiasm for my work was incredibly confidence-building; and most of all, Jonathan Freedman. His belief in me before, during, and after my graduate work at Michigan was essential to this book's creation and completion, and his own work has set the standard that I have strived to meet. I would also like to thank James Thompson, with whom I studied at UNC–Chapel Hill. His passion for a materialist approach to literature sparked an early interest for me in the relations between money and gender. For intellectual and emotional support during graduate school (and afterward), I would like to thank Susan Rosenbaum, Steve Soper, Eliza Richards, Eric Kligerman, Michael Strong, Elly Eisenberg, Kathy Pories, and Paul Crumbley. Thanks also to Adam Henderson for close friendship outside of academia.

This book was completed at Southern Illinois University, Carbondale. During this period I have been aided, buoyed, and inspired by numerous friends and colleagues in Carbondale. Foremost among them are Paula Bennett, Ed Brunner, George Boulukos, David Sutton, Beth Rowe, Sue Felleman, and Peter Chametsky. Many thanks also to various colleagues at other universities for their insightful and challenging readings of drafts of several chapters of this book, especially Teresa Goddu, David Leverenz, John Evelev, David Zimmerman, David Shields, James Shapiro, and Christopher Looby. I would also like to thank the staff at the American Antiquarian Society for their consistently generous help, especially Laura Wasowicz, Jon Benoit, Caroline Sloat, and John Hench. I also want to express appreciation to the readers commissioned by The Ohio State University Press for their insights and enthusiasm for the project, to Sandy Crooms for her initial interest in the book and her guidance throughout the publication process, and to Maggie Diehl for her thorough-going editorial assistance.

Finally, I would like to thank members of my family for their patience and support. I am particularly grateful to my mother, Judy Anthony Henderson, for her constant encouragement and unwavering love, and to Shirley and Robert Desmond, for taking me into their family. Most of all, though, I would like to thank Erin Desmond Anthony, the person whose intellect and passion I most admire. Her faith in this project has been unflagging, and her readings and insights have been invaluable. In the ensuing pages I will discuss stories in which desperate men seek after treasure, but I am the lucky one who stumbled upon a pot of gold when I met her. This book is dedicated to her, and to our son Aidan.

FANTASIES OF TREASURE IN ANTEBELLUM CULTURE

He dreamed that he had discovered an immense treasure in the center of his garden. At every stroke of the spade he laid bare a golden ingot; diamond crosses sparkled out of the dust; bags of money turned up their bellies, corpulent with pieces of eight, or venerable doubloons; and chests . . . yawned forth before his ravished eyes, and vomited forth their glittering contents.

—Washington Irving, "The Golden Dreams of Wolfert Webber," *Tales of a Traveller* (1824)

As the rays of the lanterns fell within the pit, there flashed upwards, from a confused heap of gold and of jewels, a glow and a glare that absolutely dazzled our eyes. . . . The chest had been full to the brim. . . . Having assorted all with care, we found ourselves possessed of even vaster wealth than we had at first supposed. In coin there was rather more than four hundred and fifty thousand dollars—estimating the value of the pieces, as accurately as we could, by the tables of the period. There was not a particle of silver. All was gold of antique date and of great variety—French, Spanish, and German money, with a few English guineas, and some counters, of which we had never seen specimens before. There were several very large and heavy coins, so worn that we could make nothing of their inscriptions. There was no American money.

—Edgar Allan Poe, "The Gold-Bug" (1843)

CAPTAIN KIDD AND THE GOLDEN EGGS

One of the key images in the development of antebellum sensationalism is the staging of a relationship between men and treasure. A kind of nervously repeated primal scene, in which we see men hugging hoarded piles of gold bullion, fantasizing about chests of coins and jewels, or, most often, lamenting the recent loss of such riches, these moments proliferate in the cultural production of the period, and provide readers with an embarrassed fantasy glimpse at the source of their economic origins. For Freud, the primal scene is rarely accessible by way of direct recollection; instead, only in dreams is

I

this moment available, surfacing throughout one's life as a kind of continual trauma. Literary sensationalism is the cultural repository of such dream images for the antebellum period. Repeating in fantasy form the charged scene in which a capitalist selfhood is created, they remind us that by the mid-nineteenth century, America had become a kind of fiscal neurotic, given over to insecurity, anxiety, depression, and irrational fears—all states of affect stemming from the residual question: what was the originary relationship between men and money, and how did it go so terribly wrong?

Dream moments of found treasure inform the work of canonical writers such as Washington Irving and Edgar Allan Poe. But they are more frequent in the period's pulpier material, such as urban sensation fiction, magazine stories, and melodramatic stage productions. Moreover, these moments are usually crucial to the very fabric and structure of these narratives, often providing the backdrop against which both character and plot are organized. "[H]e surveyed the prospect disclosed by the opened chest, with a glance of the deepest satisfaction," we are told at a key moment in George Lippard's best-selling novel, *The Quaker City* (1845), as the criminal Devil-Bug first views a cache of gold he has stolen with the help of his accomplice Gabriel Von Gelt. "By his side knelt the Jew, his dark eyes sparkling with delight, as he gazed upon the treasures of the opened chest . . . and over the rich stores of coin" (238). Von Gelt's comments are equally telling. "Bi-Gott!" he says. "I smellsh te gooldt already. . . . Doubloosh! Doubloosh!" (239). Lippard's unembarrassed anti-Semitism offers the Jew Von Gelt as a negative figure of greed, but the somewhat obscene covetousness Von Gelt displays is not enough to displace the more general significance and desirability of the treasure in this passage. Indeed, described as analogous to the missing "funds of the United States Bank" (200), the "rich stores of coin" are at the thematic and emotional center of the novel; representing a form of financial stability otherwise absent from the world Lippard depicts, the gold is (far more than the various imperiled women the reader encounters) the real object of desire in this novel.

As I will discuss over the course of this book, there are an even greater number of moments in which antebellum narratives pivot around the exchange of currency—for example, the dramatic moment in Harriet Beecher Stowe's *Uncle Tom's Cabin* (1852) when young George Shelby seeks somewhat naively to arrest the commodity status of his good friend, the slave Uncle Tom, by giving him his golden dollar. "*I've brought you my dollar,*" George says to Uncle Tom (171; emphasis in original). Stowe makes it clear that the gift is a direct response to the crisis of debt that has engulfed his family and forced his father to sell Uncle Tom to the slave trader Haley ("He had speculated largely and quite loosely," we are told of Mr. Shelby

[51]). But the repeated sale of Uncle Tom proves that the dollar is no match for the vicissitudes of the modern paper economy—just as George is himself unequal to the task of bettering speculative capitalism, this despite his eventual assertion of his manhood when he punches the slave trader Simon Legree (592). And as I will show, it is precisely this inequity between hard money and the speculatory economy that drives much of antebellum sensationalism, and the form of manhood it so often depicts. By way of starting, though, I want to emphasize how literary representations of treasure—money hoarded and stored, longed-for and sometimes located—retain their own special significance in the works of this period. For what they offer is a fantasy response to the very problem experienced by George Shelby. Indeed, as Lippard's mention of the U.S. Bank begins to suggest, these moments signal, both directly and indirectly, a broader set of concerns over the period's economy. Specifically, they take part in a complex meditation on the shift from a mercantilist form of capitalism, in which value is thought of as stable and linked to local trade and secure sites of gold bullion, to a sense of the world informed by the drama and dynamism of capitalist exchange. What these stories comment on, in other words, is the shift from money as treasure to money as capital. And, I will argue, this shift makes all the difference for the representation of manhood, especially as manhood was linked more and more closely to the context of the boom-and-bust economy of mid-nineteenth-century America.

"I love the paper money, and the paper money men," writes Thomas Love Peacock in *Paper Money Lyrics,* a satiric work produced in the wake of the 1837 Panic. "I hold the paper money men say truly, when they say / They ought to pay their promises, with promises to pay" (115). I want to follow Peacock, and refer here to a paper money manhood, one emerging with particular force and complexity within antebellum sensationalism. On the one hand, this designation refers simply to the speculator villains who populate so much of the period's fiction—the men whom Carroll Smith-Rosenberg, writing about the early republican period, refers to as the "corrupt new men of paper and place—the new capitalism's stock-jobbers . . . [who] live in a passionate and venal world driven by fantasy and credit, obsessed with stocks, speculation, and debt" ("Domesticating Virtue" 172). But paper money manhood also implies the far greater number of aspiring professionals who found themselves the victim of the new and unstable paper economy in the period from 1819 to 1857. As historians such as Charles Sellers, Scott A. Sandage, and Steven Mihm have shown, this period was marked by widespread economic insecurity and failure, as the increasing extension of paper forms of credit connected local communities and their inhabitants with distant, unseen markets and

as the value of paper currencies fluctuated with changes in those markets.[1] "Wherever the market extended," Sellers writes in a description of
the seemingly inevitable series of economic panics that rocked the nation
during this period, "the remorseless process of debt liquidation chastened
not only modest venturers, but also the apparently wealthy who had plunged
and borrowed most recklessly. Specie to satisfy their creditors could not be
had" (*Market* 137). Sandage puts it thus: "Nineteenth-century Americans
had to live in a new world where the sky was always falling. . . . From Wall
Street to the muddiest rural lane, failure and the fear of it left a garrulous
people at a loss for words" (*Losers* 22; 24).

The image of the specie-poor, failure-anxious citizen was particularly
poignant and especially frequent in the countless representations of fiscally imperiled professional manhood that I will be examining here. Critics
and historians have made it clear that early-nineteenth-century professional manhood was especially volatile, in particular as a new breed of men
migrated from the country to the city, and took up careers that were increasingly intertwined with and vulnerable to distant market forces beyond their
control.[2] Thus Toby Ditz suggests that the "imperiled" masculinity characteristic of the wholesale merchant classes in early republican Philadelphia
reflects "dislocations caused by the long-term transformation of markets
from temporally and spatially delimited places and events into impersonal,
unbounded, and abstract processes" ("Shipwrecked" 51). The result, she
argues, is a "precarious" form of male selfhood, one centered less and less
on an interior form of self-possession and "inner being," and increasingly
contingent on a commodified and frequently "elusive" form of reputation.
To become economically insolvent in this world, Ditz explains, is to become
"unmanned" and "feminized" (72; 66). David Leverenz provides similar
analysis of the professional male of the antebellum period. As he explains
in his seminal study, *Manhood and the American Renaissance* (1989), "The
basic class conflict between 1825 and 1850 comes with the rise of a new
middle class, for whom manhood is based much more exclusively in work
and entrepreneurial competition. Traditional norms of dignity and social
status, implying as they do a relatively stable world of small villages, can mit-
igate the basic connection between manhood and humiliation. In a world of
much greater mobility and competition, manhood becomes a more intense
anxiety" (74). For Leverenz as for Ditz, early forms of professional American
manhood were located at the uneasy dividing line between older forms of
mercantile capitalism and the new, more fluid world of the paper economy.
Indeed, as they make clear, the various versions of a dominant capitalist
manhood emerging during this period were themselves ideological, and
designed to guard against the vicissitudes of risk and competition.

Building on the work of Ditz, Leverenz, and others, Dana Nelson further complicates the capitalist manhood emerging during this period.[3] Arguing that the "radicalizing energy of local democratic practices" was "rerouted" (*National* 34) during the early national and antebellum periods into the psychological and affective energies of "market competition" (15), she suggests that the white professional manhood came to embody a new and "corporate" (21) form of national selfhood. The result, she says, is an anxious manhood constantly at odds with itself. "[E]merging models of competitive manhood, quite differently from the communal models they replaced, required individual men to internalize in terms of personal responsibility the political and economic vicissitudes of the early nation," she says. "These new 'responsibilities' propelled a substantially intensified need for management and control and a particular pattern of emotional anxiety among white men" (62).

Nelson demonstrates throughout her study the way in which the anxiety of the professional male is often projected onto figures of Otherness such as women and Native Americans. As I detail throughout this study, the period's sensationalism performs a similar logic of displacement, whereby sensational figures of financial anxiety such as the Jew and the speculator (and, more specifically, characters such as Irving's Headless Horseman and Melville's Bartleby) embody the putative "theft" of masculine wholeness and enjoyment, even as they represent the disavowed desires of the emerging professional male. But by way of starting, I want to emphasize two main points. First, and as the above critics suggest, we need to continue to extend our study of the professional male during this period, and in doing so extend our understanding of the very psychology of capitalism as it was both shifting and coalescing within the emergent professional classes. How was desire negotiated by the professional male in postmercantile America, and how did this negotiation reflect the more fluid world of paper money and credit? What was the role of fantasy in helping the professional male negotiate the shift from mercantilism to capitalism proper, and how did the very notion of fantasy change for these new men in this new world? Moreover, what do these changes tell us about mid-nineteenth-century capitalism, at least as experienced by an emerging class of professional men? And, finally, what is the role of anxiety in shaping the professional male of the mid-nineteenth century? The period was punctuated by economic panics, cataclysmic upheavals that underscored the precariousness of the paper economy. Can we read these traumatic events (especially the panics of 1819, 1837, and 1857) as triggers for a more general masculine psychology of anxiety and loss? I suggest above that we might read the sensational staging of men and treasure as a kind of embarrassing primal scene, wherein antebellum culture was able to glimpse, if unconsciously, a supposedly original relationship to money, but one tinged already with the discomfiting reality of erotics and desire. Are such dream images also informed by the anxious knowledge that, in a world of economic panics, a primary relation to money—hard money, money as treasure—is no longer possible?[4]

In seeking to answer these and related questions, I will be emphasizing the second issue I want to stress here at the outset: the fact that paper money manhood appears across the spectrum of early American cultural production. Clerks, merchants, financiers, confidence men, lawyers, bachelors, libertines, doctors, politicians, philosophers, investors, speculators, dandies: these and other figures of male professionalism are the ubiquitous but often-overlooked supporting cast of antebellum cultural production. This book argues that this cast of characters is especially important as we seek to understand the story that this culture was telling itself about itself in a period of tremendous social and economic upheaval. This book argues further that it is antebellum sensationalism that specializes in depictions of this new and quite anxious form of manhood. Over and over we see in this material the tableau of a struggling professional male negotiating the frightful—but also sometimes thrilling and titillating—world of credit and paper money. "To retrieve my fortunes so that I might marry—I speculated in stocks and lost all I possessed," says a plaintive Mark Livingstone in Dion Boucicault's hit play *The Poor of New York* (1857), a narrative that thematizes the panics of 1837 and 1857: "The poor!—whom do you call the poor? . . . [T]hey are more frequently found under a black coat than under a red shirt. The poor man is the clerk with a family, forced to maintain a decent set of clothes, paid for out of the hunger of his children. . . . These needy wretches are poorer than the poor, for they are obliged to conceal their poverty with the false mask of content" (145). A kind of white-collar *agonistes*, Livingstone here gives voice to the plight of several decades of professional men who precede him in the period's sensationalism, for whom the sense of selfhood and self-possession has become contingent on the uneven tides of the economic marketplace. Indeed, distinct from the struggles of the "red shirt" working-class male, the white-collar professional male as embodied in Livingstone is absolutely central to antebellum sensationalism, and thus to antebellum culture. For it is in the sensational representation of this figure that we see the anxieties, desires, and fantasies of antebellum capitalist culture staged for audiences who were themselves negotiating life in the paper money world of the mid-nineteenth century.

We might therefore turn to the frequent staging of a relationship between professional men and treasure in the pages of the period's sensationalism. Two useful examples are offered in the above-quoted stories by Irving and

Poe, both of which revolve around the search for treasure said to have been buried by the notorious pirate Captain Kidd. The Irving story is titled "The Golden Dreams of Wolfert Webber." Part of a series of stories dubbed "The Money Diggers" in *Tales of a Traveller,* the story centers on the increasing worry and embarrassment experienced by the title character, Wolfert Webber—the family "patriarch[]" and "rural potentate"—as his once isolated and successful family farm is gradually surrounded by the modern urban world (*TT* 228).[5] "The chief cause of anxiety to honest Wolfert . . . was the growing prosperity of the city," we are told. "[W]hile every one around him grew richer, Wolfert grew poorer, and he could not, for the life of him, perceive how the evil was to be remedied" (229). But in what follows, Webber is invigorated with hopes of economic recovery when, visiting his local pub, he hears a series of tales about buried treasure in the area. One story claims that the Dutch governor Peter Stuyvesant buried chests of gold specie when the British invaded, and continues to haunt the region. Another and more frequent story has it that the treasure was buried by Captain Kidd. The problem, however, is that regardless of who buried it, such treasure is as elusive as gold specie itself in America in the wake of the 1819 Panic. Though Webber dreams nightly of immense treasures in his garden, his increasingly desperate efforts to find the gold buried on his farmland prove futile. Worse, his search causes him to abandon his crops, with the result that he and his family are soon faced with dissolution. "Wolfert gradually woke from his dream of wealth," we are told. "By degrees a revulsion of thought took place in Wolfert's mind, common to those whose golden dreams have been disturbed by pinching realities. . . . Haggard care gathered about his brow; he went about with a money-seeking air, his eyes bent downward into the dust" (238). Late in the following story of "The Money Diggers" sequence, the apparitional Captain Kidd appears before Webber, but it is only to taunt him, and we are left to understand that, at least for Irving post-1819, found gold is merely a fantasy.

In *Sheppard Lee: Written by Himself* (1836), Robert Montgomery Bird reworks Irving's story of a debtor male's futile search for Captain Kidd's gold. "I found the whole coffin full of gold and silver, some in the form of ancient coins, but most of it in bars and ingots," he says in describing his nightly dream vision of the treasure. "Ah! how much torment a poor man has in dreaming of riches!" (35).[6] But the more famous revision of Irving's story is offered in Edgar Allan Poe's "The Gold-Bug" (1843). Like "Wolfert Webber" and *Sheppard Lee,* the tale revolves around a man marked by financial failure. "He was of an ancient Huguenot family, and had once been wealthy," we are told of William Legrand. "[B]ut a series of misfortunes had reduced him to want. To avoid the mortification consequent upon his

disasters, he left New Orleans . . . and took up his residence at Sullivan's
Island, near Charleston, South Carolina" ("Gold" 234). While on Sullivan's
Island, Legrand is bitten—quite literally—by a "gold bug," which is to say that
he finds and is bitten by a large beetle whose "scales were exceedingly hard
and glossy, with all the appearance of burnished gold" (242). But Legrand
is also bitten by the fetish for gold. As Marc Shell demonstrates, Legrand's
increasing obsession with gold echoes the similar obsessions of Democrats
such as Andrew Jackson, Martin Van Buren, and Thomas Hart Benton in
the 1830s (*Money* 5–23). Believing that, along with the beetle, he has found
a map to Captain Kidd's long-rumored and much-sought-after store of buried treasure, Legrand, like Irving's Wolfert Webber, becomes obsessed with
locating the hidden hoard of gold bullion. As he explains, the gold will, if
found, "reinstate me in my family possessions" ("Gold" 242). By story's end,
of course, we find that Legrand has been correct in his guess about Captain
Kidd's hidden gold. With the help of the narrator and his ex-slave Jupiter,
he finds $450,000 in gold specie, as well as a fortune in jewels (254). If not
quite enough to calm the more general climate of financial panic plaguing
the nation in the wake of the 1837 Panic, the treasure is certainly enough
to restore Legrand to his accustomed position of propertied manhood. But
we might consider as well the fact that, as the above quote reveals, "[t]here
was no American money" (254) among the "antique" coins found in Kidd's
treasure chest. The comment is telling, for it suggests that the chest is quite
literally filled with old money—money created, that is to say, during a time
when the new economy had yet to take hold, and when America's economic
instability was still far off in the future. What Legrand locates is thus money
as treasure rather than money as capital. I will be arguing here that this is a
crucial distinction in seeking to understand not only the form of manhood
emerging during the antebellum period but also the very nature of the stories antebellum culture was telling itself about selfhood and money.[7]

    Literary fantasies of found gold are not new to literature, of course. The
discovery by Beowulf and Wiglaf of the hoard of treasure in the Dragon's lair
in *Beowulf;* Jack's theft of the goose that lays the golden eggs in *Jack and the
Beanstalk;* the pirate treasure finally located at the conclusion of Stevenson's
Treasure Island (1883); Jonathan Harker's discovery of the Count's hoarded
gold in Bram Stoker's *Dracula* (1897): such narratives make it clear that the
dream of finding hidden stores of gold treasure is repeatedly enacted across
a range of historical periods and narrative forms, and always, it would seem,
as a means of addressing a variety of social concerns. Thus in *Beowulf,* for
example, the dragon and his treasure represent a corrupt king who with-
holds wealth from his people. Conversely, in Cotton Mather's *The Life of*

Phips (1697), the description of William Phips's search for treasure is exemplary precisely in that it acts as a lesson for Puritans concerned about the fates of their souls. As Jennifer Baker puts it, "images of payment or sudden outpourings of wealth had long suited the Puritan notion of a covenant of grace, through which Christ's sacrificial death redeems the debt of human sin for the elect" (*Securing* 35). In this sense, she argues, Mather's story of Phips's trial and doubt imparts the crucial lesson that "treasure can only be obtained through a faith that rests somewhere between the dangerous extremes of assurance and despair" (37).

But what about stories such as "Wolfert Webber" and "The Gold-Bug"? How might we understand them as reflecting the emergence of a new sort of narrative in antebellum America? More specifically, how might we understand the very notion of American literary character as undergoing a shift in such narratives? And more specifically still, how is American literary *manhood* changing in such stories? One place to begin in seeking to answer such questions is with the representation of money—and especially treasure—in the period's literature. For, and as Fredric Jameson suggests, the literary depiction of money has shifted across time and literary genre. Thus he observes that narratives such as the art-novella are quite different both in content and form than their later incarnations, precisely because of evolving conceptions of money at different historical junctures. As he explains in a passage that I want to quote at length:

> The art-novella, then, will be governed by the experience of money, but of money at a specific moment of its historical development: the stage of commerce rather than the stage of capital proper. This is the stage Marx describes as exchange on the frontiers between two modes of production, which have not yet been subsumed under a single standard of value; so great fortunes can be made and lost overnight, ships sink or against all expectation appear in the harbor, heroic travelers reappear with cheap goods whose scarcity in the home society lends them extraordinary worth. This is therefore an experience of money which marks the form rather than the content of narratives; these last may include rudimentary commodities and coins incidentally, but nascent Value organizes them around a conception of the Event which is formed by categories of Fortune and Providence, the wheel that turns, bringing great good luck and then dashing it, the sense of what is not yet an invisible hand guiding human destinies and endowing them with what is not yet "success" or "failure," but rather the irreversibility of an unprecedented fate, which makes its bearer into the protagonist of a unique and "memorable" story. (*Ideologies of Theory* 52)[8]

For Jameson, it is only with the entrance into a more advanced stage of capitalism proper—the stage Marx describes in terms of the distinction between "money as money" and "money as capital"—that success and failure become interiorized psychological conditions (*Capital* 247). Notions such as luck and fate, Fortune and Providence, or—as with Mather's narrative—the covenant of grace, are part of an earlier literary ethos, one that is simply inconsistent with the more dynamic fiscal world of the nineteenth century, in which fiscal panics are increasingly common, and in which it is the invisible hand of mysterious market forces that guides human destiny. Accordingly, it is only with a more advanced system of capital, one marked by what Marx refers to as "the unceasing movement of profit-making" (254), that writers such as Irving and Poe begin to invent characters for whom success and failure have their specifically monetary resonance.

Characters such as Wolfert Webber and William Legrand, that is to say, are the product of a new economic order. Indeed, Jameson's observations also allow us to see how the narratives produced within the context of capital can reflect a longing for an earlier, precapitalist period, even as they make it clear that such a period is permanently foreclosed. For if, as Jameson suggests, the concept of treasure signals a period that predates the vicissitudes of modern capitalism, then certainly the "golden dreams" of a character such as Wolfert Webber reflect a kind of desperate desire to escape the very psychology of success and failure in modern America. Literary treasure is in this sense a reference to the earlier moment of mercantile capitalism; even better than the "funds of the United States Bank" ironically invoked by Lippard, such stores of currency represent an immutable form of value and stability—one that, by extension, is linked to a longed-for form of fiscally secure, self-possessed masculinity. Captain Kidd's money is therefore nostalgic, precisely in that finding (or losing) such treasure is quite different from making or losing a fortune on a speculative business venture. Both represent luck and contingency, but it is the later phase of "capital proper" that produces the more internalized, anxious form of selfhood that is all but wholly based on market notions of "success" and, more often (especially in American narratives post-1837), "failure." This, then, is the payoff for Legrand in locating Kidd's money: finding the treasure means escape from a felt sense of failure, but it also provides him imagined (and, for the reader, allegorical) passage back to a very different historical moment, one that *precedes the very notion* of an individual who has "failed" in the context of the economy proper.[9] Sandage's analysis of the links between nineteenth-century ideals of manhood and ideologies of market success is especially useful here. "Failure troubled, hurried and excited nineteenth-century Americans not only because more of them were going bust," he explains, "but also because their attitudes toward ambition were changing. . . . An American with no prospects or plans, with nothing to look forward to, almost ceases to exist. . . . Failure is the lost horizon of American manhood" (*Losers* 13; 20; 87).

The above nineteenth-century narratives thus tap into an issue that would saturate American culture from the 1820s through the 1850s, and that predominates in the narratives I will examine over the course of this book: what had become of the nation's gold bullion? In one respect, of course, this was a question that occupied political economists and more general social commentators, especially during periods of economic panic, when the specie reserves of the nation's banks dwindled and the value of the paper money in circulation plummeted. Writing during the Panic of 1819, the first fiscal panic to affect the nation as a whole, James Swan put it thus: "Let us reason a little on the present scarcity of silver and gold coin: whatever be the cause of that scarcity[,] whether it be real or fictitious, whether it has been sent abroad, or been concealed at home from fear or bad intentions—we are without it" (*Address* 12). Nearly twenty years later, concerns about the nation's supplies of gold bullion had only increased in intensity. Echoing Swan's concern that America's hard currency has been siphoned away to other countries, William Gouge explained that the problem was the use of paper money as a circulating medium. As he explained in his influential treatise, *A Short History of Paper Money and Banking* (1833): "A hundred years ago, the chief feature in the commercial policy of nations, was the amassing of gold and silver, as a kind of wealth *par excellence*. Now, he is the wisest statesman, who is most successful in driving the precious metals from a country. . . . Eagles have disappeared for the same reason that dollars have disappeared. Whenever Bank notes are used, no more specie is retained in a country than is necessary for transactions of a smaller amount than the least denominations of paper. . . . It has been found impossible in England to make sovereigns and one pound notes circulate currently; and we all know that small notes in the United States have not only driven away gold coins, but also such silver coins as are of a higher denomination than half a dollar" (67; 107).

For Gouge as for many others, the demand for specie in countries that did not use paper money necessarily resulted in the inexorable exit of hard money out of the United States and into the coffers of foreign merchants and their banks. Worse, the absence of hard money within the United States resulted in economic instability. As Gouge also argued in the same text: "In foreign countries the paper of [U.S.] Banks will not pass current. The holders of it, therefore, present it for payment. The Banks finding their paper returned, fear they will be drained of coin, and call upon their debtors to repay what has been advanced to them. . . . The circle extends through society. Multitudes become bankrupt, and a few successful speculators get possession of the earnings and savings of many of their frugal and industrious neighbors" (25).

Such proclamations were the product of a long-running debate over the new economy initiated by Alexander Hamilton in the early 1790s over the vociferous objections of Thomas Jefferson, James Madison, and other Republicans. Insisting that the country needed a means of creating cash in order to compete on a world stage, Hamilton created a national bank with the powers to fund a national debt and to forward credit in the form of banknotes and paper money without relying on an actual gold standard. The Jeffersonian opposition to these measures centered on the argument that real material value inhered only in actual specie (gold and silver), while paper money and banknotes not backed by specie offered the mere illusion of value. For example, in a pamphlet titled *The Bank Torpedo, or Bank Notes Proved to be a Robbery on the Public, and the Real Cause of Distresses Among the Poor* . . . (1810), Benjamin Davies claimed, "There is nothing on which men more generally agree, than on what is called the right of property. . . . But how can he enjoy this right, while the Bankers are suffered to use paper, lieu of gold and silver [?] Does it require any more labor to fabricate a note, than to counterfeit money? Do not then the Bankers enjoy the benefit of labor without laboring themselves?" (10). Such arguments were echoed by a range of critics in the years before and after the Panic of 1819, each of whom decried a system in which a proliferating number of state banks were not backed by actual capital but instead specialized in transactions based on intangible, paper forms of value (such as banknotes and corporate stocks) and persisted in the policy begun during the War of 1812 of refusing specie payment "on demand." Even the Bank of the United States, rechartered in 1816 to rein in these state banks by enforcing specie payments, cashed in on the boom by overextending its own loan line, especially in western banks involved in land speculation. Rather than provide stability, the U.S. Bank added to a precarious and absurdly circular situation: any bank pressed for specie would be forced to demand repayment from debtors, most of whom were unable to pay except in notes held on banks that had no specie reserves.[10]

The bullionist stance was intensified in the 1830s by Andrew Jackson and his high-profile "war" against the U.S. Bank and its president, Nicholas Biddle. Backing Jackson's 1832 veto of the bill to recharter the Bank, as well as his 1833 decision to remove the federal deposits from it and redistribute them to smaller state banks, "hard money" Democrats depicted a corrupt economy floating precariously on the airy foundation of uncertain promises.

Concerns about a floating bubble economy are central to numerous satiric narratives about the tensions between paper money and gold. For example, in a pamphlet titled *Specie Humbug* (1837), the narrator relates his plan for a bank "founded on the great principle of making money out of nothing" (*Specie* 6); in "Colloquy Between a Bank Note and a Gold Coin" (1835), the two forms of currency debate theories of inherent worth while jostling around in the pocket of an unnamed citizen ("Colloquy" 45–49). But these worries are best represented by writers such as Gouge and Theophilus Fisk, the latter of whom produced two lengthy pamphlets in 1837, both of which were aimed at explaining the threat that paper money and the banking system posed to the nation's core ideals of labor and value. Writing in *Labor, the Only True Source of Wealth,* Fisk claims that the "most respected" people in the new economy are "the air bubble paper money nobility which considers honest labor fit only for serfs and bondmen" (*Labor* 5–6). Similarly, in *The Banking Bubble Burst*—where he quotes at length from Gouge and British writer William Cobbett's *Paper Against Gold* (1822)—Fisk argues thus: "Bank notes are not money—they are only 'promises to pay' money. They pass as money so long as the credit of the institution from which they are issued remains unimpaired; but this is easily deranged, and then they are comparatively worthless, having no intrinsic value whatever. . . . [P]aper money produces nothing but an army of consumers (who fabricate it) and who diminish the real wealth of the country in exact proportion to the number of those who live without labor. The president, cashiers, clerks, &c. &c., do nothing but consume the wealth others have earned; consumption is the end of production" (*Banking Bubble* 36–37; 40).

Elaborating on Jackson's warning in his 1837 Farewell Address that "[I]f your currency continues as exclusively paper as it now is, it will foster [the] eager desire to amass wealth without labor" ("Farewell" 302), Fisk depicts a dystopian society based on pure consumption. From this perspective, the notion of self-possession rooted in labor and a correspondingly reliable form of specie value has given way to a dispossessed, laborless model of selfhood, one that is not only insubstantial but also, perhaps inevitably, self-consuming.

The debates over gold were made particularly dramatic in many of the political cartoons produced in response to the period's banking controversies. For example, in an 1833 image entitled *The Doctors Puzzled or the Desperate Case of Mother U.S. Bank* (figure 1), Jackson is depicted as a wise medical practitioner who looks on with bemused satisfaction from a rear window as a corpulent U.S. Bank is purged of its specie reserves (this is the missing money Lippard refers to some years later in *The Quaker City*). Pro-Jackson in orientation, the image suggests that Jackson's 1833 order for the withdrawal of federal funds from the Bank and their placement into

Figure 1 *The Doctors Puzzled or the Desperate Case of Mother U.S. Bank.* 1833 published by Anthony Imbert. Lithograph on wove paper; 28 x 39.2 cm. Reproduced with permission of the American Antiquarian Society.

state banks (actions signaled here by the broken vials on the floor in front of the vomiting Mother Bank) will save the nation's specie from the corrupt clutches of Bank president Nicholas Biddle and return it into the hands of honest workingmen. "D—n that Doctor Jackson," Biddle says as he straddles the Bank, seeking to comfort her. "This is the effect of his last prescription." For the Biddle of this image, the loss of gold bullion means a curtailing of speculative excess; for Jackson, it means a chance to recover the nation's integrity by retrieving its lost gold.

Anti-Jackson images also relied on fantasies of treasure saved or restored. For example, in an 1833 lithograph titled *Troubled Treasures* (figure 2), we see a reversal of the dynamic offered in "The Doctor's Puzzled." Here it is Jackson who is bent over and vomiting—in this case, he is expelling his veto of the U.S. Bank, this while a devil figure makes off with the $200 million in Treasury funds that Jackson had threatened to withdraw from the Bank. The implication here is that the nation's treasure has actually been *saved* as a result of Congressional resistance to Jackson's fiscal policies. Similarly, in *Capitol Fashions for 1837* (1837), Jackson's successor, Martin Van Buren, is caricatured as wearing a cloak trimmed with "Shinplaster" banknotes, the mocking term for the small-denomination banknotes that were circulated during the 1837 Panic in an unsuccessful effort to compensate for the run on the nation's specie reserves (figure 3). "I like this cloak amazingly," says a vain Van Buren, "for now I shall be able to put into execution my designs without being observed by every quising [*sic*], prying Whig." The joke here is that Van Buren seems unaware that his hard-money banking policies have failed, and that, as America's specie reserves are being drained away, the nation is increasingly reliant on unstable paper currencies. This is driven home both by his aside that "this kind of Trimming is rather light, *not so good as Gold*" (emphasis in original), and even more so by the image to his left, in which we see a large audience streaming into a theater in order to catch a glimpse of "A Real Gold Coin The Last In This Country." Once more, it is the seeming scarcity of gold that is located at the heart of the nation's problems, both fiscal and social.

This perceived lack of gold bullion is perhaps why the fairy tale *Jack and the Beanstalk* was popular in America in the first half of the nineteenth century (the related *Jack the Giant Killer* was also a popular stage production).[11] The tale almost always begins with a description of young Jack as profligate and lazy, so much so that his widowed mother is forced to desperate measures to support the two of them. "Oh! you wicked child," she says in one text from the early 1840s.[12] "[B]y your ungrateful course of life you have at least brought me to beggary and ruin! Cruel, cruel boy! I have not money enough to purchase even a bit of bread for another day—nothing

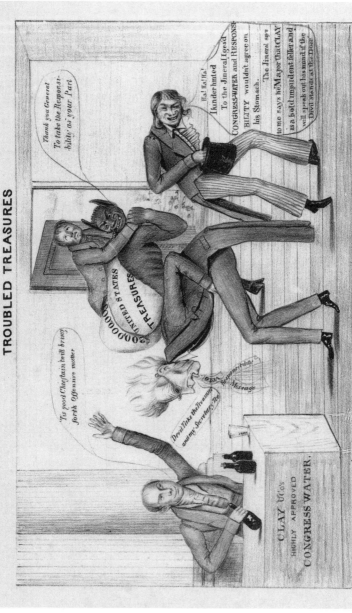

Figure 2 *Troubled Treasures.* 1833 by R. Bisbee. Lithograph on wove paper; 23.2 x 32.9 cm. Reproduced with permission of the American Antiquarian Society.

Figure 3 *Capitol Fashions for 1837.* 1837 by F. J. Winston. Etching on wove paper; 30.1 x 24.4 cm. Reproduced from the Collections of The Library of Congress.

now remains to sell but my poor cow!" (*Surprising History* 4). Made thus to feel guilty, Jack volunteers to take the cow to market, and therefore begins the difficult transition from childhood (and its link to the mother) to manhood (and its location in the commercial world of the father).[13] Hence when Jack is apparently swindled into accepting magic beans instead of money, we see an image of masculine economic failure, one that would surely have resonated in antebellum America. (In the first American version of the tale, *The History of mother Twaddle, and the marvellous atchievments* [sic] *of her son Jack* [1809],[14] the man who sells the beans to Jack is "a Jew," which is to say he is a stereotypical symbol of market corruption. "Come buy," he says, "dis rare bean for a faring / It pofsefses such virtues dat sure as a Gun / Tomorrow it vill grow near as heigh as de Sun" [H.A.C., *Mother Twaddle* 4]. I will turn more fully to the sensational figure of the capitalist Jew in chapter 3, but suffice it to say here that the deeper one travels into antebellum sensationalism, the more dramatic the examples of anti-Semitism, and the more one realizes the centrality of the Jew in American culture's attempt to imagine its relationship to money).

Jack's bad luck at market is countered, however, by the magical interposition of good fortune. Overnight a beanstalk grows to an impossible height, and when Jack climbs it he is amazed to find a castle in which resides an evil giant, who it turns out has killed Jack's father and siblings, and stolen the family fortune. "Having gained your father's confidence, he knew where to find all his treasure," the fairy tells Jack. "[Y]ou must persevere in avenging the death of your father, or you will not prosper in any of your undertakings, but be always miserable" (*Surprising History* 10; 11). In the ensuing scene, the giant's wife lets Jack into her house, and hides Jack from her flesh-eating husband in her oven. As a result, Jack manages in successive trips up and down the beanstalk to rob the giant of his goose that lays golden eggs, his sacks of gold and silver, and his magical singing harp. The image of Jack that appears in an 1857 version of the story published by John McLoughlin in New York, in which we see Jack struggling with two bags stamped with the words "SILVER" and "GOLD" (*Jack and the Bean Stalk* 8), captures the masculine fantasy of found treasure (figure 4).[15] Indeed, especially as staged in the context of antebellum America, the giant comes to represent both an Oedipal father figure who must be defeated, *and* (as with the market Jew) the abstract, devouring forces of market capitalism that have ruined his father's patriarchal agency. Jack's theft from and subsequent slaying of the giant, meanwhile, suggests a revitalized form of market manhood. In some versions Jack cuts off the giant's head, while in others he chops down the beanstalk and the giant breaks his neck. Either way, Jack's slaying of the giant amounts to a return form of symbolic castration, and successful entry into

Figure 4 Image from *Jack and the Bean Stalk*. 1857 by William Momberger. Published by John McLoughlin. Reproduced with permission of the American Antiquarian Society.

the world of both manhood and capitalism (no more hiding in the maternal oven for Jack).

Here the fairy's words to Jack at the end of an 1856 version of the story published in New York by H. W. Hewet are suggestive: "Now, my dear Jack, you may take possession of all your father's property again, as I see that you will make a good use of it, and become a useful and good man. . . . If you had remained as idle and lazy as you once were, I should not have exerted my power to help you to recover your property, and enable you to take care of your mother in your old age" (*Jack and the Bean-Stalk* 32).[16] On the one hand, the quote suggests that an Algeresque form of pluck and initiative has rescued Jack's fortunes. But it's important to note that Jack's success is possible only through the fantastical work of the fairy and her beanstalk. In fact, in early American versions of the story the fairy is often adamant in explaining to Jack that it is *her* agency, rather than Jack's, that has brought about his reversal of fortune. "By my power, the bean-stalk grew to so great a height, and formed a ladder," she says in the *The Surprising History of Jack and the Bean Stalk*. "I need not add that I inspired you with a strong desire to ascend the ladder" (11). Thus, although Jack is "indolent, careless, and extravagant" (4), his is not a story of success and failure proper. Rather, the tale is a deeply nostalgic fantasy of a premodern form of young manhood, one guided still by the sort of "Fortune and Providence" Jameson suggests. And what this suggests is that the giant's gold is quite different from the money Jack uses to pay for his beans. Discovered only through a magical form of good fortune, the giant's hoarded gold—much like Captain Kidd's treasure in Poe's story—is located outside of, and in many ways precedes, the modern stage of speculative capitalism that Jack's money inhabits.

The same form of nostalgia informs a version of the Mother Goose narrative from the early 1840s titled *The History of old Mother Goose, and the golden egg* (1840–42).[17] In this version of the story, a boy named Jack discovers that the goose he buys at market "had laid him / An egg of pure gold" (*Mother Goose* 1). Not surprisingly, his mother is delighted by this news, and tells him that he is a "good boy." But when Jack seeks to convert his golden egg into cash, his luck takes a turn for the worse. "Jack sold his egg / To a rogue of a Jew / Who cheated him out of / The half of his due," we are told. Worse still, the Jew then steals the goose itself: "The Jew got the Goose / Which he vow'd he would kill / Resolving at once / His pockets to fill" (3). Here, though, Jack's mother—Mother Goose—intercedes, and in a magical narrative resolution she flies off with the goose "up to the moon." In this fantasy, Jack can again be cheated at market (and physically beaten: we learn that the Jew "began to belabour / The sides of poor Jack" [4]), but it doesn't matter. For the narrative insists on a dream rescue of Jack's treasure from the clutches of the capitalist male (embodied once again in the figure of the Jew), a conclusion that echoes the outcomes of both *Jack and the Beanstalk* and Poe's "The Gold-Bug." In each case, we see manhood rescued from the complex and emasculating world of modern market relations. Indeed, it is only the discovery of gold that seems to satisfy such fantasy needs. This is why, in stories ranging from Charles Brockden Brown's *Arthur Mervyn* (1799–1800) to very recent novels (and their cinematic reproductions) such as Scott Smith's *A Simple Plan* (1993) and Cormac McCarthy's *No Country for Old Men* (2005), the discovery of large caches of paper money leads only to disaster and masculine failure. Paper money is in these narratives false treasure, and its dramatic discovery a false triumph that is part and parcel of the capitalist ethos that real treasure—found gold—is able to counter. Unfortunately, though, while a character such as Jack is able to find his stolen riches at the top of the beanstalk, most of America in the period 1819–57 was left to wonder who had made off with its supplies of hard money.

THEFT AND COMPENSATION:
MEN AND MONEY IN THE SENSATIONAL PUBLIC SPHERE

Canonical authors such as Irving and Poe were not the only writers seeking to tell the story of gold lost and (occasionally and with the help of tremendous luck) found. Rather, stories such as "The Gold Bug" were intimately linked with a diverse media, which included not only pulpy works such as *The Quaker City,* but also penny press newspapers such as the New York *Herald,* stage melodramas such as Boucicault's *The Poor of New York,* murder pamphlets, lithographs, minstrel songsters, and more.[18] Again and again these sensational texts stage narratives in which male characters—especially professional men—seek to negotiate the related crises of economic self-possession and gender. I thus suggest that this work consolidates within the representational space I will refer to here as the "sensational public sphere." Marked by the emergence of penny press newspapers and cheap urban-sensation novels, as well as the increasing popularity of magazine fiction, melodramatic stage productions, and political cartoons, the sensational public sphere offered a space in which an emergent professional class of men was able to see itself reflected in a whole range of narratives, virtually all of which were located at the fraught moment of transition I am describing—that which marks the shift from an older form of mercantile capitalism to the new and much less stable world of the emergent paper economy. Moreover, the various texts that compose this public sphere appeared with a frequency and an intensity that reflects what I will suggest is a profound sense of lost security. For what these stories outline is a notion of masculine selfhood that turns quite intimately on one's relationship to money. Moreover, it is a form of manhood specific to the context of the boom-and-bust economy of mid-nineteenth-century America, and thus to the various forms of cultural production seeking to respond to the shift from mercantilism to capitalism proper.

By invoking the notion of a "sensational" public sphere I am thus seeking to add to recent critical work that complicates and challenges the notion of a "rational" public sphere theorized by Jürgen Habermas in *The Structural Transformation of the Public Sphere* (1989). For Habermas, the public sphere acted as a space of discourse in which citizens were able to bracket inequalities of status and private concern, and to engage in unrestricted and rational political discussion devoted to the common good. But, and as critics such as Nancy Fraser, Mary Ryan, Lauren Berlant, Michael Schudson, and others have made clear, the idealized space Habermas conceives is exclusively white, male, and bourgeois in orientation, and is in fact structured by the exclusion of, and in conflict with, alternate publics.[19] As Fraser puts it, "[T]he bourgeois public sphere was never *the* public. On the contrary, virtually contemporaneous with the bourgeois public sphere arose a host of competing counterpublics, including nationalist publics, popular peasant publics, elite women's publics, and working-class publics" ("Rethinking" 7). I want to argue here that the sensational public sphere is a "competing public sphere" of the sort Fraser outlines (7). It is of course true that the emergent professional classes of the antebellum period were predominately white and male, as well as upwardly mobile in ways that the working classes generally were not. Accordingly, it might seem as though a discourse oriented around such a class is reasonably close to the sort of public sphere Habermas describes. But the sensationalism I am describing is the virtual antithesis of the rational-critical discourse Habermas attributes to the bourgeois public sphere. Indeed, revolving in large part around the excessive emotions, passions, and desires of the professional classes, and marked by "sensational" extremes of violence, sexuality, fear, and titillation, the sensational public sphere staged a professional selfhood in the very act of responding—often poorly, but usually in interesting ways—to the intense pressures and anxieties of life under an emergent and quite unstable capitalist economy. One might say that this counterpublic acted as the emotionally charged and often irrational underbelly of the period's more properly bourgeois public sphere. This is not, then, a "subaltern" counterpublic of the sort Fraser envisions (14), a space that gives voice to minoritized populations. Instead, the sensational public sphere provided a new, alternative space for expressing the concerns and anxieties of the very figure—the professional male—that Habermas associates with a rational sphere of discourse.

A useful example of the print discourse that characterized the antebellum sensational public sphere is offered in the lead story from an 1842
issue of *The Weekly Rake,* one of many short-lived, tabloid-style rags aimed
primarily at the young men of New York's clerking classes.[20] Titled "The
Dandy and the Soap-Fat Man," the article recounts an assault perpetrated by
a working-class Irish laborer on a "finical, conceited fop" who not only has
accrued debts throughout town but also has had the poor judgment to challenge the laborer physically (*WR* 10-1-1842). The real violence of this narrative, however, is contained in the accompanying cartoon (figure 5). Offering
a freeze-frame of Jacksonian class politics—with the Soap-Fat Man embodying the prolabor, anti-Whig posture voiced by Jacksonian critics of paper
money, and the dandy representing the fiscal recklessness of the upwardly
striving professional male and the economic market more generally—the
cartoon suggests that professional masculine selfhood is frequently staged
in terms of humiliation, disempowerment, and a general sense of class instability. But the cartoon also implies that this sensational masculinity is being
negotiated in a very public manner. For while the assault is viewed by the
many clerk types who have gathered to cheer the dandy's embarrassment,
it is also subject to re-presentation within the very pages of *The Weekly
Rake*—something made overt by the figure of a newsboy in the foreground
of the cartoon, watching the assault and carrying a bundle of the paper's
recent issues. The interest the newsboy takes in the action thus tells us what
we already know: that the city's fast-growing market for sensational media
was organized to a great extent around the vociferous class politics of masculine conduct and sensibility. In *Public Sentiments* (2001), Glenn Hendler
argues that "[a]s early as the 1840s, when the ideology of gendered separate
spheres was being forcefully inscribed in American culture, sentiment and
male embodiment were already being deployed together as part of a public discourse of political reform and masculine self-fashioning" (43–44).
Whether packaged as "sentimental" (Hendler's primary focus), "gothic," or
"sensational," the masculine postures of affect and self-fashioning Hendler
describes are everywhere in evidence within the sensational public sphere.
And again, they counter the ideal of the traditional bourgeois public sphere,
in which a bourgeois male public could supposedly debate political questions in a purely rational and abstract fashion. Instead, by offering a space
for the depiction of masculine affect, class violence, and fiscal crisis, the
sensational public sphere was forwarding vexed questions of class, gender,
and self-possession into public discourse in new ways.[21]

At present, most of the critical work on antebellum sensationalism
builds on the historical work of Sean Wilentz's *Chants Democratic* (1984)
and examines its working-class orientation. For example, this perspective is
poignantly argued by Michael Denning in his seminal work on dime-novel

Figure 5 Cover image from *The Weekly Rake*. 10-2-1842. Reproduced with permission of the American Antiquarian Society.

sensationalism, *Mechanic Accents* (1987). "Who read these stories and what did they think of them?" he asks (27), and goes on to suggest that the majority of these readers were working-class laborers. "The dime novels were part of the popular culture of the 'producing classes,' a plebian culture whose metaphoric centers of gravity were the 'honest mechanic' and the virtuous 'working-girl'" (46). Denning's reading is echoed by critics such as Eric Lott in *Love and Theft* (1993) and Shelley Streeby in *American Sensations* (2002). Extending the work of Denning as well as that of historians such as David Roediger and Alexander Saxton,[22] both Lott and Streeby argue that working-class whiteness was the central issue in antebellum mass culture. Focusing on blackface minstrelsy, Lott argues that the minstrel show provided a kind of fantasy space onto which white, working-class male audiences could project anxieties about desire and embodiment, while at the same time gaining vicarious access to these same repressed modes of feeling. As he explains, "[W]hite pleasure in minstrelsy was . . . a willed attempt to rise above the stultifying effects of capitalist boredom and rationalization. . . . It was a rediscovery, against the odds, of repressed pleasure in the body" (148–49). For Streeby, meanwhile, the many imperial narratives that appear within antebellum sensationalism—especially those that revolved about the U.S.–Mexican War—represent a complex negotiation of class, gender, and nativism for (primarily male) working-class readers. "[I]nterest in the material and the corporeal makes sensationalism an aesthetic mode that supports an emphasis on laboring bodies and the embodied relationships that workers have to power," she says. "[S]ensationalism is the idiom of many nineteenth-century working-class cultures" (15; 27).

These and other studies are invaluable to our understanding of the cultural work performed by antebellum sensationalism. But, and as I have been suggesting, a great many of the stories we see in the period's newspapers, magazines, cheap novels, plays, and (now) canonical fictions revolve around professional men, whether merchants and clerks or speculators and confidence men. Sometimes these characters are depicted as positive, morally striving members of the community and nation; other times they are corrupt villains whose proximity to the economic market have left them materially and ethically vitiated. Either way, they act as the "center of gravity" of the sensational public sphere, the representational space that revolves around the career of the professional classes—and especially the professional male—emerging during the antebellum period. I thus echo Paul Gilmore's suggestion in *The Genuine Article* (2001) that the focus of critics such as Lott on "mass culture as exclusively (or nearly exclusively) working class" works to "obscure[]" the active presence of professional and middle-class audiences (4), as well as a "mass cultural sphere" that "responded to and helped to figure" the period's dramatic economic and social upheavals (6). As he puts it in describing the emergence of entrepreneurial sensational- ist venues such as P. T. Barnum's American Museum, "In their synthesis of middle-class respectability and Bowery-born sensational entertainments, such as minstrelsy, these more middle-class-oriented mass cultural arenas provided a model for combining older artisanal and genteel paradigms of gender ideals within a highly commercialized realm" (6). For Gilmore, this mass cultural sphere was particularly noteworthy for the way in which the representation of race and racial difference worked to bolster a white middle-class formation he terms "literary manhood." I will also pursue the sensational representation of race in several chapters of this study. But I am arguing more generally that the sensational public sphere was the discursive representational space in which a professional manhood was being staged in an extended and quite vexed relationship with the stage of "capital proper" described by Jameson. More specifically, it was the sensational public sphere that made most evident a form of manhood for which success and failure have become interiorized psychological conditions.

Exact dates of origin are difficult to pin down, but I argue that the sen- sational public sphere took shape in April 1836, with the dramatic sales of penny press newspapers in New York City during the coverage of the Helen Jewett murder trial.[23] As I discuss at length in chapter 4, the case, in which a young male office clerk was accused of murdering a high-priced female prostitute, became an immediate sensation, fueling intense but also quite lurid media coverage and rivalry between papers such as the New York *Her- ald* and the New York *Sun*. These papers took up competing postures toward the case, offering as they did so a long-running debate about an emergent white-collar masculinity, about male and female sexuality, and about politi- cal economy more generally. Sales of the city's penny papers soared, and a tabloid-style form of sensationalism was born. Very quickly, writers such as Poe, Lippard, George Thompson, and Ned Buntline, as well as Nathaniel Hawthorne and other "highbrow" writers, all began to adopt the titillating and affecting mix of gothic horror and sentimentality deployed by the *Her- ald,* the *Sun,* and other papers, as well as their obsessive interest in the career of the professional male.[24]

In designating a sensational public sphere, I therefore hope to encom- pass the range of material that consistently tapped into the psychological undercurrents—the desires, fantasies, and anxieties—of antebellum capital- ist culture, especially as experienced by the emerging professional classes that were so often the central subjects of this material. In doing so, I am arguing that much of this psychological work revolves around a fairly par- ticular logic, wherein sensationalism seeks to rewrite masculine insolvency by providing what I will term "compensatory fictions." Indeed, the central premise of this book is that the sensational public sphere offers narratives that engage in a kind of psychic trade-off, wherein the absence of American gold (or "American money," as Poe puts it) is countered with other, compensatory forms of currency and value. And what these alternate forms of currency provide is a kind of fantasy redress for the failed or imperiled manhood of the new paper economy. Thus while characters such as Wolfert Webber and George Shelby are forced to discover the compromised and vulnerable nature of manhood in the era of paper money, the fiction itself seeks to provide readers with alternative solutions to the crisis of male selfhood everywhere evident in this material. For, in fact, the narrative of treasure actually found that we see in tales such as "The Gold-Bug" or *Jack and the Beanstalk* is relatively unusual: amidst the climate of financial unrest, antebellum writers were inventing new ways of imagining a stable (and usually male) selfhood, one that might rewrite the sense of failure faced by so many of the professional men depicted within the period's sensationalism.

In "Reification and Utopia in Mass Culture" (1979), Jameson suggests that works of mass culture must of necessity offer some "genuine shred" of fantasy content to consumers as they confront the alienating effects of life under capitalism (144). For Jameson, this means giving voice to "genuine social and historical content," or, more abstractly, to what he describes as the "deepest and most fundamental hopes and fantasies" of a social order longing for collectivity or Utopia (144). Thus he suggests that part of the lure of a mass culture phenomenon such as Steven Spielberg's *Jaws* (1975) lies in its ability to tap into the image of an older, more traditional America (figured in the salty World War II veteran and small business owner Quint)—even as this image of national cohesion is killed off by the giant shark as leviathan, and replaced by the new alliance between technological corporate capitalism and bureaucratic law enforcement (embodied in the characters Hooper and Brody). Similarly, he suggests that films such as *The Godfather* (1972) and *Godfather II* (1974) hinge on the fantasy content of the ethnic family, even as it displaces the role of corporate capitalism onto the scapegoated Mafia. This sort of reading might well be available in the works of various antebellum writers (for example, the famous "A Squeeze of the Hand" chapter in *Moby-Dick* certainly offers a counter to the ruthless drive of the American capitalism Ahab embodies). But I am more concerned with the way antebellum sensationalism often seeks to compensate readers with narratives in which male characters heal the psychic wounds of fiscal crisis. For in doing so, what these narratives reflect is a longing for the kind of stable selfhood—and indeed the social cohesion—that have been "stolen" by modern capitalism and the new economy: hence, again, the lure of treasure in so many sensational narratives. But in the absence of treasure found, antebellum sensationalism seeks to answer to the felt sense that American manhood has lost a precious, essential part of itself—its very potency—by imagining alternate forms of male selfhood. Thus, while I am not engaging with notions of a collective unconscious according to Jameson, I am interested in the way mass culture—and especially the sensational public sphere of antebellum America—engages readers with compromise strategies that offer fantasy solutions to life in capitalist culture, solutions that often tap into libidinal psychological currents running beneath the surface level of conscious modern life.

My thinking here takes off from the following insight David Leverenz offers in *Manhood and the American Renaissance,* one we might take as axiomatic for the literary and cultural production of the early national and antebellum periods: "[A]ny intensified ideology of manhood is a compensatory response to fears of humiliation." Thus, for Leverenz, "manhood becomes a way not of dominating, but of minimizing maximum loss" (4; 73). I want to extend Leverenz's insight to show how the sensational public sphere is one of the key sites within which such compensation is offered, and the dramatic losses of the paper money period are "minimiz[ed]." Other critics of nineteenth-century sensationalism have suggested related readings. For example, in *Mechanic Accents* Denning suggests that the mid- and late-nineteenth-century dime novel revolves around a specific form of fantasy compensation for working-class readers, in which "powerlessness" finds imagined redress in stories of social alchemy. "The dime novels that elicit allegorical readings in order to make sense of them are novels of disguise," he argues. "[T]he stories of tramps who are discovered to be heirs, and of working girls who become ladies. All depend on magical transformations to compensate the impossibility of imagining 'realistic' actions by powerful agents" (74). Thus, for Denning, dime-novel sensationalism rewrites the story of working-class disempowerment by repeatedly staging narratives that are not unlike the sorts of fairy tales I cite above. Just as Jack magically ascends the beanstalk in order to retrieve his lost family fortune, the characters Denning examines perform impossible shifts of class status and agency as a means of answering to the fantasy needs of working-class readers unable to achieve such change in their own lives.

This book suggests that the sensational public sphere is engaged in a similar process of fantasy resolution. Specifically, I show how sensationalism performs a kind of dual task, in which readers see both economic crisis, and its compromise resolution. One of my main goals is therefore to demonstrate how this material seeks tirelessly to project fiscal crisis—and more specifically, capitalist desire—onto figures of Otherness such as the

Jew and the speculator, suggesting thereby that it is they who have stolen away the kind of fiscal security that went along with the nation's supplies of gold bullion. This, indeed, is one of the prime forms of cultural work performed by the sensational public sphere, and it is without doubt one of the primary reasons this material was so popular. Quite simply, these texts allowed a reader to see his own complicity in the capitalist system embodied in a figure of recognizable alterity: not only the speculator and the Jew, but also the libertine and rake; the always sexually charged black male; the female prostitute and other threatening females; gothic figures of Otherness such as Irving's Headless Horseman; even Melville's Bartleby. These are all sensational characters who absorb, crystallize, and help manage the forms of pleasure and enjoyment that we see circulating, often madly and excessively, within the world of sensationalism, and the sensational public sphere more specifically. Indeed, they are a kind of symptom, one expressed widely and variously throughout the sensational public sphere in what we might think of as the messy psychological aftermath of the primal scene staging the embarrassing intimacies of men and treasure.

In *The Clerk's Tale* (2003), Thomas Augst examines a range of diaries maintained by young professional men in the antebellum period, and argues that they reflect the painstaking efforts of the period's emergent class of white-collar men to fashion an interior and disciplined form of selfhood. Arguing that the clerk's life was measured, often obsessively and frequently quite anxiously, against the presence of his "moral Other," he suggests that "[f]or middle class men, free time was not merely a privilege, but a moral test" (58; 62). And certainly the period's advice books for young men stress the need for self-control. Again and again writers such as Henry Ward Beecher, William Alcott, Daniel Wise, and Timothy Shay Arthur warned against excess expenditure of finances, sexual energy, and even emotion. "ALWAYS LET YOUR EXPENDITURE BE LESS THAN YOUR INCOME," writes Daniel Wise in an altogether typical passage from these tracts. "*Deny thyself,* in little as in great things, is a necessary condition of prosperity" (*Young* 146; caps and emphasis in original). But the period's sensational public sphere suggests that many if not most young professional men failed the test Augst describes. For what this material performs is a panicky and often guilty unease about the very excesses, lusts, and appetencies said to have supplanted the putative security of a gold-backed form of selfhood. Indeed, from the mercurial Ichabod Crane in Irving's 1819 "The Legend of Sleepy Hollow" (whose "devouring mind's eye" signals his desire to sell off the Van Tassel estate "for cash" [*SB* 279; 280]), to the racy pages of *The Weekly Rake,* to the notorious Mr. Tickels in George Thompson's gritty 1849 urban gothic novel, *Venus in Boston* ("one of the those wealthy beasts whose lusts run riot on the innocence of young females" [11]), male desire and capitalist desire are the *sine qua non* of the period's sensationalism.

And this goes for the many characters (persecutory creditors, misers and hoarders, and so on) whose obsessive, clutching relationship to money—especially gold bullion—is excessive, even disgusting, precisely because of its negative relationship to circulation. This negative form of avarice is often embodied in the figure of the Jew, and usually the Jewish usurer. The above passage depicting Gabriel Von Gelt gazing with delight upon a chest of gold partakes of this tendency, as does the "rogue of a Jew" who swindles Jack and tries to steal his goose in the *Mother Goose* narrative. But Gentile figures such as the "old miser" in Melville's *The Confidence-Man* (1857) are represented as equally negative and problematic. "My gold, my gold! Ugh, ugh, ugh!" the miser cries out after being duped into giving over his "ten hoarded eagles" to "the stranger" without receiving a receipt for his supposed investment (104). Indeed, Jew or otherwise, the miser and similar figures of hoarding place us in the terrain of "filthy lucre," that site which Freud famously outlines in theorizing the symbolic links between money and excrement. "We know that the gold which the devil gives to his paramours turns into excrement after his departure," Freud says, "and the devil is certainly nothing else than the personification of the repressed unconscious instinctual life. We also know about the superstition which connects the finding of treasure with defaecation, and everyone is familiar with the figure of the 'shitter of ducats'" ("Character" 9: 174). "Gold," he goes on to say in a related discussion of dreams in folklore, "is seen in the most unambiguous way to be a symbol of faeces" ("Dreams" 12: 187). Christopher Herbert suggests that the contradiction Freud points to, in which an object as socially significant as gold is linked with that culture's most repulsive form of filth, reflects the fact that "Christianity idealizes poverty and anathematizes money" ("Filthy" 190). Quoting the biblical moment when Paul in the First Epistle to Timothy says that a pious man must be "not greedy of filthy lucre," Herbert explains that "The Victorian worship of money, rooted though it is in Protestant culture, is shot through with the dread and aversion that such passages enjoin upon all faithful believers" (190).

Herbert's discussion is useful for understanding the seeming contradiction we often see in antebellum American sensationalism. Though, as I have been suggesting, gold was for many the longed-for embodiment of fiscal and social stability, its accumulation could also be perceived as unclean or pathological. This was especially true for Whig-Republicans opposed to the hard-money postures of Jackson, Van Buren, and other Democrats. Consider, for example, the strain of humor that informs political cartoons such as *Treasury Note* (1837) and *Cleansing the Augean Stable* (1844) (figures 6 and 7). In each, the joke revolves around the imagined relation between

Figure 6 *Treasury Note.* 1837 by Napolean Sarony. Printed and published by H. R. Robinson. 25 x 44.2 cm; lithograph on wove paper. Reproduced with permission of the American Antiquarian Society.

Figure 7 *Cleansing the Augean Stable.* 1844 by H. Bucholzer. Lithograph with water color on wove paper; 30.1 x 44 cm. Reproduced from the Collections of The Library of Congress.

feces and the "mint drop" coins issued by Van Buren during the Panic of 1837, in response to a shortage of hard money after the suspension of specie payments by New York banks on May 10, 1837. In the image to the right of "Treasury Note," we see Jackson depicted as an ass excreting mint drops as Van Buren collects them in a hat. In "Cleansing the Augean Stable," presidential candidate Henry Clay and various other Whigs, such as Daniel Webster and John C. Calhoun, shovel piles of mint drops from the floor of the newly vacated White House. Clearly, for some, the Jacksonian fetish for gold was no better than the excess greed of the speculator. Indeed, as a "shitter of ducats," Jackson is here guilty of a relationship to hard money that is both morally corrupt *and* pathological. Thus, whether male capitalist desire was represented in relation to paper money (the speculator) or hoarded money (the miser and usurer), what we see within the period's sensationalism is an attempt to negotiate the problem of desire—and especially male desire—under capitalism.

The forms of psychological management and negotiation I am describing within sensationalism—in which we see projected onto sensational figures of alterity the linked and sometimes contradictory anxieties about (on the one hand) the felt theft of an older, mercantilist way of life and (on the other hand) the excess desires of capitalism—are usefully captured in the dynamic of projection Slavoj Žižek terms the "theft of enjoyment." As he explains in a well-known passage:

> What we gain by transposing the perception of inherent social antagonisms into the fascination with the Other (Jew, Japanese . . .) is the fantasy-organization of desire. The Lacanian thesis that enjoyment is ultimately always enjoyment of the Other, i.e. enjoyment supposed, imputed to the Other, and that, conversely, the hatred of the Other's enjoyment is always the hatred of one's own enjoyment, is perfectly exemplified by [the] logic of the "theft of enjoyment." What are fantasies about the Other's special, excessive enjoyment—about the black's superior sexual potency and appetite, about the Jew's or the Japanese's special relationship towards money and work—if not precisely *so many ways for us to organize our own enjoyment?* Do we not find enjoyment precisely in fantasizing about the Other's enjoyment, in this ambivalent attitude toward it? (*Tarrying* 206; emphasis in original)

Žižek's insights about this process of "theft" are especially interesting when thinking about the fiscal anxieties of the antebellum period. As I have been suggesting, it is the very notion of theft or loss that informs this culture's relationship to money, and to the economy more generally. How else to explain the continuing obsession with treasure and lost gold during the period? Gold, that illusive and quite magical substance, represents the very way of life that has been (or is believed to have been) "stolen" by the new economy. Hence, one suspects, the power for antebellum readers of *Jack and the Beanstalk,* the story of a voracious, flesh-eating giant who has stolen the family fortune, and whose greatest pleasure is to count the stolen coins each night before bed. Like the figure of the Jew or the speculator, the giant is the excessive Other who has stolen "our" lost enjoyment.

And yet Žižek makes clear that this ideology of theft *also* allows for much that is pleasurable within sensationalism. Indeed, the constant staging of Otherness that sensationalism specializes in allowed antebellum readers to fantasize about their own outré forms of desire and enjoyment even as they denied that this link existed. Thus, although as Žižek argues, "*The hatred of the Other is the hatred of our own excess of enjoyment*" (*Tarrying* 206; emphasis in original), *reading* about the sensational Other is another matter altogether.[25] For what sensational reading provided is a kind of indirect access to the libidinal world of capitalist desire that is both anxious-making and, simultaneously, quite titillating. The many depictions of Jack gazing longingly at the giant's gold are in this sense ironically revealing reminders that the giant's obscene covetousness is in fact a mirror image of Jack's *own* excessive greed—greed that is of course linked to the youthful capitalist manhood that Jack, especially in American versions of the story, embodies. "If Jack was pleased at the sight of the silver, how much more delighted he felt when he saw such a heap of glittering gold!" we are told in *The Surprising History of Jack and the Bean Stalk* (19), a passage highlighted by a telling image of Jack peering over the giant's shoulder at a pile of coins (figure 8). This, I would suggest, is a somewhat embarrassing moment when the ideology of "theft" and stolen enjoyment gives way, and we receive a glimpse of the very excesses it is supposed to mask.

We should therefore understand that while the professional male of American sensationalism was seeking to deny his own relation to the desires and appetencies of the paper economy, he was at the same time involved in an often desperate effort to retrieve this very enjoyment back from the figures of Otherness who have stolen it away from him. This, of course, is one way to read Jack's return theft of the giant's stolen treasure in *Jack and the Beanstalk.* In the majority of the period's sensational texts, however, we see a different process at work, which revolves around the logic of compensation I am describing. For what antebellum sensationalism much more frequently provides is the fantasy of enjoyment retrieved, but also—via a version of the alchemy Denning describes—a fantasy of an enjoyment *purged of its more troubling relations to capitalist desire.* Indeed, though antebellum sensationalism is obsessed with figures of Otherness who embody capitalist desire, it

ed with new guineas, and the other with new
shillings.

They were both placed before the giant, who
began reprimanding his poor wife most severely
for staying so long; she replied, trembling with
fear, that they were so heavy that she could
scarcely lift them; and concluded at last, that
she would never again bring them down stairs;
adding that she had nearly fainted, owing to their
weight.

This so exasperated the giant, that he raised
his hand to strike her; she, however, escaped,
and went to bed, leaving him to count over his
treasure by way of amusement.

The giant took his bags, and, after turning
them over and over, to see that they were in the
same state he left them, began to count their contents. First, the bag which contained the silver
was emptied, and the contents placed upon the
table. Jack viewed the glittering heaps with de-

Figure 8 Image from *The Surprising History of Jack and the Bean Stalk*.
1842–45[?] published by Turner and Fisher. Reproduced with
permission of the American Antiquarian Society.

is just as obsessed with inventing narratives through which readers might see capitalist desire cleansed of its most troubling aspects, and thus returned to its male characters in safer—perhaps "laundered"—form. Put another way, antebellum sensationalism frequently repackages and defuses male desire in ways that make its link to capital difficult to see. This compensatory masculinity thus acts as an *alternative* to the form of manhood we might associate with an earlier, mercantilist period—regardless of whether this form of manhood ever existed. It is not, in other words, manhood directly linked to gold and treasure. Rather, knowing that treasure à la William Legrand's discovery in "The Gold-Bug" is unlikely, the sensational public sphere seeks to forge other, compensatory forms of currency and value—differing versions of a gold standard—for the professional men of the antebellum period. This, it seems to me, is the corollary to the fantasy of found treasure, and it is one of the primary fantasies driving the sensationalism of the antebellum period.

An example from one of the ensuing chapters might clarify what I am suggesting here. This is from chapter 2, "Shylock on Wall Street: The Jessica Complex in Antebellum Sensationalism." Here I show the compensatory logic at work within the many antebellum sensation narratives that reimagine the Shylock and Jessica story from Shakespeare's *The Merchant of Venice*. In particular I argue that the economic tensions that inhere in American versions of the Shylock character—his tendency to hoard and withhold, as though he has himself stolen the nation's missing gold bullion; his excessive and sometimes perverse forms of pleasure and desire—are perhaps most complex when played out in the many texts that reimagine the romantic life of his daughter. Distant cousins of the Jessica narrative, in which Shylock's daughter, having stolen her father's ducats and jewels, elopes with the Christian Lorenzo, these sensational stories recur throughout the period, and are important in two ways. First, they suggest a fantasy strategy by which the Gentile male might reappropriate the forms of economic potency and manhood that have been stolen and hoarded by the sensational Jew. Simultaneously, these updated Jessica stories provide a means of imagining how the otherwise problematic and alien forms of passion and desire housed in the Jew might be "converted," and smuggled back into the capitalist world of Gentile culture in less threatening form. Here, in other words, it is the figure of the Jew that fuels the compensatory logic I am describing. Streeby shows how sensational narratives about the U.S.–Mexican War and other mid-century imperial encounters, especially as produced in the urban northeast by writers such as Buntline, tapped into nativist sensibilities in order to appeal to a working-class audience. I show here how the language of anti-Semitism offered by Buntline and myriad other writers performed a similar form of "cultural work" in imagining the relationship during this period between professional manhood and the economic market.

As this example suggests, the sensational logic of masculine compensation cuts across a range of issues, and comes in a variety of packages. But in each case what we see emerging from the welter of material that comprises the sensational public sphere is a fairly specific logic whereby professional manhood is reimagined in terms of an altered relationship to desire. Over and over again sensationalism stages scenarios in which men are threatened by a figure of menacing Otherness (the Headless Horseman; creditors, etc.), *even as* these texts provide a titillating mix of readerly anxiety and pleasure. But, and somewhat surprisingly, the result is a narrative convention whereby we see the *conversion* of male desire. The goal, of course, is a conversion of paper money desire into a form of desire somehow associated with a gold standard—a bullionist desire in which value and desire are imagined as proximate. But in the chaotic world of sensationalism (to say nothing of the real world of antebellum America), this form of exchange isn't possible. Instead, the narratives of the sensational public sphere offer a form of fantasy compensation whereby the excess passions of the professional male are traded for categories of selfhood—Gentile; middle-class; white—that are themselves the new and improved markers of "success" and value in corporate America.

But even this is uncertain. For, and as I show in several of the ensuing chapters, some texts suggest that fantasy compensation is either difficult to achieve, or unavailable entirely. The result in such cases is a sort of narrative crisis, where we see the ideological strain that fantasy resolution actually requires. The most famous such example is Herman Melville's "Bartleby, the Scrivener: A Story of Wall-Street" (1853), which I discuss in the epilogue to this study. Here, the unnamed attorney's narration reflects a kind of desperate effort to retrieve from his enigmatic clerk some portion of his own lost enjoyment, and to thus rewrite his uneasy sense of Wall Street manhood. But Bartleby, of course, is a figure of alterity more radical even than the capitalist Jew, and what we see is that he is in fact resistant to any form of fantasy closure. And yet this sort of text is, I will argue, just as interesting and just as important as those that provide what we might think of as "successful" forms of compensatory fiction. Indeed, the fact that sensationalism of the sort I am describing is uneven and contradictory is simply to be expected. Less a coherent aesthetic space than an amalgam of materials that addressed the sorts of issues—professional manhood, commerce, desire—that I have been describing, the sensational public sphere was not ideologically consistent.

The other chapters of this study take up a similar line of analysis. In chapter 1, I read Washington Irving's "The Legend of Sleepy Hollow" and a range of other stories, novels, and plays from the 1819 period in the context of the Panic of 1819. Arguing first that the chronically nervous and highly gullible Crane is an early embodiment of sensational paper-money manhood (especially given his desire to sell off the Van Tassel estate for cash in order to invest in speculative ventures on western lands), I argue further that the ghostly figure of the Headless Horseman embodies the felt theft of masculine wholeness and potency experienced by American men in the 1819 era. Following my discussion of Americanized versions of the Shylock–Jessica narrative in chapter 2, I turn in chapter 3 to the role of emotion in the negotiation of a capitalist male selfhood. Looking at a range of urban sensation produced in the wake of the 1837 Panic (*The Quaker City* in particular), I show how this material repeatedly seeks to transform the crisis of excessive masculine expenditure into problems of masculine emotion and self-management. Affect and humiliation, that is to say, become in the urban narrative (especially the urban gothic) a new and compensatory form of male "specie," one that brings with it the cultural prestige of a sentimentalized and recognizably middle-class manhood.

I pursue a related narrative about masculine anxiety in chapter 4, with a discussion of the 1836 penny press news coverage of the Jewett murder, which I describe above. Focusing in particular on the obsessive coverage of the murder in James Gordon Bennett Jr.'s New York *Herald*, I suggest that the prostitute Jewett acted for Bennett as a figure of sensational Otherness and "theft" much like the Headless Horseman, the Jew, or the paper money con man, in particular as she came to embody the period's frightening paper economy. But I suggest as well that the murderer Robinson acted as a kind of male proxy for Bennett in his imagined efforts to "retrieve" the very manhood that she has stolen, a fact that complicates his depictions of the murder considerably. Nor, I argue, is Bennett's an isolated representational strategy. As I show in a concluding section of this chapter, Nathaniel Hawthorne's *The Blithedale Romance* (1852) stages a similar form of market allegory, in which female characters such as Priscilla (especially as the Veiled Lady) and Zenobia act as overwhelming and at times monstrous versions of the speculative economy for many of the novel's male characters.

I continue my examination of Hawthorne in chapter 5, as I look at a sensational subgenre I refer to as the "bank romance." Reading Hawthorne's *The House of the Seven Gables* (1851) alongside urban Wall Street novels such as by J. B. Jones's *The City Merchant; or the Mysterious Failure* (1851), I suggest that the sensational black body so frequently deployed within this material acts as a site onto which to project fears about the capitalist male, and thus about economic failure. Here, in other words, the black male plays the role performed by the Jew and other figures of Otherness in antebellum sensationalism; simultaneously, the category of whiteness comes to act as a kind of compensatory gold standard for masculine selfhood. But I show as well how sensational narratives that promise fantasy forms of whiteness also reveal the blurred edges at the boundaries of such racial categories. For just as the gold standard is in truth illusory—an agreed-upon fiction—so too is the sensational fantasy of whiteness a cultural myth, one writers such as Hawthorne seem to both believe in and undermine in their fictions.

As this overview suggests, it is the attempt to render the excesses of capital somehow comprehensible that is really the key mark of sensationalism as I understand it. Sensationalism—especially the material offered within the sensational public sphere—acted as a key fantasy space for members of the professional classes in antebellum America. Indeed, I would suggest that, as a whole, sensationalism does work fairly similar to that of fairy tales such as *Jack and the Beanstalk*. Here again I turn to Denning's provocative comparisons of working-class dime-novel narratives to fairy tales such as *Cinderella*. Suggesting that the "magical transformation" often offered within these stories (from working girl to heiress, for example) responds to the "powerlessness" of working men and women, Denning argues that such forms of "wish-fulfillment" offer a "utopian vision of reorganized society" (*Mechanic* 195–96). The sensationalism I am describing, while targeting a different demographic than Denning's working-class material, is also committed to strategies of wish fulfillment and fantasy resolution as a means of redressing a pervasive sense of social powerlessness. We are not here in the realm of the "liberating magic" Walter Benjamin ascribes to the fairy tale (*Illuminations* 102), but it may be that we are close to the qualities Ernst Bloch suggests when he says that they provide "an immature, but honest substitution for revolution" (*Hope* 368). The tales within the sensational public sphere are often similarly immature, but they also offer a similar form of alternative to social upheaval. What they offer is compensation. Return payment for a felt sense of loss, sensationalism helps imagine an adaptive selfhood, one "reorganized" to confront the troubling realities of life in mid-nineteenth-century America. In this, sensationalism acknowledges that, as Sandage puts it, "the only identity deemed legitimate in America is a capitalist identity" (*Losers* 5). But, I argue, it also allows its consumers to envision an imaginary resolution to the problem of masculine failure so pervasive under the sign of capitalist identity.

This compensatory logic is why the oft-staged fantasy glimpse of America's fiscal primal scene—the embrace of men and treasure—is so important and so interesting. For it reminds us of America's very deep-seated and libidinal relationship with the economic system of capitalism, and the role that sensationalism played in representing and negotiating this relationship. Like a primal scene, antebellum sensationalism often provides us with a discomfiting glimpse of our economic origins—a glimpse, that is to say, of the origins of a selfhood based on the market-inflected ideologies of "success" and "failure." The ensuing chapters will focus on the logic of compensation I am describing here, but it is worth reiterating that this logic stems directly from these primary fantasies about treasure and male selfhood. Indeed, while, in a fantasy of masculine ascension, most nineteenth-century American versions of *Jack and the Beanstalk* imagine Jack and his mother living "happily ever after" following the death of the giant, the sensationalism of this period reflects the knowledge that the modern, paper money male must resort to alternative narratives of male success. This book examines some of the more prevalent versions of these alternatives. Fantasies in their own right, they militate against the specter of economic failure—something every bit as terrifying as the giant that Jack is able in his great luck to slay.

"Sleepy Hollow," Gothic Masculinity, and The Panic of 1819

[L]egerdemain tricks upon paper can produce as solid wealth as hard labor in the earth, [making it impossible] to reason Bedlam to rights.

—Thomas Jefferson, Letter to Charles Yancy, 1-6-1816

So that when we see a wise people, embracing phantoms for realities, and running mad, as it were, in schemes of refinement, taste, pleasures, wealth and power, by the sole aid of this civil *hocus pocus;* when we contemplate paper gold, and paper land, paper armies and revenues; a paper government and a paper legislature; we are apt to regard the Fairy Tales, the Travels of Gulliver, and the Arabian Nights Entertainment, as grave relations, and historical facts. . . . We have heard of the Golden, Silver, and Iron ages of the poets; the present, to mark its frivolity, may be called the *Paper Age.*

—*Niles Weekly Register*, 1819

Humiliation and Horror

Like vast numbers of his contemporaries, the Washington Irving of *The Sketch Book* era (1817–19) was haunted by the twin specters of credit and debt. "Various circumstances have concurred to render me very nervous and subject to fits of depression," he wrote to his close friend Henry Brevoort in 1819 about the "humiliating alternative" of bankruptcy after the family business which he and his brothers ran collapsed under the weight of over-extended credit. "My mode of life has unfortunately been such as to render me unfit for almost any useful purpose. I have not the kind of knowledge or the habits that are necessary for business" (*Letters* I: 549–50; 516). Sounding a similar note of unease in an earlier letter, Irving writes, "I would not again experience the anxious days and sleepless nights which have been my lot since I have taken hold of business to possess the wealth of Croesus" (432). It was a theme he returned to repeatedly in the years leading up to the financial stability that would come with the publication of *The Sketch Book* in 1819. Irving famously contends that his literary career—and *The Sketch Book* in particular—acted as compensation for such anxiety and humiliation, allowing him his only chance of "acquiring real reputation" (550). But *The Sketch Book* also acts as a crucial barometer for understanding the increasingly "nervous" and "anxious" form of masculinity emerging in the period leading up to and following the devastating financial Panic of 1819, the first widespread financial crisis in American history and a watershed moment in the nation's growing awareness of its own complex and often uneasy relationship to commerce. Critics and biographers have demonstrated that Irving was himself Federalist in orientation during this period, and he is clearly seeking throughout *The Sketch Book* to provide a kind of lament for a lost era of what Linda Kerber refers to as "statesmanship of the highest order," one embodied in George Washington and one said by Federalists to have vanished with Jefferson's election in 1800 (*Federalists* vii). Even more specifically, however, we might read *The Sketch Book* as reflecting a nostalgic longing for a period predating the modern period of commerce and credit, one that found an anxious Irving financially embarrassed and decidedly out of place.

This is particularly true of the most anxiety-laden text within *The Sketch Book,* "The Legend of Sleepy Hollow." Organized around the overtly gendered humiliation suffered at story's end by the mercurial Ichabod Crane, "Sleepy Hollow" depicts in Ichabod a new form of masculinity as it was taking shape in the 1819 period, one that Irving and many others saw as the direct manifestation of the perceived trauma brought about by the shift from a mercantilist to a paper economy. Writing about the shift in eighteenth-century England toward a credit-based, paper economy, J. G. A. Pocock suggests that since property was during this period "acknowledged as the social basis of personality, the emergence of classes whose property consisted not of lands or goods or even bullion, but of paper promises to repay in an undefined future, was seen as entailing the emergence of new types of personality, unprecedentedly dangerous and unstable." Entire nations, he continues, "seemed to have been placed at the mercy of passion, fantasy, and appetite. . . . It was the hysteria, not the cold rationality, of economic man that dismayed the moralists" (*Virtue* 235; 112–13). The form of masculinity embodied in the property-less and emotionally mercurial Ichabod—whose plan is to marry the landed heiress Katrina Van Tassel and then sell off the estate for cash, apparently for investment in speculative ventures on western lands and "shingle palaces in the wilderness"—does much to capture an early American variant on the new form of selfhood Pocock describes (*SB* 280). Ichabod, that is to say, represents the mindset of commerce. Romantic desire for him is inextricable from economic desire and a market-oriented form of "imagination."

Jennifer Baker provocatively suggests that the propensity for imaginative dreaming we see in Irving characters such as Ichabod and Rip Van Winkle reflects what is actually a laudable form of speculation (both artistic and financial). Performing "acts of masculine daring" quite unlike the "conformity and risk aversion" we see in female characters such as Dame Van Winkle and the Old Dutch Wives of Sleepy Hollow, these men are, she argues, dreamers who are in fact charting the path of future growth and prosperity for their communities and the nation more generally (*Securing* 161; 162). Indeed, in Baker's view, early American writers as varied as Cotton Mather, Benjamin Franklin, Charles Brockden Brown, Judith Sargent Murray, and Irving were performing a "civic function" by imagining the positive potential of credit and speculation (17). But, at least as it applies to Irving and the 1819 period with which Baker concludes her study, this argument is difficult to square with the obvious fact that Ichabod is in his dreaming so easily duped and humiliated, especially by Brom Bones in his imposture as the ghostly Headless Horseman. I will thus be suggesting instead that Ichabod is a figure for the many thousands of American men who, "embracing phantoms for realities" in the manner described in the above quote from *Niles Weekly Register,* were *deceived* by the fantastical nature of the period's economy, and suffered thereby a psychological trauma that sensational literature spent the next forty years addressing. Much as with Ichabod when he learns that the monstrous apparition that assaults him is merely the local prankster Brom Bones, these investors were left in the 1819 period with the realization that they had invested in an apparition—a "civil *hocus pocus*"—whose value was sustainable only as long as everyone believed in it.

The rhetorical links between the ghostly world of the gothic and an apparitional paper economy were captured as early as 1786, in Thomas Paine's observation that "paper money issued by an assembly *as* money . . . is like putting an apparition in the place of a man; it vanishes with looking at it, and nothing remains but the air" ("Dissertations" 176). Striking a note of concern similar to that expressed in the above *Weekly Register* quote about a "wise people, embracing [economic] phantoms for realities," Paine voices the fear that the paper economy was turning the self-possessed individual into a substanceless and thus possibly ghostly being. A related scenario is offered in a satiric 1808 lithograph titled *The Ghost of a Dollar, or the Bankers* [sic] *Surprize* (figure 9). Here the powerful Philadelphia merchant Stephen Girard (described as "Stephen Graspall, Banker and Shaver") is represented as mesmerized by the ghostly image of an 1806 Spanish dollar hovering in front of him. According to Girard, "If thou art a real dollar do drop in my

Figure 9 *The Ghost of a Dollar, or the Bankers* [sic] *Surprize.*
1808 by W. Charles Del et Sculp. Etching on wove paper; 37.8 x 26.7 cm.
Reproduced with permission of the American Antiquarian Society.

till and let me hear thee chink. As I have been sued for repayment of part of my notes in Specie I must collect some to pay them for quietness sake or the game would be up at once." On one level the joke here is that the gold bullion "Graspall" sees hovering before him is as illusory as the notes he has been circulating. But on another and perhaps more serious level, the lithograph suggests that Girard, famous for speculations in the Caribbean and later a leading backer of the Second Bank of the United States, is haunted by a kind of return of the repressed, one that forces him to confront the illusory nature of his own sense of fiscal and material self-possession. Irving extends images such as *The Ghost of a Dollar* by making the paper economy overtly horrific: embodied in the specter of the Headless Horseman, modern, credit-based commerce confronts Ichabod with the terrifying implications of the increasingly alienable form of male selfhood emerging in the 1819 period.

One part of my argument in this chapter is thus that Ichabod acts as the embodiment of a "gothic" form of literary manhood emerging in relation to the new economy. As critics have demonstrated, the gothic fiction of writers such as Ann Radcliffe, Charles Brockden Brown, and others during this period often reflects what Andrea Henderson terms a "market-based model of identity" (*Romantic* 39). Built up on the radical contingencies of modern social and market relations rather than the stable foundations of rank or property, this gothic selfhood embodies not only the breakdown in distinctions between an interior, feeling subject and a superficial social self, but also, like the commodity form itself, the increasingly attenuated distinction between use value and exchange value in a commercial economy. As Teresa Goddu puts it in language that echoes Paine's, "The commercial man, who in manipulating money seemingly fashions himself out of nothing, is an apparition" (*Gothic* 34). Such analyses are especially useful in examining the contestation over manhood we see enacted in "Sleepy Hollow." For as I will suggest, the central drama—the encounter between Ichabod and the apparitional Headless Horseman—revolves around crises of property relations, social rank, and, most strikingly, gender. And as I will also suggest, this drama offers a crucial touchstone in the literary representation of paper money manhood in mid-nineteenth-century America. Indeed, in Ichabod we see the seeds of a variety of sensational characters, both "gothic" and otherwise. Poe's William Legrand, Stowe's Mr. Shelby, Melville's attorney-narrator of "Bartleby": these and a host of lesser-known (and unknown) characters are Ichabod's sensational descendants, something most evident as we see their anxious efforts to negotiate the vexed terrain of the antebellum paper economy. In this sense the distinction between the gothic and other sensational genres is a false one, for what we see staged throughout virtually all of the sensational public sphere is exactly the "market based model of identity" in which the gothic so specializes. The early gothic according to Irving is, that is to say, a useful primer for reading the various later strands of American sensationalism.

The other part of my argument here is therefore that the mysterious and terrifying Headless Horseman acts as a similarly key figure in the early history of the period's sensationalism. Indeed, the Headless Horseman has specific resonance for the sensational narratives about professional American manhood that would emerge for the next thirty-five years or so (or up until the Panic of 1857 and the publication of Melville's *The Confidence Man*). Indeed, the Headless Horseman is perhaps *the* central figure of gothic or sensational Otherness in American literature, so much so that he has taken on a fairy-tale-like quality not unlike the giant in *Jack and the Beanstalk* (whom I discuss in the introduction). Hence the many filmic remakes of this narrative, including the Disney cartoon versions from the 1940s and 1950s, and Tim Burton's more recent adaptations (one of which, *Edward Scissorhands*, I discuss in a short coda to this chapter). For while the Headless Horseman is, as I will suggest, a terrifying figure out of Ichabod's unconscious, he is also a similarly frightening figure out of an *American* unconscious, especially as this psychological space has developed under capitalism. And one place to start in interpreting the Horseman is to view him as a figure of stolen enjoyment, one similar to the sensational figure of the Jew invoked by Žižek. Indeed, as the "dominant spirit" of the "enchanted region" of Sleepy Hollow (*SB* 273), as well as the chief subject of local folklore and gossip, the Headless Horseman seems to have access to a sort of secret code or logic—perhaps a way of life—so elusive to Ichabod, especially in his role as foreign interloper into Sleepy Hollow. This might, in fact, explain Ichabod's "fearful pleasure" in hearing stories about the Horseman while passing "long winter evenings with the old Dutch wives" (277): hurtling through the night, immensely powerful but also elusive and mysterious, the Horseman gives shape to the ghostly, apparitional world that, as speculative dreamer, Ichabod longs to access. And perhaps this goes for an American audience as well, knowing as it does that Sleepy Hollow is a prelapsarian dream space to which it cannot return except in fantasy narratives such as Irving's.

But as a figure that is as much a part of Ichabod's (or our) unconscious as he is a "real" being (Brom Bones or otherwise), the Headless Horseman is also a figure of the uncanny, one who registers for Ichabod precisely to the extent that he mirrors his own repressed sense of fiscal disempowerment and impotence. Indeed, forever conducting a nightly "quest of his head" (273), the Horseman is in many ways a figure of frustration, failure, and—ultimately—castration.[1] As critics have pointed out, the Horseman is *himself* an outsider in Sleepy Hollow, having come to the valley as part of a force of

Hessian troopers seeking to win Sleepy Hollow for the British army. From this perspective the Horseman is a kind of double for Ichabod, a ghostly figure who is no more at home in Sleepy Hollow than the story's hapless protagonist. We might thus say that the horror Ichabod experiences in his encounter with the Headless Horseman has to do with his repressed knowledge that, as Žižek puts it in discussing the logic that drives the ideology of the theft of enjoyment, *"we never possessed what was allegedly stolen from us: the lack (castration) is originary"* (*Tarrying* 203; emphasis in original). The Horseman is, in other words, a projected figure of loss and dissatisfaction. And in this he is the projected image of capitalist passion itself, returning in unrecognized form to haunt Ichabod, and to remind him of the excesses within *himself* as a subject under the emergent paper economy. But this, of course, is what Ichabod cannot see, any more than the American public can see this as a key reason for its continuing fascination with this story. Instead, the Headless Horseman is simply an external image of Otherness, one that haunts Ichabod with the knowledge that he has lost a precious part of himself, and isn't likely to get it back.

Certainly the gothic link between the period's paper economy and a dispossessed, anxious masculinity is something that appears elsewhere in Irving's fiction. A fairly overt example is "The Devil and Tom Walker," another story from the "Money Diggers" sequence in *Tales of a Traveller* that revolves around the search for Captain Kidd's long-rumored store of buried treasure (I discuss "The Golden Dreams of Wolfert Webber" in the introduction). The narrative relates the bargain that Tom Walker makes with the Devil in exchange for the location of Kidd's gold. Hounded by a greedy wife whom Irving depicts as far more castrating even than the famously shrewish Dame Winkle, Walker eventually agrees both to the sale of his soul and to a new profession as a moneylender. According to the story's narrator, Diedrich Knickerbocker, "It was a time of paper credit. The country had been deluged with government bills; the famous Land Bank had been established; there had been a rage for speculating; the people had run mad with schemes for new settlements; for building cities in the wilderness; land jobbers went about with maps of . . . Eldorados, lying nobody knew where, but which everybody was ready to purchase. . . . As usual the fever had subsided; the dream had gone off, and the imaginary fortunes with it; the patients were left in doleful plight, and the whole country resounded with the consequent cry of 'hard times'" (*TT* 223). In this story Walker takes great pleasure in the abject postures of his many debtors. "In proportion to the distress of the applicant was the hardness of his terms," we are told (224). But in the end the increasingly "anxious" protagonist is himself carried off by a Satanic figure dubbed "the black man" (224; 225). In a scene strongly echoing Ichabod's persecution by the Headless Horseman, Walker is thrown "like a child into the saddle" and whisked away "on a horse that galloped like mad across the fields" (225). More telling still, we are told that the "gold and silver" that once filled Tom Walker's chest is transformed into "chips and shavings" (226). Here as elsewhere in America, gold suffers a kind of negative alchemy, transforming into paper and leaving only masculine humiliation and panic in its wake.

But whereas in 1824 Irving was able to clearly vilify a character such as Tom Walker ("[l]et all griping money brokers lay this story to heart," we are instructed [226]), his 1819 treatment of Ichabod Crane is considerably more vexed, perhaps even ambivalent. And a primary reason for this may well be that during this period Irving himself was still immersed in financial difficulties that would find resolution only with the eventual success of *The Sketch Book*. Representing both the predatory threat of speculation and the often manipulative effeminacy associated with the new professional classes (his is the "labor of headwork," we are told [*SB* 276]), Ichabod embodies the vexed nature of manhood as it was evolving—both for Irving and for America more generally—under the sign of the unstable paper economy in and around 1819. Based on trauma and loss, this new personality reflects a widespread understanding that, by 1819 in America, accounts cannot be balanced, and a return to a site of Edenic wholeness such as Sleepy Hollow is impossible. Indeed, what Irving stages here is the crisis that will haunt U.S. sensationalism in the decades following publication of *The Sketch Book*, as we see characters such as William Legrand seek either treasure or, more often, alternative forms of value and compensation for the sense of loss inherent in the new capitalism.

But in Sleepy Hollow (and the story of the same name), compensation is hard to come by. Here, in other words, I am tracing the literary antecedent to the sensational public sphere and its logic of compensatory manhood. The nervous male subject we see in "Sleepy Hollow" reveals in mirrored form the sensational, or even "gothic," nature of masculinity as Irving (and thousands of men like him) was experiencing it in the everyday world of 1819 America. Fantasies of recuperation would have to wait.

"GONE DISTRACTED": THE PANIC OF 1819

The Panic of 1819 marked the close of a three-year-long economic boom that had followed the end of war with England in 1815. As Europe unloaded its stockpile of goods into American markets at discount rates and paid high prices for American products, entrepreneurs found seemingly limit-less opportunities for growth and investment. Simultaneously, federal land sales increased from approximately five hundred thousand acres in 1813 to almost four million in 1818, a boom enhanced by new steamboat tech-nology that allowed for the increasingly widespread sales of market goods from abroad and for the transportation of cotton to market centers. But as Charles Sellers puts it, soon "[s]olid prosperity was turned into specula-tive saturnalia [as] [g]littering investment opportunities created insatiable demands for capital. Chronically short of capital, venturesome Americans knew how to manufacture the next best thing, credit, through the marvelous device of banking" (*Market* 132). The result was an unprecedented increase in the production both of bank charters and banknotes. From 1815 to 1818, for example, the number of state-chartered banks nearly doubled, increas-ing from 200 to 392. The problem, however, was that frequently these new state banks were not backed by actual capital. Instead, they specialized in transactions based on intangible, "paper" forms of value such as banknotes and corporate stocks. These same state banks, having suspended specie pay-ments during the war, tended to persist in the practice of refusing specie payment "on demand." Extending ever greater amounts of paper currency into the market, these banks were able to earn considerable interest—usu-ally from twelve to twenty percent—on notes backed by very little actual hard currency (132–34).

The difficulty of attaining actual specie (and thus a reliable form of monetary value) from state banks is satirized usefully in *The History of a Little Frenchman and his Bank Notes. "Rags, Rags, Rags!"* (Sanderson 1815), a short pamphlet narrative depicting the travails of a French traveler who has exchanged his $8,000 in gold for paper notes from a Georgia bank, only to find that he cannot redeem them again for anything but increasingly devalued paper notes. "The funds of the bank—le diable est aux vaches!" he exclaims to his American friend. "[H]ave you not told me they have no funds but paper rags, and consequently cannot pay any else[?] In what do their funds consist?" (10). The American's response is to the point: "[M]onsieur, the basis of all this enormous issue of paper bank notes, is only paper notes of hand. The man that happens to be in possession of the rags, as you are pleased to call them . . . will go to the bank and demand payment, [and] they will give him the choice of rags belonging to other banks, but no money" (11). What the French traveler learns, in other words, is that in shifting away from strict adherence to a "gold standard" of specie convertibility (or what the "Citizen of Pennsylvania" refers to in an 1816 pamphlet as "the *Bankometer*" [*Examination* 7]), the U.S. economy had become dependent

on a fiscal system that was itself floating on the airy promises of future profits rather than a dependable system of value rooted in "hard money" and
labor.

In a vitriolic response to *The History of the Little Frenchman* and other
antibank treatises (*Little Frenchman* went through numerous reprintings
from 1815 to 1819 and was apparently quite popular), Thomas Law com-
plained in *The Financiers* [sic] *A, B, C, Respecting Currency* (1819) that
"[B]ullionists denominate the advocates for a national [paper] currency
crackbrained chimerists and selfish speculators, and with a parrot's perti-
nacity, cry out rags! rags! rags! or, sometimes changing their notes, exclaim,
specie! solid stuff! ready rhino! When asked how it is to come, they are
silent, or argue . . . that ten millions of dollars will answer all the purposes
of an [sic] hundred million" (8).[2] But as it became obvious that many of
the nation's economic woes were the direct result of fiscal recklessness and,
more often than not, actual corruption, such defenses of the paper money
system were increasingly hard to support. As Hezikiah Niles put it in his
newspaper, *Niles Weekly Register* (generally regarded as the most informed
publication on economic matters during the period), "Paper—credit—a
directorship or a cashiership in a bank, or a father, brother, cousin or friend,
who was a director, or a cashier, was the test of respectability! Sign away,
was the word—and it was generally calculated that one debt might be paid
by the creation of another! The people were wild—they acted as if a day of
reckoning never would come" (*NWR* 6-12-1819).

The bitterness and cynicism marking such texts was especially evident
in discussions centering on the role of the Second Bank of the United States
in regulating the economy. Chartered in 1816 by "New School" National
Republicans eager to reverse Republican tradition and take up an entrepreneurial posture that backed expansion and manufacturing, the U.S. Bank
cashed in on the boom by overextending its own loan line, especially in
western banks. Soon the Bank had so many of its own notes in circulation
that it was unable to force state banks to make specie payments without
having to do the same itself. This contradiction was assailed by numerous
critics who saw the Bank as an institution created primarily for the benefit of the wealthy. As the anonymous "Brutus" put it in William Duane's
staunchly "Old School" Philadelphia *Aurora*, the Bank's directors were a
"cabal" of self-interested "stock-jobbers" whose greed echoed the decadence
and luxury of European nobles. "[T]heir object was *speculation* from the
outset," he argues. "[T]hey had subscribed for stock beyond their means,
and to pay for it, it was necessary to enhance its value to a *bubble;* the bank
charter was purposely contrived for *speculation;* and the men suited to the
purpose, were placed upon the ticket, who of course composed a majority

of *brokers, shavers,* and *speculators*" (*Aurora* 1-24-1818). Similar sentiments were voiced in Old School Republican newspapers throughout the eastern part of the country, such as the New York *National Advocate,* Philadelphia's *Democratic Press,* Richmond's *Enquirer,* and Baltimore's *Weekly Register,* each of which voiced distrust both of the Bank and the newer, more entrepreneurial, elements of the Republican party that had created it. The liveliest and most incisive of these papers was the *Niles Weekly Register.* For example, commenting on the Bank's incorporation, Niles wrote with characteristic scorn that "Sundry projects were set on foot to remedy or restrain the 'paper system' until at last we had the bank of the United States *incorporated.* This was to do everything—to restore the golden age, and strew the highways with silver dollars. . . . [B]ut in regard to its own internal construction, it was soon discovered that it had mightily increased the amount of ideal money— that its stock, which was to have been composed of the precious metals and national securities, was in a great degree *paid* by promises to *pay*—that it had introduced a new system of gambling to demoralize and defraud the people" (*NWR* 7-17-1819; emphasis in original).

Federalist publications, dismayed by the challenge to more traditional forms of landed aristocratic authority, took similar stances against the Bank and the new paper economy and thus found themselves in unexpected alliance with Old School Republicans.[3] This was often reflected in longtime party affiliates such as the *Columbian Centinal* in Massachusetts (perhaps the country's leading Federalist paper), but a mixture of outrage and anxiety was especially evident in upstate New York papers such as the *Northern Whig,* the *American,* and the *Independent American.* The *American* is particularly representative of such postures. Started in 1819 in an effort to unseat New York's Republican Governor DeWitt Clinton and to "purify" the Federalist party, the *American* made it clear that one of its main concerns was quick-fix "paper" solutions to the country's financial crisis. For example, deriding the suggestion put forth by the Kentucky legislature to allow banks to suspend both specie payments and "calls" for debts, the editors warned that "[a]ny wild schemes of experimental finance, however pernicious, will find advocates among . . . [l]and speculators, negro speculators, and all kinds of speculators, who bought at high prices, [and who] must lose." The key to fiscal safety, they urged, was to "avoid the evils of a legalized paper currency" (*American* 6-9-1819). New York's *Independent American* was even clearer in detailing the way in which a paper currency was artificially sustained by banks. As the editors put it in an 1818 editorial, "[T]he present circulation in the state principally consists of the notes of those banks whose nominal capitals are small, and composed principally of the notes of the individual stockholders called stock notes; so that the security of the public consists of the private fortunes of individual stock-holders, and those fortunes, in a great measure, consist of the stock, for which they have given their notes; so that the bank is enriched by holding their notes, and they are enriched by holding the stock of the bank. And as these banks make large dividends, many rapid, and what are considered solid fortunes are made" (*Independent* 4-1-1818). Echoing Republican complaints voiced in the *Aurora,* the *Weekly Register,* and elsewhere, such commentaries reflect the growing awareness that, rather than provide stability, the U.S. Bank had added to a precarious and absurdly circular situation: any bank pressed for specie would be forced to demand repayment from debtors, most of whom were unable to pay except in notes held on banks that had no specie reserves.

Such precariousness was also captured in popular responses to the failing economy, many of which represented financial collapse in terms of a crisis of manhood. A good example is offered in Vermilye Taylor's *The Banker; or Things as they have been!* (1819), a three-act farce that thematizes the 1819 Panic. Here an honest man named Heartwell finds himself destitute when his banker refuses specie payment on the $5,000 he holds in the bank's bills. "After speculating for years upon the industrious and laborious class of the people," the banker says, "I must give the finishing stroke, by plunging those very men, who have trusted to my honour and promises, into misery and want. . . . [B]ut, as I did not compel them to receive my bills, they shall not compel me to redeem them—unless in *promises!*" (1). The problem for Heartwell is exacerbated by the fact that the scheming broker Shaveall, having gotten wind of his financial problems, now refuses to allow Heartwell to marry his daughter, Emily. Instead, Shaveall plans to marry Emily off to a monied dandy named Tim Shallow. As he puts it in a brief soliloquy, "[T]o speak the truth, I believe [Heartwell] has more the appearance of a *man,* than that fellow Shallow, with his corsetts [*sic*] and meal-sack pantaloons—but, egad! he has another appendage, which Heartwell . . . is in danger of losing—that is, a *full purse*" (7). Equating a man's "appendage"/phallus with the possession of actual specie ("a full purse"), Shaveall operates according to a logic in which masculinity is intimately tied to the economic market. Unable to convert his paper notes into material capital, Heartwell finds himself disabled—and symbolically castrated—on the market of gender and romance.

A similar if more fraught narrative is offered in Thomas Holcroft's *The Road to Ruin,* a popular five-act production performed in Philadelphia and New York in 1819. Much as with Taylor's *The Banker,* the play centers around the impending collapse of the "great banking house" Thornton and Co. as a result of the debts brought on by the firm's profligate junior partner—also the wayward son of the firm's owner and namesake. "Nothing less than a miracle can save the house," the young Thornton is told. "The purse of Fortunatas could not supply you." The young man's response amounts to a cynical rejection of a bullionist economy: "No. It held nothing but guineas. Notes, bills, papers for me!" (13). But in what follows, we see Thornton's repentant son trying to save his father's financial house by marrying a rich and much older widow well known for her utter lack of morals (or beauty). "I want an old mistress, with her old gold," explains the reformed son (60), a line he expands on with the following proclamation to the widow: "Thou hast bought and paid for me, and I am thine: by fair and honest traffic thine" (64). The humiliation and submission the young Thornton seeks to embrace here is telling, for it suggests that "old gold" is attainable only if accompanied by such postures of emasculation. (Similarly, in an 1821 novel by Thomas Gaspey titled *Calthorpe; or, Fallen Fortunes*—set in London but published and sold in Philadelphia—the dishonest and eventually bankrupted proprietor of a financial house dubbed "Messrs. Export and Riskall" continually has his manhood challenged by his one-eyed and overtly castrating wife, whom he sarcastically refers to as "the female Cyclops" [33]. The misogyny here is clear, but so too is the link between speculation and a disempowered form of masculinity).

Perhaps not surprisingly, given the fairly radical nature of young Thornton's masculine humiliation, "The Road to Ruin" concludes with the wayward junior partner narrowly averting a life as male concubine. Just before the wedding ceremony it is discovered that the widow is in league with a Jewish usurer named Silky, who is in possession of a missing will left by the widow's husband, one that forbids her to remarry on pain of losing her inheritance; simultaneously, the elder Thornton obtains loans sufficient to save his banking house. The marriage is called off, father and son are rejoined, and the climate of economic crisis is provided a highly sentimentalized solution. Yet while, once again, the period's fiscal woes are here displaced onto the convenient figure of the Jew ("Bait [Satan's] trap with a bit of guinea, and he is sure to find you nibbling," one character says to the usurer, one of many lines that imply that Silky has hoarded the majority of the economy's missing bullion; [49]), the postures of masculine anxiety and submission the play has foregrounded cannot be so easily forgotten. Indeed, the eventual plot resolution hinges on the son's very willing emasculation, and one senses in this play and in the period's culture more generally an anxiety that such postures were beginning to seem unavoidable, regardless of one's rank or station.

Indeed, by early 1819 the dire predictions of anti-Bank fiscal doomsayers had proved painfully accurate.[4] With the last of its specie reserves being drained away, the U.S. Bank began calling in its loans to state banks, requiring each branch to redeem its own notes. By this time the Bank had reduced its loans from $22 million to $10 million, and its circulating notes from $10 million to $3 million; simultaneously, the Bank increased its specie reserves from $2.5 million to $8 million. The process saved the Bank, but state banks and their debtors were hit particularly hard, especially after a collapse of commodity prices in Europe (*Market* 134–35). The result was the Panic of 1819, the first market collapse far-reaching enough to cause devastation on a widespread scale. Almost overnight, businesses failed, property prices plummeted, and paper notes became devalued to the point of worthlessness; simultaneously, unemployment soared, and homelessness became acute. As John Quincy Adams put it in 1820, "There has been within these two years an immense revolution of fortunes in every part of the Union; enormous numbers of persons utterly ruined; multitudes in deep distress; and a general mass of disaffection to the government" (*Memoirs* 5: 128). The crisis Adams describes is captured in particularly telling ways by his depiction of General Samuel Smith, co-owner of the leading commercial house in Baltimore (itself the national center for the speculative market and the target of almost daily editorials in the *Weekly Register*). Described by Adams as "[g]one distracted" and "dangerously ill in bed," Smith—much like the "nervous" Irving poised on the brink of bankruptcy, or like the hapless protagonists of "The Banker" or "The Road to Ruin"—embodies the distressed form of masculinity emerging within an increasingly unstable paper economy (*Memoirs* 4: 382). In search of "old gold" of the sort invoked by the younger Thornton in Holcroft's "The Road to Ruin," the nation's men were finding instead that their very manhood had been stolen by the specterlike new economy. This is the drama that Irving addresses in his famous short story about the hapless Ichabod Crane.

NOSTALGIA AND COMMERCE IN *THE SKETCH BOOK*

In "Sleepy Hollow," Irving's concern about the caprices of the period's economy is first evident in the depiction we receive of Sleepy Hollow itself, a small valley seemingly insulated against the rapid advances of the economic market. Located some two miles from a "rural port" commonly known by the appellation "Tarry Town" for the tendency of its men to "linger about the tavern on market days," Sleepy Hollow is described approvingly by Knickerbocker as "one of the quietest places in the world." As he explains, "[I]t is in such little retired Dutch valleys, found here and there embosomed in the great State of New York, that population, manners, and customs remain

fixed; while the great torrent of migration and improvement, which is making such incessant changes in other parts of this restless country, sweeps by
them unobserved" (*SB* 274). Within Sleepy Hollow itself, the heart of this
"fixed" stability is the large estate owned by "a thriving, contented, liberal-
hearted farmer" named Baltus Van Tassel (278). With a barn "every window
and crevice of which seemed bursting forth with the treasures of the farm"
and a farmhouse depicted in terms that suggest the sumptuous display of
a seventeenth-century Dutch still-life painting (279–80), Van Tassel's land
seems to be a virtual Eden of agrarian abundance, one that, like the specie-
sensitive "Bankometer" referenced by the "Citizen of Pennsylvania," is an
entity by which the forces outside of Sleepy Hollow might be measured in
their various degrees of market-based corruption.

The Van Tassel estate might thus be understood as an at least wished-for
Federalist retreat from the forces of economic change and turmoil lurking
just miles away at the port city of Tarry Town. Similarly, Van Tassel—"thriving, contented, liberal-hearted"; "satisfied with his wealth, but not proud of
it"; and concerned more with the "abundance" rather than the "style" of his
"paternal mansion"—is himself a figure of dignified Federalist masculinity
(278–79). In fact, *The Sketch Book* abounds with this form of manhood, in
particular as it is expressed in the longing for a period when the men of
the landed aristocracy embodied the "statesmanship" Kerber describes, and
acted as the nation's natural leaders. This is perhaps most evident in the
Squire of Bracebridge Hall, whom we see in the book's extended "Christ-
mas" section. As the Squire's son explains to the touring Crayon, "My father,
you must know, is a bigoted devotee of the old school. . . . He is a tolerable
specimen of what you will rarely meet with now-a-days in its purity, the
old English country gentleman; for our men of fortune spend so much of
their time in town, and fashion is carried so much into the country, that
the strong rich peculiarities of ancient rural life are almost polished away"
(159). An advocate of both "chivalry" (172) and the avoidance of "modern
effeminacy and weak nerves" (171), the Squire is probably the closest to Van
Tassel in terms of the propertied, Federalist masculinity Irving offers in *The
Sketch Book*.

But as Michael Warner suggests, the obsessively nostalgic tone of *The
Sketch Book* is bound up not only with Irving's anxieties about modernity
but also with his concerns about patriarchal masculinity. "Irving idealized
patriarchy just at the moment when it was clearly being displaced by modernity," he says ("Posterity" 776–77). Indeed, as Warner also makes clear,
Irving's lifelong status as bachelor reflected his vexed relation to notions of
patriarchy based primarily on reproduction and "the succession of fathers"
(776), especially as that succession is grounded in the transmission of

property through inheritance (as a younger son, Irving was not able to count on an inheritance to secure his financial future). For Warner, Irving's entire career reflects an effort to instantiate a kind of "surrogate" patriarchy (794), one based on literary "reproduction," and one that might compensate for his own felt inadequacy about his failure to inhabit the category of a reproductive masculinity. My own sense is that, especially in the context of the 1819 Panic and his personal economic failures, Irving was *also* seeking to work out his anxieties about a form of manhood that is reproductive neither biologically *nor* economically. Borrowing from an already anachronistic past of dignified, propertied manhood of a Federalist stamp, Irving seeks to pay his debt to a future that no longer accepts his notes of exchange. It is as though there has been a run on the hard currency held in Irving's (national) bank of propertied masculinity, and he has been left nervously unable to make himself into the "self-made man" of a modern era of commerce. The nostalgia for the sort of manhood valorized in the Squire of Bracebridge Hall—what Warner refers to as "a peculiarly American redaction of Burkean conservatism" (781)—is thus compensatory, a kind of nervous Federalist effort to rely on an "old gold" of male selfhood that is no longer in effect.[5]

This is why the patriarchal manhood we see in the Squire is almost inevitably expressed in *The Sketch Book* in terms of decline and nostalgia for a form of masculinity unscathed by the forces of commerce and market corruption. For example, in "The Country Church," Crayon praises "a nobleman of high rank" for his "real dignity," but he turns almost immediately to a longer and more troubled description of a "wealthy citizen" who has "amassed a vast fortune" and "purchased the estate and mansion of a ruined nobleman in the neighborhood" (*SB* 80). "Looking about him with the pompous air of a man accustomed to rule on change and shake the stock market," the wealthy citizen embodies "the aspirings of vulgarity" that Crayon (and Irving) associates with the new economy (82).[6] The short sketch "Roscoe" offers a similar form of antimarket nostalgia. For although Roscoe is praised by Crayon for his ability to maintain a "union of commerce and the intellectual pursuits," he has nevertheless been "unfortunate in business" (18). The result, Crayon soon learns, is that one of Roscoe's mansions has been sold off; worse still, his large library has "passed under the hammer of the auctioneer" (19). "The good people of the vicinity thronged like wreckers to get some part of the noble vessel that had been driven on shore," Crayon says, clearly disgusted over the market value assigned Roscoe's literary collection. "We might picture to ourselves some knot of speculators debating with calculating brow over the quaint binding and illuminated margin of an obsolete author" (19). Indeed, as Crayon continues, it seems evident that Irving is making connections between Roscoe's compromised economic state and his own. "The scholar only knows how dear these silent, yet eloquent companions of pure thoughts and innocent hours become in the season of adversity," Crayon says, speaking still of Roscoe's books. "When all that is worldly turns to dross around us, these only retain their steady value" (19). Echoing complaints such as that voiced in an 1819 editorial in the *Weekly Register* that "reason seemed topsy turvey. . . . The sober and discreet were thrown aside as vulgar folks . . . [while] the *borrower* of $100,000 was a gentleman of rank" (*NWR* 6-12-1819), Crayon finds in Roscoe a figure who has become anachronistic both culturally and financially—but who, as Warner points out, is thus valued for his very resistance to modernity. Like Rip Van Winkle, such men have awakened from their extended slumber to find they no longer fit into an American society that has exchanged the "dignity" of a Federalist manhood rooted in property for the insubstantial "paper" masculinity of the credit-based commercial world.

In "Sleepy Hollow," the character most threatening to the "dignity" and paternal authority of the landed gentry—and the one most closely tied to the corruption of the new paper economy—is of course Ichabod Crane, an interloper from Connecticut who arrives "with all his worldly effects tied up in a cotten [*sic*] handkerchief" (*SB* 275). "From the moment Ichabod laid his eyes upon these regions of delight," we are told of his first visit to the Van Tassel estate, "the peace of his mind was at an end, and his only study was how to gain the affections of the peerless daughter of Van Tassel" (280). Seeing in Katrina the key to economic advancement, Ichabod might be understood as the embodiment of the ever-expanding economic market that threatens to invade the enclosed environs of Sleepy Hollow. Indeed, Ichabod's prodigious appetite, a quality stressed repeatedly throughout the tale, itself figures the voracious nature of postwar capitalism.[7] "[H]e was a huge feeder, and, though lank, had the dilating powers of an Anaconda," we are told at one point (275), a description echoed when Knickerbocker depicts his "devouring mind's eye" (279), or describes how Ichabod's sexual desire for Katrina is realized through fantasies about "dainty slapjacks, well-buttered, and garnished with honey or treacle, by the delicate little dimpled hand of Katrina Van Tassel" (278). Threatening to swallow whole not only the fecundity and virtue of Sleepy Hollow but also the bullionist posture on which it is based (the latter represented usefully by the "ornaments of pure yellow gold" that Katrina wears [278]), Ichabod embodies the appetitive "economic man" Pocock describes, as well as an (albeit comic) variation on the similarly voracious figure of the libertine as depicted throughout the 1790s in texts such as Hannah Webster Foster's *The Coquette* (1797), Charles Brockden Brown's *Arthur Mervyn* (1800–1801), and Sarah Wood's *Dorval; or the Speculator* (1801).[8] By 1819 libertine discourse had largely fallen out of vogue, but the period's many anticommerce editorials make it clear that the language of deception and seduction associated with the rake was still available in staging critiques of the period's economy.[9] For example, in an 1820 denunciation of state banks by the *Independent American,* the editors argue that such banks "enable the designing, unprincipled speculator, who in fact has nothing to lose, to impose on the credulity of the honest, industrious, unsuspecting parts of the community, by their specious flattery and misrepresentation, obtaining from them the borrowed notes and endorsements, until their ruin is consummated, and their farms are sold by the sheriff" (*Independent* 3-25-1820).

The "unprincipled speculator" imagined in this editorial echoes quite closely seductive and chronically indebted characters such as Foster's Major Sanford or Brockden Brown's Welbeck, but he also parallels the obsequious Ichabod as he attempts to ingratiate himself into the Van Tassel world of wealth and prosperity. Ichabod is of course laughably unsuccessful in his efforts to seduce Katrina, but he nevertheless represents a potentially threatening form of masculine agency—one best understood in relation to his desire, similar to that noted by the *Independent American,* to liquidate the material value of the Van Tassels and invest in speculative ventures on land in the western United States (the Yazoo-style "Eldorados" Irving invokes in "The Devil and Tom Walker"). Here is the full passage from which I quoted earlier: "[H]is heart yearned after the damsel who was to inherit these domains, and his imagination expanded with the idea, how they might be readily turned into cash, and the money invested in immense tracts of wild land, and shingle palaces in the wilderness" (*SB* 280). While male characters from *The Sketch Book* such as the Squire of Bracebridge Hall represent and literally embody a Federalism grounded in property and lineage, Ichabod, like his libertine antecedents, represents a form of desire seemingly inextricable from the paper economy, one that is utterly unconcerned with history or tradition, especially as grounded in the fixed material value of property. Indeed, in language strikingly similar to that offered here by Knickerbocker, Thomas Jefferson (himself a victim of the 1819 crash) wrote in 1819 that speculative excitement had resulted in "a general demoralization of the nation, a filching from industry its honest earnings, wherewith to build up palaces, and raise gambling stock for swindlers and shavers, who are to close their career of piracies by fraudulent bankruptcies" (*Writings* 122). Quite unlike the Van Tassel estate, the "palaces" imagined by Ichabod and Jefferson represent a corrupt and insubstantial form of value, one based on "chimerical" paper profits decried by bullionists, rather than the inherent value said to be contained in a monetary system based on specie.

We might in this sense understand Ichabod's commerce-based imagination as directly tied to his tendency to read Sleepy Hollow through the "gothic" lens of the supernatural. Indeed, the various descriptions we receive of him early on in the story make it clear that he is highly susceptible to tales regarding exactly the kind of supernatural events said by Knickerbocker to predominate within the region. "He was an odd mixture of small shrewdness and simple credulity," Knickerbocker explains. "His appetite for the marvellous, and his powers of digesting it, were equally extraordinary; and both had been increased by his residence in this spellbound region. No tale was too gross or monstrous for his capacious swallow" (*SB* 277). As with his extraordinary appetite for food, Ichabod is apparently an ideal "consumer" of fantastical narratives—tales we might understand as metaphoric nods to the many stories of speculative riches awaiting timely investors. But perhaps nowhere is the connection between Ichabod's shared faith in things supernatural and things speculative so powerfully illustrated as the moment when, reflecting on the riches awaiting him if only he can manage to marry the rich heiress Katrina Van Tassel, he looks out at the late-afternoon beauty of the sun setting over the Hudson river. "A sloop was loitering in the distance, and as the reflection of the sky gleamed along the still water, it seemed as if the vessel was suspended in the air" (286). The illusion of weightlessness the image provides, with what is likely a merchant's vessel seeming to defy the laws of gravity and reason, certainly speaks to the "witching power" said by Knickerbocker to "hold[] a spell over the minds of the good people [of Sleepy Hollow], causing them to walk in a continual reverie" (273). But, especially as conjoined with Ichabod's dreams of economic prosperity *vis-à-vis* marriage to Katrina, the image also captures the seemingly magical quality of the credit-based U.S. economy during the postwar years, and Ichabod's fervent desires to cash in on it. Patrick Brantlinger suggests that the weightless homes of the citizens of Laputa in Jonathan Swift's 1726 *Gulliver's Travels* (built from the roof downward) are part of Swift's thoroughgoing critique of "the fantastic basis of public credit" in England in the wake of the South Sea debacle (*Fictions* 71). The "vessel . . . suspended in the air" that Ichabod imagines provides a parallel moment, in which Irving (who in the 1807–8 *Salmagundi* had used the image of Laputa in mounting a Federalist critique of Jefferson's intellectual idealism) provides wry satire on the putatively weightless nature of America's political economy in 1819.

But while this basic tension between the new paper economy and an old-world Federalism (one linked by implication with a gold standard) certainly informs "Sleepy Hollow," it is somewhat less clear where to place Irving himself in relation to this narrative. For Ichabod also acts as a kind of double for Irving. It is perhaps a critical commonplace to suggest that both Irving and Ichabod are creative and highly gullible dreamers who struggle to fit into society. Jeffrey Rubin-Dorsky suggests, for example, that "Sleepy Hollow" "comically exaggerates Irving's projection of himself as artist parasite" (*Adrift* 109). If, however, we understand their shared fantasy life as linked to the seemingly fantastic world of economic success available in the new economy, a picture emerges of an old-world Federalist unable to take up a disciplined life of business or labor, but similarly lost within the world of the new paper economy. The relationship between Irving and Ichabod is only furthered when we realize that *The Sketch Book* itself was a kind of speculative project for Irving, one he was hoping would lift him out of his debtor embarrassment. This is something Irving makes clear in an 1817 letter to Breevort, in which he refers to his early plans for *The Sketch Book:* "I am waiting to extricate myself from the ruins of our unfortunate concern, after which I will turn my back on this scene of care and distress. . . . I have a plan which, with very little trouble, will yield me . . . a sufficient means of support. . . . I cannot at present explain to you what it is—you would probably consider it precarious, & inadequate to my subsistence—but a small matter will float a drowning man and I have dwelt so much of late on the prospect of being cast homeless and pennyless upon the world; that I feel relieved in having even a straw to catch at" (*Letters* 486). Irving's desperation here is certainly echoed in Ichabod's as he seeks to court Katrina Van Tassel, so much so that one senses that Irving may well be mapping his anxieties onto his hapless protagonist, even as he critiques him for his foolish embrace of the illusory paper economy.

One other letter from Irving to Breevort about financial anxieties, this from 1816, is worth citing in this context. After complaining that he has been "harassed & hagridden by the cares and anxieties of business for a long time past," Irving shifts to a tone of lament in writing the following: "It is not long since I felt myself quite sure of fortune's smiles, and began to entertain what I thought very sober and rational schemes for my future comfort and establishment[.]—At present, I feel so tempest tossed and weather beaten that I shall be content to be quits with fortune for a very moderate portion and give up all my sober schemes as the dream of fairy-land" (450). The "fairy-land" of fiscal stability Irving describes here is echoed in Ichabod's belief in the dreamlike possibilities contained within Sleepy Hollow; but as the bitter edge to Irving's various complaints makes clear, such dreams of economic and masculine wholeness are often frustratingly deceptive. Indeed, Ichabod's eventual realization that Katrina Van Tassel is the "sham" practitioner of "coquettish tricks" (*SB* 291) might be thought of in relation to the figure of "Lady Credit" described by Daniel Defoe in his *Review* in the early eighteenth century. According to Defoe, "Pay homage to this idol, I say, and be very tender of her; for if you overload her, she's a coy mistress—she'll slip from you without any warning, and you'll be undone from that moment" (*Review* 6-14-1709). As Sandra Sherman suggests, Defoe's Lady Credit is no lady (*Finance* 40), but neither is Katrina Van Tassel, at least according to the apparent standards of Ichabod (and perhaps of Irving): coquettish and productive of economic passion, she, like Lady Credit, threatens men such as Ichabod with emasculation once they realize they have been deceived. It may seem contradictory to read the heiress to an old-world estate as embodying an unstable form of modern commerce, but in the world according to Ichabod—for whom everything is apparently for sale—Katrina's refusal can mean only one thing: that he is himself devalued on the fluctuating but also competitive market of romantic exchange.

"[N]ightly quest of his head": Castration and Other Anxieties

The lingering threat of emasculation associated with the period's economy makes it doubly significant that the spirit that presides over Sleepy Hollow is "the apparition of a figure on horseback without a head" (*SB* 273). "[H]urrying along in the gloom of night, as if on the wings of the wind," the horseman reflects the same weightless quality attributed to the rest of the region (273). In fact, given that the Horseman represents the central narrative circulating throughout Sleepy Hollow, and the one that ultimately proves so devastating to Ichabod, it is he—more so even than Ichabod—who acts as the embodiment of the period's speculative economy. But the Horseman, forever repeating a "nightly quest of his head," is also very tellingly a figure of castration, one that haunts Ichabod with his own repressed awareness of his failures in Sleepy Hollow, and in 1819 America. And what this suggests is that we are being prompted to understand the period's panic-prone, speculation-based economy and a castrated form of masculine identity as related notions. In each case, the central crisis is a perceived loss of wholeness (figured alternately as a gold standard and as embodied forms of masculine self-possession and agency), a trauma that results in the nervousness and anxiety that so characterizes Ichabod.[10] The radical alterity embodied in the Headless Horseman thus reflects Ichabod's own desperate efforts to understand the Hessian Trooper as the figure who has stolen from him the very forms of enjoyment he has so clearly lost out on—not just in his rejection by Katrina Van Tassel but also as a subject under the emergent paper economy. But again, this felt sense of loss—experienced by Ichabod as fear of castration—is original to him as a paper money man in the 1819 moment he represents. Indeed, we might go further, and say that the sheer excess embodied in the Headless Horseman is in fact the projected image of Ichabod's very relationship to the desires and appetencies of the new paper economy. But this, of course, is something Ichabod cannot see. Instead, the nightmarish assault he receives from the Headless Horseman acts as the very means by which he experiences his sense of failure and impotence.

But if Ichabod is plagued by a kind of castration anxiety, it is a fear that stems in part from the often virulent forms of male homosocial struggle that mark negotiations over class and manhood within Sleepy Hollow. This is reflected early on, in Ichabod's ready willingness to "flourish the rod" (275) in establishing discipline among the young boys in his classroom. "[H]e administered justice with discrimination rather than severity, taking the burden off the backs of the weak, and laying it on those of the strong," we are told (275). Ichabod's excuse to the children's parents for these sometimes "appalling act[s] of justice" (284) is that he is simply "doing his duty" (275). But one suspects that such acts of violence are in fact a form of retribution for the humiliations Ichabod suffers at the hands of Brom Bones and the Sleepy Hollow Boys. Jealous over Katrina's seeming interest in the schoolteacher, Brom is overheard by Ichabod as he threatens to "double the schoolmaster up, and lay him on a shelf of his own school-house" (283). In response, Ichabod enacts an "obstinately pacific system" that thwarts the "rough chivalry" and "open warfare" preferred by the more physical Brom. But within the close confines of Sleepy Hollow he is unable to evade the "whimsical persecution" of his rival (283). The result is that Ichabod is repeatedly harassed in ways that make it clear that Brom is engaging Ichabod in a struggle in which rank and property are collapsed into a contestation over masculine vulnerability. Indeed, Brom's threat, emphasizing as it does his ability to dominate Ichabod and place him in a vulnerable, "feminized" posture (doubled up and laying prone), coupled with his various pranks, suggests that gender is here understood in terms of postures of sexual dominance and submission.

Toby Ditz emphasizes a similar dynamic in her analysis of the often vociferous homosocial rivalries amongst merchants in 1790s Philadelphia. "As the merchants negotiated the meaning of a rather elusive masculinity with one another," she observes, "they frequently triangulated their position with reference to a heavily symbolized femininity. . . . [F]ailed merchants and the unscrupulous colleagues who were held responsible for the failure of others became feminized or ambiguously gendered figures: violated, weeping victims and harpies" ("Shipwrecked" 53–54). The gendered and "feminizing" rhetoric Ditz uncovers is everywhere in evidence in the rivalry between Brom and Ichabod (as well as that between Ichabod and the Headless Horseman). For what is at stake in each instance is the relative status of a masculinity that is itself contingent on the vicissitudes of an unstable market economy. Thus, while, on the one hand, the Hessian trooper embodies Ichabod's repressed knowledge that illusions of economic prosperity have been traded in for the hard fact of masculine humiliation, he represents on the other an abject form of sexuality, one that returns to haunt the itinerant schoolteacher precisely because of his ambivalent status within the shifting and unstable hierarchies of class and manhood in 1819 America.

And this, of course, is most dramatically demonstrated near story's end, in the actual assault on Ichabod following the party at the Van Tassel estate. Believing himself followed by the Headless Horseman, Ichabod tries unsuccessfully to outrun his persecutor. Here is the description of the now famous chase: "[T]he goblin was hard on his haunches; and (unskilful [sic] rider that he was!) he had much ado to maintain his seat; sometimes slipping on one side, sometimes on another, and sometimes jolted on the high ridge of his horse's backbone, with a violence that he verily believed would cleave him asunder" (SB 294). Focusing as it does on Brom's assault from the rear ("hard on his haunches") and Ichabod's own panicked sense that he will be physically split open by this assault ("cleaved asunder" and unable to "maintain his seat"), the description intensifies the allusions to sexual violation used in describing Brom's initial threat against Ichabod, and makes the threat of male rape all but explicit. Earlier in the text we are told that Ichabod brings "pliability and perseverance" to the competition with Bones, qualities linked fairly overtly to sexual agency: "though he bowed beneath the slightest pressure, yet, the moment it was away—jerk! he was as erect, and carried his head as high as ever" (282). But while Ichabod is able to rebound from the majority of Brom's threats and pranks, it is, tellingly, the assault involving Brom's imposture as the Headless Horseman that moves Ichabod from persecuted to disempowered and humiliated ("castrated"). Nor should this come as a great surprise: after all, the late-night attack on Ichabod is as much psychological as physical, and as such the apparitional appearance of a figure such as the Headless Horseman (threatening physical assault, sexual humiliation, and the theft of enjoyment) signals a regulatory check on Ichabod not only as he is vying for ownership of the Van Tassel estate but also at the very moment he is emerging as a social type—the paper money man of the new economy—in early national America.

The gothic atmospherics of paranoia and hysteria that inform this tale thus reflect a mode of affect—a "structure of feeling"—organized around a form of policing at the levels of sexuality, class, and desire. Indeed, the crucial issue here is that, as Eve Sedgwick puts it, "what *counts* as the sexual is . . . variable and itself political" (*Between* 2). And to be sure, one of the things we see over the course of this story is how by 1819 in America, masculinity and male sexuality were increasingly implicated in and influenced by the vicissitudes of the emergent paper economy, so much so that to be disempowered, economically, was *inter alia* to be subject to an all-but-perpetual anxiety over humiliation at the levels of gender and of sexuality. And as Ichabod's competition with Brom and the Headless Horseman suggests, this fear extended to a felt panic over the blurred relations between economic competition and manhood. Ichabod thus acts as the axis for related registers of "panic." With the period's context of financial crisis intersecting with his more personalized form of gender trouble, Ichabod provides a map for a new and identifiably "gothic" male subject emerging in early national America; haunted by the apparitional nature of a paper economy that has made self-possession an increasingly elusive dream, but similarly haunted by anxieties at the levels of gender and sexuality, he is in his various states of panic and hysteria a figure for whom postures of terror and humiliation are becoming the norm.

Thus, whereas a sketch such as "Roscoe" deploys the relays of sentimentality and sympathy in evoking nostalgia for the social cohesion of Federalist-style community and fiscal conservatism, "Sleepy Hollow" utilizes the affect of gothic horror as a means of exploring the ruptures and instabilities of masculinity and class forced by an inherently panic-prone paper economy. Nor is this instability limited to the likes of Ichabod. As unpropertied interloper, Ichabod is of course quite vulnerable both to Brom's assaults and to the vicissitudes of the economy more generally. But we might consider that Brom too is quite vulnerable, if not to physical assault from Ichabod, then certainly to the long arm of the increasingly capricious economy—a force that, again, is embodied in Ichabod himself. A "rustic" known for his "Herculean frame and great powers of limb" (*SB* 281), Brom is a laborer in a world in which labor-based forms of value are clearly in decline—even as the "labor of headwork" that Ichabod performs is itself marked as perilous. Indeed, though Sleepy Hollow is usually read as a space set outside the forces of market intrusion, the strangely narcotic atmosphere that pervades the valley might itself be indicative of the seductive and apparitional magic of a speculatory economy that has *already* made its way into Sleepy Hollow. As the narrator explains early on, "Certain it is, the place [is held] under the sway of some witching power, that holds a spell over the minds of the good people, causing them to walk in a continual reverie. . . . However wide awake they may have been before they entered that sleepy region, they are sure, in a little time, to inhale the witching influence of the air, and begin to grow imaginative, to dream dreams, and see apparitions" (273–74).

The spectral presence of the paper economy within Sleepy Hollow thus reminds us that Brom is all but entirely reliant on Katrina's "vast expectations" (278) for his future support. Yet with the Panic reaching to all corners of the United States in 1819, even the Van Tassel estate is subject to possible ruin—something confirmed by frequent mention in both Republican and Federalist newspapers during the period of farmers who have lost their property as a result of speculatory schemes (the above 1820 editorial in the *Independent American* is a typical example). And what this suggests is that the contest between Ichabod and Brom is one pitting two forms of unstable masculinity against one another. Similarly cut off from the supposedly secure certainties of a bullionist economy, the two men are in effect struggling for dominance over a radically uncertain—and in 1819, fairly bleak—future. Ditz suggests that the financial "man in distress" in 1790s Philadelphia was subject to new and radical contingencies of value and gender ("Shipwrecked" 53). Ichabod Crane reflects the way in which, by 1819, manhood was if anything more unstable, as well as subject to increasingly virulent forms of regulation through the mechanisms of gender panic. Indeed, in the gothic world of Sleepy Hollow, financial panic and male panic seem virtually synonymous, and Ichabod represents the kind of hystericized and humiliated manhood inevitably resultant from an affective "investment" in the ghostly world of market finance.

Again, then, "Sleepy Hollow" is an important first step in understanding how various forms of literary sensationalism—here the gothic—were responding both to the emergent paper economy, and to the paper money manhood that was its byproduct. In the following chapters I will show how antebellum literary and cultural sensationalism—especially as these forms intersected in the sensational public sphere—tended to provide readers with various kinds of fantasy compensation to crises of the sort faced by Ichabod Crane. Here, though, Irving seems primarily interested in mapping out a sensational form of manhood, one haunted by a felt sense of loss and anxiety in the rapidly changing world of 1819 America. On the one hand, of course, Ichabod's expulsion from Sleepy Hollow suggests that the world of agrarian abundance is still secure. But in terms of reading the professional manhood Ichabod represents, there is little available in the way of fantasy compensation. Indeed, although we hear of a rumor that Ichabod goes on to a professional career as attorney, politician, and judge, it's easy to imagine that, even far away from the haunted precincts of Sleepy Hollow, he still whistles nervously in the dark, worrying—knowing—that he is still being stalked by the uncanny figure of the Headless Horseman.

CODA: FROM SLEEPY HOLLOW TO SUBURBIA—
THE CASE OF *EDWARD SCISSORHANDS*

I want to conclude this chapter with a brief analysis of one of the various contemporary revisions of Irving's "Sleepy Hollow": Tim Burton's 1990 film, *Edward Scissorhands*. A stricter, more literal reading might require examination of Burton's 1999 film, *Sleepy Hollow,* which is of course a more explicit remake of Irving's story (though here Ichabod is a detective investigating a series of murders in upstate New York). But I would suggest that *Edward Scissorhands* is in fact closer to the mark, especially in terms of Irving's desire to articulate the vicissitudes of manhood under emerging forms of commerce and capitalism. For what we find in the enclosed suburban landscape of Burton's film is the very inverse of Irving's Sleepy Hollow: here the figure of alterity must be driven out so that commerce can *retain* its stranglehold over the benumbed residents of a world drained of male potency.

The story begins with the discovery of the teenage Edward—a young man with scissors for hands—by a woman named Peg Boggs (Dianne Wiest) as she is making her rounds one morning in an effort to sell Avon products. "Avon calling!" she says in a comic moment as she enters the gothic environs of Edward's castle. Edward, it turns out, has been living alone in this castle (located both absurdly and suggestively at the end of a suburban cul-de-sac) ever since his father passed away, years before. Worse, Edward's father (played in a flashback by Vincent Price) died before he could "finish" Edward, and provide him with actual hands to replace his scissorhands. For the catch is that Edward is an artificial being, one who, we see later in the film, is literally the product of an assembly-line production (though he seems to be one of a kind). This form of monstrosity is startling to Peg, but only momentarily. Almost immediately, she and Edward are in her car and headed back to her house, where she intends to care for him as a member of her middle-class suburban family. The rest of the film traces Edward's vexed efforts to assimilate into Peg's home and the community more generally. In particular, the film focuses on Edward's efforts to win the hand of Peg's daughter, Kim (Winona Ryder). In this scenario Kim becomes a benign suburban version of Katrina Van Tassel, while her boyfriend, Jim (Anthony Michael Hall), stands in as an aggressive and hostile version of Brom Bones. Near film's end Edward is chased out of town, not just by Jim-as-Brom, but also by a mob of angry neighbors, for whom Edward has become an easy scapegoat for the failures and frustrations of modern suburban life.

But Edward is not simply an updated version of Ichabod Crane. Indeed, we might also think of him in relation to the Headless Horseman, especially in that Edward haunts the suburban community of this film much as the

Headless Horseman haunts Sleepy Hollow. Part man and part machine, he represents a modern—and distinctly suburban—version of capitalist alienation. Literally separated from the work of his hands, he is clearly meant to represent a kind of return of the repressed for the community we see so comically depicted by Burton. With the cars of the neighborhood's commuters all departing and returning at exactly the same time, and with each house a carbon copy of the next (bold differences in color notwithstanding), the neighborhood is the bland world of suburban boredom created by the very forms of capitalism so threatening to the inhabitants of Irving's Sleepy Hollow almost two hundred years earlier. Peg's futile efforts to peddle her Avon products highlight this, but in a way that suggests that these are people at the far limit of the fearful capitalist desire we see in "Sleepy Hollow." These people are so desensitized that they don't even *respond* to new products. More telling is the fact that the community of women who represented a potentially utopian collectivity—the Old Dutch Wives of Sleepy Hollow— are here reduced to backstabbers whose desires are either for empty sex with dishwasher repairmen, or for newsworthy information to circulate in the intense local economy of telephone gossip.

Yet despite his seeming monstrosity as he emerges from the shadows of his overtly gothic home, Edward is not a threat to the community in the way that either Ichabod or the Headless Horseman is threatening. Instead, Edward represents the longing for community and value that the residents of this community seem to have long since repressed and forgotten. It's no mistake that Peg first catches a glimpse of Edward's castle in her car's side-view mirror: his castle represents all that she has put behind her and repressed in her efforts to conform to the empty suburban lifestyle represented by her job as an Avon salesperson. Her visit to his castle is in a sense a visit to her own—and her culture's—unconscious. We might think of Edward's castle as quite similar to that other famous gothic edifice, the Transylvanian castle inhabited by Bram Stoker's Count Dracula. In each case, middle-class characters enter an inverted fantasy space in which they confront in uncanny form the very things they have tried to repress in forging a middle-class, professional selfhood. For Jonathan Harker, this means an encounter with the sexuality locked away in the forbidden portions of Dracula's castle. But Peg Boggs discovers something different: when she finds Edward cowering in the upstairs space of his father's home, she encounters a figure of enjoyment and pleasure, one whose profound artistic talent—evidenced in the topiary sculptures he has created in the castle's front yard—allows him to *transcend* the stranglehold that commerce and capitalism have placed on his neighbors. Peg's sense of awe and reverence as she walks through the front gate of Edward's gothic mansion and discovers the topiary—"it's so beautiful," she says—suggests that she has managed, if briefly, to return to a prelapsarian state of Edenic beauty. My sense here is thus that Burton is linking Edward's garden space to the still-isolated and pristine space of Sleepy Hollow itself: we might say that both Edward's topiary garden and Sleepy Hollow represent a now "stolen" space of wholeness and plenitude that characters such as Peg and Ichabod simply cannot return to after America's "fall" into the modern world of commerce and paper money—especially as cut loose from a gold standard of reliable value, *and* from the forms of community and rural life that cushioned one against economic failure.

In bringing Edward home, Peg is thus attempting to give expression to this sense of longing in her own life. But the fact that she immediately attempts to assimilate him into her suburban world suggests that she doesn't really understand what he actually represents to her. Indeed, what we find is that she immediately attempts to outfit Edward in old clothes of her husband's—a move that suggests a felt desire to *gender* him as a middle-class male subject. Indeed, prior to his awkward attempt to put on these clothes (his scissorhands make this laughably difficult), Edward, whose tight leather clothing acts almost like a kind of skin, seems decidedly gender-neutral, the implication being that it is commerce itself that mandates specific forms of masculinity and masculine sensibility. This point is driven home in the aggressive sexual advances a confused Edward receives from one of the local housewives, Joyce (Kathy Baker): Edward, it seems, must be taught certain forms of desire and manhood. This is even more evident at the picnic held by the Boggs family shortly after Edward's arrival to the neighborhood: here Edward is surrounded by the neighborhood wives and literally force-fed the various desserts they have made. The scene provides a telling reversal of the overwhelmingly appetitive desire we see in Ichabod, whose "dilating powers of an anaconda" of course signal the voracious nature of capitalism as it seeks an inroad into Sleepy Hollow. Here, Edward's mouth is stuffed with desserts in what seems like a desperate—and eroticized—effort to *create* that very form of desire in Edward. This desperation extends to the manner in which the neighborhood wives race to have Edward cut their hair with his scissorhands: the haircuts quickly become eroticized commodities, the result of which is that Edward's possible transcendence of the commercial logic that predominates in this suburban world is subsumed into the market itself (it is in this sense fitting that Peg even convinces Edward to apply for a loan in order to open his own hair salon—she too feels he needs to put his talents up for sale).

But the interesting thing here is that Edward is ultimately unable to acquire the form of desire necessary to assimilate into this suburban community, and is thus unable to achieve the type of masculinity necessary to function within this world. And yet he doesn't experience the sort of symbolic castration and emasculation suffered by Ichabod in "Sleepy Hollow." Indeed, though he is chased out of the neighborhood much as Ichabod is chased out of Sleepy Hollow, it is *Edward* who prevails over his rival, stabbing Jim with one of his scissorhands and pushing him out of his castle window. But perhaps this shouldn't come as a great surprise: with scissors for hands, Edward—like the Headless Horseman—is the virtual embodiment of castration anxiety for the men of Burton's suburbia. For to be sure, it is the men of this community who have lost a precious part of themselves, and who seem utterly incapable of ever retrieving this lost sense of wholeness and selfhood. It is, that is to say, Edward who ends up "stealing" *their* enjoyment.

Edward's victory over his male rival is therefore not the signal that he will assimilate into the world of middle-class ennui that would await him in a marriage to Kim. Instead of such a marriage, Edward retains what we might think of as a kind of resistant capacity, one that ensures that he will continue to live at the edges of modern America's suburban landscape. By the end of the film Edward is back in his castle, making snow for the residents of the neighborhood he has been forced to flee. Edward is thus like a figure in a dream, a rarely glimpsed reminder of a lost enjoyment that is available to us if only we would—or could—step outside the middle-class world of commerce that has come to seem so incredibly natural, when in fact it is as false as the paint on the suburban homes Burton depicts in his film. This is what Irving's original gothic sought to show us in the expulsion of Ichabod from Sleepy Hollow, and perhaps this is why his story is if anything more popular today than it was in the early nineteenth century: because we are like the residents Burton's suburbs, knowing we have lost something and occasionally aware of what that something might be, but too repressed and too neurotic to find our way back to it.

CHAPTER TWO

SHYLOCK ON WALL STREET

THE JESSICA COMPLEX IN
ANTEBELLUM SENSATIONALISM

"Your daughter spent in Genoa, as I heard / one night fourscore ducats."
"Thou stick'st a dagger in me. I shall never / see my gold again."

—Exchange between Tubal and Shylock in
Shakespeare's *The Merchant of Venice*

───

THE JEW'S STOLEN MONEY

One of the more common narratives circulating during the banking panics and fiscal depressions of the 1830s, '40s, and '50s was that the Jews had
stolen the nation's missing gold bullion. Early versions of the urban legend
in America, these narratives provided, at least on one level, a convenient
rationale for why the economy was in a continual state of crisis, this despite
Andrew Jackson's "war" against the fiscal corruption of the U.S. Bank and its
president, Nicholas Biddle. According to this logic, Jackson's efforts to curb
the nation's addiction to credit and speculation by enforcing a specie-based
monetary policy were too late: the nation's hard currency had *already* been
siphoned off and stored away by avaricious Jews whose fiscal instincts had
kept them one step ahead of Jackson and his mostly Democratic counter-
parts.

These dynamics are literalized in a number of political cartoons produced during the 1830s period. For example, in an 1834 lithograph by T. W.
Whitley, *The People Putting Responsibility to the Test* (figure 10), the reader
receives an image of the disastrous consequences ensuing from Jackson's
decision to withdraw federal funds from the Bank in late 1833. Depicting in
the background an unruly mob of laborers and farmers waving signs that
read "Broken Bank" and shouting demands such as "Recharter the Bank!"

Figure 10 *The People Putting Responsibility to the Test.* 1834 by T. W. Whitley. Lithograph on wove paper; 28.5 x 36.8 cm. Reproduced with permission of the American Antiquarian Society.

as Jackson himself flees, stage right, the lithograph foregrounds an exchange between a sailor and a Jewish broker named Levi (lower left). "I say Moses give us some ballast for this here bit of rag," the sailor says, referring to the fact that in the wake of Jackson's bullionist fiscal policies, his paper money is fast losing value. "Mine Got that ish one of the Pet Bankhs I'll give you one Dollar for the Ten," Levi says. Borrowing from the stereotype of the Jew as greedy and opportunistic, the lithograph suggests that, because he is in possession of actual bullion, he is able to take advantage of the unstable market by buying up what he assumes will be the somewhat reliable currency of Jackson's pet state banks. Echoing a slightly earlier image by E. W. Clay titled *The Downfall of Mother Bank* (1833), in which Mordecai Noah, the oft-maligned Jewish editor of the pro-Bank New York *Enquirer,* flees the collapsing Bank with a bag of gold bullion,[1] Whitley's lithograph suggests that Jackson's efforts to curb the paper economy have actually benefited the Jew, who now more than ever is in possession of the nation's hard currency (note that the bag Levi clutches is filled with bullion similar to the dollar coin he holds out in his hand).

Such visual images took more complex form in a variety of post-1837 sensational or "urban gothic" narratives that star the figure of the Jew. Invariably modeled on Shakespeare's Shylock, the sensational Jew acts as a consistent—and consistently exaggerated—foil in the many sensational narratives produced during this period that revolve around crises of finance, class, and gender. As Lawrence Levine and Louis Harap have shown, *The Merchant of Venice* and related comic spin-offs, such as John Brougham's 1858 *Much ado about a merchant of Venice,* were a staple of the period's theatrical productions.[2] But it is in the period's sensational literature that Shakespeare's story of a grasping, usurious Jew seems to have taken deepest and most complex hold in antebellum culture. Indeed, while all but completely absent from the canonical literature of the antebellum period,[3] each of the period's best-selling urban gothic writers (George Lippard, George Thompson, and Ned Buntline), as well as numerous less successful and for the most part unknown sensation writers, turned to the Shylock figure as a means of articulating and negotiating the anxious terrain of capitalist expansion and manhood at mid-century.

The following exchange from an early moment in *The Merchant of Venice* suggests why Shylock answered to the period's linked concerns about political economy and masculinity: "I owe you much, and like a willful youth / That which I owe is lost," says the plaintive debtor Bassanio to his friend Antonio (1.2.146–47). Antonio replies thus: "Neither have I money, nor commodity / To raise a present sum. Therefore go forth. / Try what my credit can in Venice do" (1.2.178–79). Emphasizing as it does a fiscally insolvent and disempowered form of professional manhood (Bassanio has squandered his money and gone into debt, while Antonio as speculator can only rely on whatever credit he can gain), the exchange seems to have resonated in the financially turbulent Jacksonian era. Antonio's plan, of course, is to borrow against his various speculative ventures in foreign trade. But what we find is that, unable to pay his debt to Shylock after the agreed-upon three months, Antonio faces certain death when Shylock demands the pound of flesh Antonio has promised as collateral. The play provides dramatic resolution to the crisis in the form of Portia's mock-legal intervention, but the specter of Shylock—of the merchant Jew—haunts the pages of U.S. sensationalism throughout the early national and antebellum periods. For, possessed of the money that men such as Bassanio, and later Antonio, so desperately need and yet reviled for his own more open enjoyment of money ("I did dream of money bags to-night," he tells Jessica at one somewhat comic moment [2.5.18]), Shylock is the very agent of masculine anxiety and fiscal disempowerment—both for Renaissance audiences, and, I want to argue, for antebellum readers as well.

Certainly the use of the Shylock figure in America precedes the banking crises of the mid-1830s. For example, in 1795 Richard Cumberland's play *The Jew: or, Benevolent Hebrew* was touring through eastern cities such as Boston and New York, and offering audiences a complex reprise of Shylock's character in *The Merchant of Venice*. "[T]hou hast horded wealth, till thou art sick with gold even to plethory," one character tells the Jew Sheva, an early indication that market-based anti-Semitism will be integral to the period's efforts to come to terms with the vicissitudes of the new economy. "[T]hy bags run over with the spoils of usury; thy veins are glutted with the blood of prodigals and gamblers" (*Jew* 13). We see this as well in 1812, when the Jew Ishmael appears "counting his gold" at the outset of James Ellison's play *The American Captive; or, the Siege of Tripoli*. "Vat comely form!" he says. "The world talks of *peauty*, or *woman's* peauty! Spshaw! compared with this, 'tis all *deformity!*" (*American Captive* 29). Ishmael's erotic relationship to his gold bespeaks not only his greed, but a perverse form of desire for hard currency, one that turns him inward upon himself and his money in a solipsistic embrace.

Such images only multiply in the post-1837 period, as we see the sensational Jew emerge with greater frequency, and in ever closer relation to his money. A primary example is Gabriel Von Gelt, the "Jewish dwarf" from Lippard's *The Quaker City*. "Bi-Gott! . . . I smellsh te gooldt already!" he whispers in a line I also quote in the introduction, as he and an accomplice steal a chest of gold doubloons. "Toubloonsh! Toubloonsh!" (239). The kind of visceral response Von Gelt displays in this scene (he "thrust[s] his hands eagerly into the chest" and then "holds it in the embrace of his arms" [239]) is, I would suggest, at the very heart of the period's urban sensationalism, and perhaps even of antebellum culture more generally. For what we see in his very sensory and affective relation to this cache of bullion is a form of desire that allows capitalist Gentile culture both to displace its many anxieties about the emerging paper economy onto a figure of alterity, and to organize its own complex relationship to the various forms of passion and desire that were part and parcel of that new formation. Nor is this simply an excessive aberration on the part of Lippard. Again and again early-nineteenth-century sensationalism offers images of Jews passionately clutching stores of gold bullion, often as preferred substitute for actual emotional or physical interaction with other human beings. For example, the plot of James Maitland's *The Lawyer's Story; or, the Orphan's Wrongs* (1853) hinges on the fiscal decisions of an old Jewish usurer named Mordecai, who late in the novel is described by his son Jacob (also a moneylender) in the following terms: "[M]any friends he never did have, gold was always the friend he most loved and reverenced, and he has found his reward in its adhering to him when all others have failed; but he must soon leave even his gold, and as he feels the hour of parting drawing near, he clutches it faster and clings to it with more intensity of devotion" (*Lawyer's* 159–60). Mordecai's intense relationship with his gold is echoed in J. B. Jones's *Border War. A Tale of Disunion* (1859), one of several novels in which Jones deploys the moneylending Shylock character as a foil for the business operations of professional Gentile men.[4] Here a Jewish usurer named Solomon Mouser has grown rich by "shaving money from poor men and women" (*Border* 156), but in the novel's present we see him watching over a stockpile of cash that has been hidden away by a corrupt policeman named Bim. As Mouser puts it to Bim at one point, "I have been watching and starving over it for days and nights. Oh, father Abraham." Bim's response confirms the Jew's abnormal (but in this case quite useful) relationship to money: "What a fool you are, Tuppeny! You can lie in rags all your life and hug a pile of gold, and when you die you can't even take it to the devil with you. But here—I'll leave the greater part of the money. I'm not afraid you'll spend it" (167).

The lack of concern displayed here by the policeman Bim—his confidence that the usurer Mouser will guard his hoard of money rather than spend it—speaks to the way in which the Jew stages a problematic relationship to hard money and its circulation. By charging usurious interest rates and drawing money out of circulation, the sensational Jew—or rather, the Jew as depicted within antebellum sensationalism—practices a form of fiscal management that runs counter to the needs and demands of the period's economy. Indeed, it's worth noting both that a number of the period's economic treatises cite usury as a major factor behind the lack of hard money in circulation, and that these texts often refer to Shylock as a means of making their point.[5] Equating value with its material manifestation in actual gold bullion and coins ("gold was always the friend he most loved and reverenced"), the Jew of these narratives is clearly an antagonist to the modern economy. Indeed, like the miser described by Georg Simmel—the one who "finds bliss in the sheer possession of money, without proceeding to the acquisition and enjoyment of particular objects" ("Miser" 179)—the Jew of such narratives has a relationship to money that inverts the capitalist's dogma of value being attained via the placing of money into circulation. Marx puts it thus: "The ceaseless augmentation of value, which the miser seeks to attain by saving his money from circulation, is achieved by the more acute capitalist by means of throwing his money again and again into circulation" (*Capital* 254–55). The advice Sheva receives in Cumberland's *The Jew* is in this sense predictive of the tensions that surround the sensational Jew of the antebellum period. "[S]ay nothing," Sheva is told when he complains about the abuse heaped upon him by Christian society, "*but spend your money like a Christian*" (*Jew* 9; emphasis added). Cumberland's Christian characters do not say what such expenditure might look like, exactly, but Sheva himself seems to answer this question when he is discovered to be the generous benefactor of several of the play's main male characters. The result is that Sheva is categorized as a kind of non-Jew: as one character puts it, "[H]e is no Hebrew, no more a Jew than Julius Caesar; for to my certain knowledge he gives away his money by handfulls [*sic*] to all the consumers of hogs-flesh [*sic*]" (22). This may sound like an enlightened counter to the Shylock stereotype, but we might also consider whether Sheva is simply the exception that proves the rule. For though Sheva clearly represents an effort to forge an anti-Shylock version of the capitalist Jew, the notion that Sheva is so radically unusual works to reinforce the "Hebrew" category of miser and usurer from which Shylock and his literary cousins spring. Indeed, it's worth noting in this context an 1806 review of Cumberland's play, in which the author writes, "[I]t has sometimes been made a question whether Shylock or Sheva, is the truer delineation of nature. . . . *Sheva* we fear will be found to have few parallels in existence; while *Shylock* can claim consanguinity with a large fraternity."[6]

Thus, while Cumberland's Sheva provides an indirect answer as to how one spends money "like a Christian," he also suggests what it might look like within antebellum fiction to spend money "like a Jew." In many ways the answer is a simple negative, for the sensational Jew doesn't spend at all; rather, staging a kind of radical mercantilism, he hoards. Starving rather than spending for sustenance, forgoing pleasure for the perverse enjoyment of renunciation, the miserly, hoarding Jew of antebellum sensationalism lurks at the edges of the expansive capitalist economy, drawing from it but seemingly unwilling to add to it.

But the cultural work performed by the Jew within this material is more complex still. For while he is certainly a figure of blame and disavowal, it is equally important to understand how the Jew is a figure through whom the new forms of desire and pleasure made possible by the period's emerging form of capitalism might themselves be negotiated on a psychological level. Here we might think again of Žižek's discussion of the "theft of enjoyment," a felt anxiety he links directly to the psychic work of anti-Semitism. For while, as he explains, "We always impute to the other an excessive enjoyment: he wants to steal our enjoyment (by ruining our way of life) and/or he has access to some secret, perverse enjoyment" (*Tarrying* 203), this felt theft is in fact a form of projection that often involves the figure of Otherness most directly tied to the psychology of capitalism: the Jew. Indeed, imagined as excessive in a variety of mysterious ways (his self-denying fetish for his hoarded gold; his erotic relationship to money; etc.), the Jew was perhaps *the* central figure of "theft" in antebellum culture. Having been accused of making off with the nation's money supply, the sensational Jew was also, implicitly, understood as the figure that had stolen the very "way of life" that, prior to banking crises such as the panics of 1819, 1837, and 1857, was supposedly secured by a stable supply of gold bullion in the nation's banks. Certainly this is part of the moral contained in the American versions of fairy tales such as *Jack and the Beanstalk* and *The History of old Mother Goose, and the golden egg,* which I briefly discuss in the introduction. As the visual images from the stories suggest (figures 11 and 12), the Jew is the active and quite exaggerated figure of economic threat to the young would-be capitalist Jack (and thus to the more general culture Jack represents—presumably the antebellum America of these editions). In both cases, of course, the Jew is thwarted in his attempts to undermine Jack's access to his golden treasure, but this does little to diminish the function of the Jew as the figure of theft in these narratives.

But, and simultaneously, the Jew was also a central figure through whom antebellum culture was able to deny its *own* relationship to the excesses of capitalism. For although the nation's apparent lack of hard currency was perceived as a central problem for the national economy, it was the overextension of credit and the recklessness of speculatory investments that was perhaps more central to the climate of fiscal panic that predominated during the antebellum period.[7] The Jew thus served a kind of dual function in antebellum culture, one Žižek's discussion of stolen enjoyment helps us understand: accused on the one hand of stealing and hoarding the very stuff of fiscal security (literally, the nation's gold bullion), the Jew was on the other hand the projected figure of capitalist excess, one reviled precisely

When Jack got to the Town and round him was staring:
"Come buy"cried a Jew "dis rare bean for a faring,
It pofsefses such virtues dat sure as a Gun,
To-morrow it vill grow near as high as de Sun.

Figure 11 Image from *The History of Mother Twaddle, and the marvellous atchievments* [sic] *of her son Jack.* 1809 by William Charles. Reproduced with permission of the American Antiquarian Society.

because he was the uncanny figure of Gentile desire. "[I]s the anti-Semitic capitalist's hatred of the Jew not the hatred of the excess that pertains to capitalism itself, i.e., of the excess produced by its inherent antagonistic nature?" Žižek asks. "Is capitalism's hatred of the Jew not the hatred of its own innermost, essential feature?" (206).[8] This vexed reciprocity between Jew and Gentile is something Marx points to in his infamous text, *On the Jewish Question* (1843). Here Marx critiques the "free inhabitant of New England" in that "*Mammon* is his idol which he adores not only with his lips but with the whole force of his body and mind. In his view the world is no more than a Stock Exchange" (49). But Marx is quick here to shift the very sensual form of greed he depicts here onto the figure of the Jew.

Figure 12 Image from *The History of old Mother Goose, and the golden egg.* 1840, printed and published by William Raine. Reproduced with permission of the American Antiquarian Society.

"The Jew has emancipated himself in a Jewish manner," he says, "not only by acquiring the power of money, but also because money has become, through him and also apart from him, a world power.... The Jews have emancipated themselves in so far as Christians have become Jews" (49).[9] This logic, whereby it is the Jew who has infected the Christian world (here antebellum America) with capitalist desire, helps explain how Jews of the sort depicted in the above lithographs (to say nothing of the more free-floating referent provided by Shylock) act as images of the Jacksonian Jew more generally. For, as in Marx's essay, the sensational Jew is deployed as a means of helping capitalist culture disavow its own excessive relationship to capital.

Consider in this sense an 1840 lithograph entitled *Shylock's Year, or 1840 with no Bankrupt Law* (figure 13). A critique of Congress's failure to pass a national bankruptcy law in 1840, the image extends the above pictorial narratives by suggesting that in the absence of such legislation, professional men are vulnerable to the sort of persecution displayed here by the Jewish moneylender, whose demand of "Pay me what thou owest" echoes the refrain professional men were hearing everywhere during this period. Indeed, with one hand around his debtor's throat and his other clutching a long cane, the Jew here seems possessed of a phallic potency that the Gentile male is unable to match in his present state of indebtedness. But the Jew depicted in this lithograph—excessive, even irrational, in his very avariciousness—should in fact be read as the embodiment of the uncontrolled passions of capitalism *itself,* returned here in almost uncanny form to persecute the debtor male and his own penchant for excessive credit and expenditure.

This sort of projection can also be seen in the many sensational narratives that depict the Shylock figure as a kind of closeted voluptuary, surrounded (always in secret) by the almost unimaginable riches and spoils that have come with his career as moneylender. Utterly representative of this ethos is a scene from S. B. Beckett's "The Jewess of Cairo," a short story appearing in the *Ladies Home Companion* in 1840 and 1841. Here an American tourist is led to the outwardly modest Jerusalem home of a Jew named Absalom whom he has befriended in Egypt, only to be surprised by the riches he finds inside: "[A] blaze of splendor burst upon the gaze of the young adventurer, which made him start back in utter surprise.... He could hardly help fancying himself in fairy land.... The figured tapestry, the golden chandeliers ... the ruby, the aqua-marine, the other precious stones, the costly paintings, the vases of agate and porphyry, the silken carpet, the gilded ottomans and sofa couches, the immense mirrors, which reached almost from floor to ceiling, multiplying every object, formed a *tout ensemble* of magnificence, such as had never met his gaze" (275). Like numerous other Jews in the period's

Figure 13 *Shylock's Year, or 1840 with No Bankrupt Law.* 1840 published by John C. White. Wood-engraving on wove paper; 34.8 x 24.7 cm. Reproduced from the Collections of The Library of Congress.

fiction, the Absalom of this tale hides his wealth from the jealous eyes of the surrounding community. But what the reader sees, of course (along with occasional Gentiles such as the American tourist he has befriended), are outré forms of pleasure that are simply the flip side of the avariciousness depicted in the above lithograph "Shylock's Year." In each case, the Jew acts a figure for the debtor's own economic passions, passions that he has projected onto the figure of the Jew.

Again, then, the sensational Jew collapses a twin set of concerns for antebellum culture. Acting on the one hand as a scapegoat for the nation's concerns over fiscal instability (understood by many as centered in a crisis of hard money), he was on the other hand a figure of disavowal and projection: it was the Jew who embodied the new and troubling forms of masculine passion and desire emerging along with the paper economy at mid-century. But perhaps the most poignant aspect of the myriad sensational versions of the Shylock figure in antebellum culture is the desperation they reveal. For what the sensational Jew *also* provides antebellum culture—and especially the antebellum male—is a way to cover over the knowledge that, as Žižek suggests (*Tarrying* 203), he *has never possessed* the form of gold-backed security that was supposedly taken from him by the Jew in the first place. From this perspective, the way of life that the antebellum male believes himself to have lost with the onset of the paper money economy—the felt sense of castration we see in a text such as Irving's "Sleepy Hollow" (chapter 1) or the similar form of masculine disempowerment staged in an image such as "Shylock's Year"—was imagined into being only at the moment of its perceived threat by the new economy. But again, this is something the antebellum male, especially as represented within the period's sensationalism, was incapable of admitting. Instead, this material continued to conjure up fantasies of Otherness and theft for the very purpose of covering over the still deeper sense of loss operating at the core of the period's paper economy.

THE JESSICA COMPLEX

But this is only half the story. For the tensions that inhere in the sensational Jew's negative form of political economy—his tendency to hoard and withhold; his excessive and sometimes perverse forms of pleasure and desire—are perhaps most complex when played out in the many antebellum sensation narratives that explore the romantic life of his daughter. Distant cousins of the Jessica narrative in *The Merchant of Venice*, in which Shylock's daughter, having stolen her father's ducats and jewels, elopes with the

Christian Lorenzo, these sensational stories appear throughout the antebellum period, and are important in two ways: first, they suggest at least one of the strategies by which the Gentile male might balance accounts, as it were, and reappropriate the forms of economic potency and manhood that have been stolen away and hoarded by the sensational Jew. Simultaneously, these updated Jessica stories suggest how the otherwise problematic and alien forms of passion and desire housed in the Jew might be "converted" and smuggled back into the capitalist world of Gentile culture in less threatening form. In various religious tracts produced during the period—with titles such as *The Dying Jewess* (1839–45?)—conversion is sentimentalized, often coming in deathbed scenes, and the motive is clearly the celebration of Christianity.[10] But the period's sensationalism is decidedly secular, emphasizing instead issues of finance and gender, and staging what I want to refer to as a "Jessica Complex," a process whereby the conversion of the Jessica character acts as a fantasy path to a reconstituted form of capitalist manhood. Indeed, stealing the Jew's daughter provides a kind of redress for the fiscal humiliations brought about by indebtedness to the Jew (in stealing his jewels and "bag of ducats" and converting to Christianity, Jessica famously performs a symbolic castration of her father[11]), but this "theft" *also* allows the very forms of capitalist passion the Jew embodies—his stolen enjoyment—to be assimilated, perhaps "laundered," and reincorporated into the professional middle classes.

Thus in A. J. H. Duganne's *The Tenant House* (1857), a desperately indebted libertine named Charles Richmond seeks to "possess a usurer's wealth" by means of seduction. "He sought the Jewess only as the adopted daughter of Mordecai Kolephant—the heiress of a millionaire," we are told. "[H]is purpose was to hold her as a captive bird, till the . . . decease of the usurer . . . should give him . . . her large possession as his own, by right of conquest" (167). This sort of libertinism is less common than narratives in which, following the example of Jessica and Lorenzo, the Gentile male and female Jew actually fall in love. But the naked desire we see in a character such as Richmond is important, in that it provides a raw glimpse of the way in which the Jessica character is a crucial component in the efforts of the Gentile male to regain the sense of potency and self-possession that has been lost to the vicissitudes of the new economy.[12] Indeed, this story is particularly revealing in that it also stages an equally aggressive—and quite literal—theft of *another* Jewish daughter: in this story line, we see the usurer Mordecai seek to locate his lost daughter, who, ten years previous, was "stolen from her nurse's arms" (161). The dilemma here is summed up by a woman named Mona Maria, who has raised the girl as a Christian, and who beseeches her to resist the urge to return to a life of Judaism with her father: "Wouldst thou go with the rich ones, who claim thee, to their grand palace, and be dressed in silks, and waited on by servants, while Mona Maria starves?" she asks. "Curses on the silken dresses, and on the gold of the heretics!" (446). As with many characters in the period's sensationalism, Mona Maria's anti-Semitism is anchored less by religious faith than by the notion that Jews such as Mordecai possess a tainted form of gold, one that not only deprives Gentiles of their comfort and security but that can be countered only by the theft—whether literal or figurative—of the Jew's daughter.

And yet, and as with all fantasies within the period's sensationalism, stealing the Jessica character is also quite fraught. Frequently, of course, the Shylock figure seeks to prevent such a union. "[I]f Miriam hes cast the eye of affection upon a Gentile, she must die the death," exclaims the Jew Mike Moss in Ned Buntline's *Agnes; or, the beautiful milliner* (1860s–70s?), one of a series of urban gothic novels in which Buntline stages the obsessive efforts of a Jewish father to cordon off his daughter (always named Miriam) from contact with Gentile men (*Agnes* 48).[13] Similarly, in an anonymous 1848 story titled "The Jewess of Constantina," an enraged father reacts as follows when his daughter tells him that she has converted to Christianity out of love for a Christian soldier: "Christian! Christian,—oh! to have my race dishonored by you; you have signed your own death-warrant, miserable child!" (36). But the real problem has to do with the Jessica character herself. For often it is as though the very passions she represents cannot be successfully contained, or as though her very difference from Gentile culture cannot be scrubbed completely clean even in the process of marrying her and having her convert to Christianity.[14] Consider thus the hapless Mr. Garame in Henry Ruffner's *Judith Bensaddi: A Tale,* a serial novella that appeared in the *Southern Literary Messenger* in 1839.[15] After meeting the title character in South Carolina as she is traveling from Europe with her brother, Garame falls in love with her, this especially when he realizes that her tendency toward excessive emotion and sensibility matches his own penchant for melancholy. But when Judith returns to Europe for several months, Garame has time to reflect, and begins to find her Jewish heritage not just disturbing, but disgusting, precisely because he links it to stereotypes about urban Jews as filthy and connected to the vagaries of the economic market. "Am I really in love with the daughter of a Jew?" he asks. "Am I to connect myself with that accursed race? . . . Yes, a Jew is to be my wife. My children are to be half-blooded Jews. My neighbors are to point at her as we pass by and say 'That is the Jewess' . . . I groaned with horror at these reflections. . . . Faugh! The squalid occupants of suburbs and streets, where a decent passenger is nauseated by their filth! The bearded venders of old clothes! . . . The malignant Shylocks of the money market!" (124–26).

Garame's dilemma here—he is repulsed by the thing he most loves—
reminds us of a central problem surrounding the Jessica narrative: what
happens to her Jewishness once she has married her Christian lover? Or, as
James Shapiro puts it in a discussion of the Jessica story in *The Merchant
of Venice* and various subsequent British retellings, "[H]ow is it possible to
preserve the fantasy of winning and converting the rich and beautiful Jew's
daughter without belatedly introducing a host of problems that arise once
she enters the Christian community as wife and potential mother? . . . When
Jessica converts to Christianity, does any *trace* or *residue* of her Jewishness
remain? . . . Will a residual Jewishness somehow emerge and assert itself,
the baptismal waters incapable of permanently washing it away?"[16] Antebellum sensationalism wrestles with the same problem, usually in ways that
reflect intense ambivalence. For again, the antebellum Jewess acts as the
figure that mediates not just between Gentile culture and Jewish culture, but
between Gentile capitalist culture and its projected Other, the Jew as moneylender. The Jessica figure, that is to say, is less a go-between than a form
of currency, one that mediates and is exchanged between the two cultures in
ways that are quite charged. To marry and convert the Jew's daughter—that
which he hoards and most values—is to gain access to the very forms of
pleasure and desire that the professional male has had to cast off in denying
his relationship to the period's expanding and increasingly unstable form of
capitalism. But at the same time, these pleasures are themselves overwhelming, sometimes even fearful and repulsive, to the Gentile male.

This is why a popular narrative such as J. H. Ingraham's 1845 *The Clipper
Yacht; or, Moloch the Money Lender!* (retitled later the same year *Moloch the
Money Lender; or, the Beautiful Jewess*) makes a certain sense, despite its obvious revision of the Shylock–Jessica narrative. For though the novel tells the
story of the Jewish usurer Moloch seeking actively to marry his niece Rachel
into Gentile culture (he is unmarried and childless, but he is raising her as a
sort of daughter substitute), it turns out that his motive is revenge, and that
his niece has been raised as a willing participant in Moloch's war against
Gentile culture. "There is nothing I will shrink from to serve you and do
injury to the Christian," she says to Moloch when he suggests that she marry
Tudor Dauling, the son of a rich duke (*Clipper* 20). Ingraham's description
of the beautiful girl's face at this moment does considerable cultural work,
especially as it underscores the latent threat that the Jewess is said to pose:
"As she spoke her dark eyes flashed and her lip curled with the proud hatred a
beautiful Jewish woman only can express when she speaks of the persecutors
of her race" (20). Similarly, in an anonymous story titled "Mina Lowe. The
Pretty Jewess" (1842), the narrator is humiliated when he learns that Mina
and her "Jew banker" (277) father have a long history of luring Gentile men

into false and inevitably costly and embarrassing relationships with the beautiful young Jewess. Such stories reflect the intensely desirable nature of the Jessica character for Gentile culture, but they also remind us that such desire is tinged with anxiety.

What we see in this material is thus a complicated extension of the Shakespearean Jessica narrative as circulated within antebellum culture. The beautiful Jessica figure and the Gentile male frequently fall in love, but a variety of sensational narratives make it clear that accessing the Jewess is an anxious proposition, one that must be negotiated carefully by the young men wishing to marry the alluring Jewess. For while stealing Jessica leaves Shylock shamed and emasculated, Jessica herself often threatens the Gentile men who desire her with a similar fate. The result is a series of narratives that explore and usually seek to resolve the tensions that inhere in the Jessica character, this as a means of bolstering and reinvigorating the imperiled form of professional manhood we see everywhere in the pages of the period's sensationalism. We might group these texts under the heading of "conversion romance." A small subgenre of antebellum sensationalism that, usually via the machinations of a complicated familial drama, imagines the union of the Jewess and the Gentile male, the conversion romance provides a kind of fantasy solution to readers interested in imagining not just the perverse pleasures of the Jew but, more dramatically, the reverse theft of the very pleasures that Gentile culture believes itself to have lost under the sign of the new economy.

Paradigmatic of the texts narrating the conversion of the Jessica character is the above-cited short story by S. B. Beckett, "The Jewess of Cairo." Like numerous other novels and pieces of magazine fiction from the period, the narrative follows the career of an American male who, displaced in an orientalized middle east, falls in love with an exotic Jewish woman. The story begins with a dramatic scene in which the American tourist in Egypt, Frank Wingate, saves a young Jewish woman from being abducted for inclusion in the local Pacha's harem. Soon afterward, however, Wingate and his friend are themselves imprisoned by the Pacha's men in the palace dungeon, and left there to await torture and execution. Tellingly, Wingate sums up the dilemma as a form of gender crisis: "[T]o be smothered in a pent up hole like this, with none but our murders [sic] being aware of our fate, this is what saps the manhood from me" (271). That night, Wingate finds respite from his anxiety in an erotic dream, in which he is approached by the woman he has saved. It was, the narrator, explains, "a gentle and confiding creature, lovely as a Hebe—it was the young Jewess—she had conferred her heart's affection on him, and a world of sunshine and flowers was open before him" (272). As though on cue, Wingate's dream is realized when the girl steals into the palace and frees him, and then sneaks off with the parting words, "Farewell, remember the Jewess, Naomi" (272). Wingate's manhood is thus restored via the intercession of a fantasy version of the Jewess as the beautiful savior. Perhaps inevitably, the two quickly fall in love. "We will leave this hapless country," he tells her, "where the iron heel of the oppressor crushes all the manlier feelings of our natures in the dust, and in the far land of freedom, find a home of peace, of domestic tranquility" (277).

But despite the fact that Naomi herself was raised in Charleston, South Carolina ("Naomi is an American, too!" Wingate exclaims upon hearing this news [276]), and despite her assurance to Wingate that she shares his belief in Christianity ("as for your belief, in my heart it is but my own" [277]), she insists that her father will never agree to their marriage. And indeed, when Wingate returns to Absolom's sumptuous home for a second visit, the American finds that Absolom has taken his daughter and vanished, and that behind its now locked doors, the house is completely empty. The result is that Naomi again becomes a part of Wingate's fantasy life. "If he thought of Naomi, it was as of one in a dream," we are told as he returns from Egypt to America. "Indeed, at times, he began to look upon his whole intercourse with her as a dream" (279). Moving in and out of Wingate's Gentile psyche, Naomi thus acts as a tantalizing image of desire, one Wingate is unable to fully access while abroad in Egypt. And this goes for Absolom's money as well, for although the rich Jew offers Wingate a fortune in railroad stocks in gratitude for saving his daughter from the Pacha ("You know not the wealth of the Jew Absolom!" he says matter-of-factly [277]), Wingate the American magnanimously refuses to accept any money from him.

Once back on American soil, however, things change for Wingate. First, he discovers that Absolom has surreptitiously placed the railroad stock in his bank account, and that he is now quite wealthy. Next, and more dramatically, he learns that Naomi is also living in New York, where she has moved following the death of her father, who has succumbed to the plague in Syria. With Absolom out of the way, Wingate is able thus to realize a new and safer form of fantasy, one in which he gains access both to the Jewess on American soil, and to her father's dazzling riches—the "*tout ensemble* of magnificence" he earlier viewed inside Solomon's home. Naomi's clothing at the marriage ceremony reflects the ideal turn of events for Wingate: whereas in the middle east Wingate was put off by "the awkwardness of [Naomi's] immense turban—the only ungainly article in the dress of the Oriental Jews" (276), in America she accedes to his request to wear "a priceless sprig of brilliants, instead of the awkward turban fashionable in Syria" (281). In abandoning her turban, Naomi is of course beginning a process of assimilation into Wingate's Christian culture, one she has already signaled with her comment that "as for your belief, in my heart it is but my own." But we might also say that Absolom's money has undergone a similar process of assimilation. No longer located in the mysterious world of harems, dungeons, and sumptuous hoards of splendor—a world where "the manlier feelings of our natures" are undermined—the fortune that falls to Wingate will now, we can assume, be spent in ways that are far less exotic and considerably more conducive to bolstering the manhood that was threatened while abroad in Naomi's middle east. Accordingly, Naomi as Jewess allows for the transfer of an otherwise excessive form of desire into the world of American domesticity. Indeed, the key element to this story might well be the railroad stocks themselves. For while in the hands of Absolom they represented a troubling, even tainted kind of currency, one connected to speculation and the excesses of the market, the stocks seem far less problematic once ensconced in Wingate's private bank account. Much like Naomi's removal of her turban, the transfer of Solomon's railroad stocks to America has removed the oriental taint from his money, this despite the obvious fact that its actual market value has remained the same. Clearly, though, value for Wingate is contingent, hinging on the delicate distinction between the Jew as a figure of orientalized fantasy, and an assimilated embodiment of what are now relatively neutralized forms of passion and desire.

Numerous other narratives imagine how the Jewess might provide Gentile men a means of negotiating the fraught terrain of fiscal insolvency and stolen enjoyment. A useful example is Mary E. Lee's "Aaron's Rod; or the Young Jewess," a short story that appeared in the *Southern and Western Literary Messenger* in 1846. Here the narrative revolves around a chronically infirm and financially impoverished young Christian man named Augustus Halm, who has fallen in love with Esther, the beautiful daughter of a rich Jew named Mr. Aaron. Early on, Halm is deeply humiliated when Aaron informs him, "Your worldly prospects are not the brightest, for a sick man is unfitted to much exertion" (555), and proceeds to offer him "a bag of ducats" (556) if he will help Aaron convince his daughter to marry one of the many Jews who have been courting her. For Aaron, the offer is a logical transaction: increasingly aware that his daughter is "ashamed of her Jewish origin" and fearful that she might "[forsake] the faith of her fathers" (556), the Jew hopes to cash in on the close friendship between Halm and Esther. But for Halm, the offer is infuriating as well as emasculating. On the one hand, this is because Aaron is accurate in assessing Halm's future prospects. As the narrator puts it at one point, "[H]e was just now entirely unable to make any exertions for the replenishment of his almost exhausted funds" (556). But this is also because Halm has himself fallen in love with Esther. Accordingly, much as Jessica's theft of Shylock's "bag[] of ducats" and jewels in *The*

Merchant of Venice leaves her father with a form of symbolic castration ("A sealed bag, two sealed bags of ducats / . . . And jewels—two stones, two rich and precious stones / Stol'n by my daughter!"; 2.8.18; 20–21), Aaron's offer here seems to remind Halm that it is only the Jew who can provide him with the currency (both literal and figurative) necessary for masculine self-possession. It is as though Aaron holds the symbolic equivalent of Halm's physical "jewels"—his testicles—and is offering to "return" his manhood with the proviso that Halm abandon his love for Esther. Hence Halm's "blush of honest indignation" (555) and his refusal to accept Aaron's offer, despite his desperate situation.

But what we find is that Aaron is correct about his daughter's waywardness. For she is in fact in love with Halm, something she makes clear when, as she and her father are leaving town for an extended journey, she secretly places "two packages of gold coins, neatly folded and carefully secured" (557) inside a pot of Aaron's rod flowers that she gives him as a farewell gift. Halm soon discovers the money, and is overjoyed both at her concern for him, and at the financial relief the money provides. "Oh, Esther, blessed and benevolent being!" he exclaims (557). Esther's money thus signifies quite differently for Halm than her father's "bag of ducats." Indeed, in what follows, Halm is able to use Esther's money to heal himself at a mineral spring, and, in the course of two years, transform from a "pale and sickly youth" to "a young man possessing all the proportions of manly grace and strength" (559). The implication is that it is the Jessica character who must launder the Jew's money, transforming it from debased and emasculating coin into the form of currency that will bolster the imperiled manhood of the Gentile male. This logic of conversion is only furthered when Halm is reunited with a still-unmarried Esther at story's end, and discovers that her father has died, and that she has converted to Christianity. "It was the happiest moment of his whole life!" we are told. "Esther a Christian and unmarried!" (559). The two are soon married, and in the story's final paragraph we are told that they are eventually surrounded by "a group of lovely children, in whose faces are softly blended the traits of the Christian and Jewish races" (560). The image is one of harmony between Christian and Jew, but we should understand that the text's conclusion depends in large part on Esther's conversion to Christianity. Unlike Naomi in "The Jewess of Cairo," Esther is not overtly exotic or threatening, but her conversion is important nevertheless. For, coupled with her earlier gift of gold coins to Halm, the conversion from Jew to Christian provides the Gentile male with access to the very forms of enjoyment—figured in this story as both money and masculine potency—"stolen" by the story's Shylock character. Indeed, the gift of gold coins also insures that Halm will be in possession of the symbolic agency in the marriage between Gentile and Jew. It will be the Lorenzo figure, that is to say, rather than Shylock or Jessica, who holds the "bag of ducats" in this relationship.

The elimination of the Shylock character that we see in the above two texts is in fact a commonplace in the conversion narrative, suggesting that his death is crucial in allowing the Gentile male to access the forms of desire and cash housed in the Jessica character. In *The Merchant of Venice,* of course, Shylock actually joins Jessica in converting to Christianity at play's end (4.5.376–92). But American sensationalism has little interest in this story line. Thus, while a British novel circulating in America such as Catherine Gore's 1843 *Abednego, the Money-Lender. A Romance* pivots around the discovery that the Jew Abednego has converted to Christianity ("Abednego the Money-lender was only in name and practices a Jew!" exclaims the young Gentile vying for the hand of the Jessica figure [60]), American writers relied fairly heavily on Shylock's death as a means of distancing Jessica from her Jewish heritage, and freeing up Shylock's money for Gentile appropriation.[17] For example, in B. Perley Poore's *The Mameluke* (1852), a young American marries "the only child of a wealthy Jewish merchant at Smyrna" (9), but only after "the Old Jewish Banker" (26) is stabbed and killed while walking in the street with the American Lorenzo character. We see a similar set of events in "The Daughter of Israel," an 1845 short story in the *Ladies National Magazine* and set in fifteenth-century Spain. Here a young Jewish girl named Miriam has fallen in love with a "penniless" student named Salvado, "a Christian of the old blood . . . who had inherited all the high intellect and manly courage of his ancestors" (174). With Salvado's influence, Miriam has secretly converted to Christianity, but she is afraid to tell her father, knowing that "he would sooner have seen her in the grave than wedded to a Christian" (174). Miriam's dilemma is solved, however, when an anti-Semitic mob, drawn by her father's wealth, sacks her family home (175). In a melodramatic scene, her father suffers a heart attack and dies in her arms, but Miriam is spared when Salvado rides in on a horse and shows the mob that she is wearing "the jeweled cross that he himself had given her" (177). Salvado is unable, however, to stop the mob from plundering Miriam's house and making off with the riches her father has stored there.[18] But in "The Daughter of Israel," it turns out that the loss of the Jew's riches is relatively unimportant. For what we see is that "the death of a distant relative" has allowed Salvado to "come into possession of title and a large estate" (178). Miriam is thus distanced from both her father and his money. We might in fact say that the Jew's money has been somewhat magically transformed into the very fortunate inheritance that descends upon Salvado. This story's Jessica figure is thus provided a smooth assimilation into Christian culture. Indeed, with the aid of Salvado's inheritance, she is able to act now as a sort of benign stand-in for the forms of pleasure and enjoyment that Salvado's Christian culture has been unable to retrieve directly from Jewish moneylenders such as Miriam's father.

But there are instances when even the removal of the Shylock character is an insufficient solution to the kinds of problems projected onto the Jew and his daughter. This is reflected in the melodramatic tragedy we see staged in Theodore Sedgwick Fay's *Sidney Clifton* (1839). For what we see here is that even the Jessica character must be eliminated for the Gentile male to achieve a full sense of comfort and self-possession. Tellingly, in apparent reference to the 1837 Panic, the novel is set on the eve of a national fiscal crisis. As one character puts it, "the crash that I have predicted is at our doors[;] . . . national and individual ruin stares us in the face. . . . [T]oo soon, the wheels of commerce will pause on their axles [and the] mercantile community and the moneyed institutions will become bankrupt" (106). In order to allegorize the looming threat, the novel follows the career of an indebted libertine named De Lyle, whose fiscal and sexual profligacy parallels the similarly reckless national economy. One narrative strand of De Lyle's excesses revolves around his seduction of Rachel Samuel, the beautiful Jewish daughter of his creditor, the rich Wall Street moneylender Isaac Samuel. The "envied possessor of millions in the funds" who is regarded as the "monarch" of Wall Street (143; 148), Isaac, we are told, "loved his child with an affection as ardent as his grasping nature could conceive for *any* object" (164). Again echoing Shylock's famous equation of his daughter with his ducats, the lines emphasize Isaac's greed (as does the description of him as suffering from "tremulous nerves prematurely shattered by continual apprehension of pecuniary loss" [142]). But this description of Isaac also prepares us for Rachel's desire to leave her father's house and enter Gentile culture with De Lyle. De Lyle's plan is to seduce Rachel and thereby gain access to Isaac's money, but his scheme is foiled when a woman he has previously seduced into a counterfeit marriage warns Rachel that he is in fact a rogue libertine (158). When Rachel learns she has been deceived, she falls into a melodramatic swoon, "the blood flowing copiously from her mouth, it being evident that the shock had caused the rupture of a blood vessel" (133). In a dramatic twist to the Jessica narrative, Rachel soon dies, and the moneylender Isaac is left to mourn over the fact that "for filthy lucre he had ministered to the depraved appetites of De Lyle, and thus indirectly been the cause of her misery" (136–37). Shortly thereafter, Samuel hunts down De Lyle in Europe, kills him, and then commits suicide.

For at least one character, a man named Shafton, Isaac's actions smack of insincerity. "Oh, aye, I perceive," he says, "the Jew's cunning has converted the debt into a *debt of honor*" (204). But Isaac's conversion of avarice into affect in avenging his daughter is more complicated than this character allows. For, staged in direct relation to the looming specter of economic panic, his murder-suicide provides an imagined solution to the coming "crash" that is predicted early in the novel. To this way of thinking, the "unbridled passions" (34) of the chronic male debtor will no longer threaten the nation with fiscal instability, just as the Jew's usury will no longer act as a drag on the nation's economy. But a similar logic also applies to Rachel's death. For if the Jewess embodies the excessive and dangerous pleasures of the new capitalism, hoarded by the Jew but potentially available for a kind of reverse "theft" by Gentile culture, then her melodramatic demise suggests that, at least in this narrative, the qualities she represents are simply too volatile for successful assimilation into the Gentile world of finance. Like the death of the Shylock character here and in other narratives, the death of the Jessica character is thus another form of fantasy resolution, one that imagines the Jewess into being only to provide the readerly satisfaction of seeing her eliminated from the fraught social context in which she has been placed.

One more text will have to suffice in showing the dual imperative of killing off the Shylock character and performing a kind of symbolic castration of his daughter. This is a long short story titled "The Wheel of Life." Serialized in *The Southern Literary Messenger* in 1845 and set in Poland, the story features Leah Ithraim, a young Jewish woman who has become well known throughout Warsaw for both her great beauty and her piety. Referred to as the "converted Jewess" for her good deeds (which apparently set her apart from other Jews), Leah stands in sharp contrast to her father, a rich moneylender named Nathan Ithraim. Described by one character as a "Shylock" who is "the greatest usurer and most sordid miser belonging to his justly despised race" (131), Nathan has ties to and control over virtually all of the important men in the city (something signaled by the iron box filled with "heavy gold coins" he keeps hidden beneath the marble slabs of his house [135]). The plot of this story centers on the relationship between Leah and one of her father's debtors, a young Gentile libertine named Victor Lauriston. Lauriston has pledged his love to Leah, but is in fact engaged to a rich Catholic woman, whom he soon marries for her money. Ithraim is enraged by Lauriston's deceptions ("[I]t is not to be wondered that we should shrink from all amalgamation with the heretical and oppressive Gentiles," he tells Leah [132]), and proceeds to plot Lauriston's familial and financial ruin. But what we find is that Leah, true to her moniker of "the converted Jewess," is forgiving of Lauriston's sins. Indeed, when at story's end Lauriston comes to her, destitute and near death, and begs her to adopt his young daughter, she agrees to his request. Leah thus becomes a kind of foster mother to Lauriston's Gentile child, a fantasy scenario in which the Gentile gains access to the Jewess, but without actual sexual contact with her. The description we receive of Lauriston's earlier disavowal of Leah to his fiancée is thus telling: "Victor Lauriston, above all others, could never forget the great line of separation drawn between her race and his own untarnished heritage" (131). Lauriston is staged here as a conniving anti-Semite, but Leah's role as adoptive mother suggests that the text acknowledges and seeks to negotiate the same "line of separation" that the libertine describes.

This seemingly unconscious textual anxiety about the Jew is also reflected in the fate of Leah's Shylock father. For what we also learn at story's end is that Nathan Ithraim has died, but so suddenly that he is unable to tell Leah about the "vast treasures" (293) that he has hidden under his floors of his home. Instead, in a fairly strained narrative twist, the money is located by Lauriston's uncle, a rich count who we learn has been searching for information about his missing niece (having heard rumors that his son brought the girl to Leah Ithraim just before his death, he ends up searching through her father's home for clues and finds the cache of gold coins). And what we see is that the Jew's money goes to Lauriston's child as part of her inheritance from the count, rather than to Leah herself. Again, then, the Jessica character helps facilitate the transfer of Shylock's tainted money over to Gentile hands. Indeed, although Ithraim's goal in his career as usurer has been to "enrich my child—yea, to give her beauty power" (135), it is apparently not in the best interests of the Gentile community to leave such power in the hands of a Jew. In fact, given Ithraim's vast influence over the Gentile world of commerce, we might understand this transfer as an imagined return of fiscal security to Gentile culture more generally. But, and of course, this security is also dependent on the successful negotiation and assimilation of the Jessica character. Here, the role of the "converted Jewess" is particularly noteworthy, for despite her tremendous beauty, Leah joins the ranks of "old maids" in the community, thus ensuring that hers is a sort of absent presence, one whereby the forms of desire and enjoyment housed in Shylock and his daughter might be realized in a safe and mediated form.

Again, then, the period's mass culture seems invested in narratives about the Jew's daughter that provide various ways to ameliorate the period's anxieties about political economy and, simultaneously, masculine passion. These are fantasies of conversion—conversion not just of the Jew into a Christian, but of the Jew's money into Christian money, and, by extension, the Jew's putatively excessive passions into less troubling forms of masculine passion. This form of romance—we might, again, call it the "conversion romance"—therefore does a consistent kind of work within the pages of antebellum sensationalism. For though these stories require considerable narrative pressure to bring about their desired conclusions, they allow the capitalist Gentile access to the very market desires that he has projected onto the Jew. Returned to him in the altered form of the converted Jewess, however, these desires are purged of their most threatening qualities, and transformed into the very means of establishing the masculine self-possession lost to the forces of antebellum capitalism.

"Dark, and yet not dark": Race and the Conversion Romance

But perhaps the most vexed versions of the conversion romance are those that revolve around issues of race. As the eastern settings of stories such as "The Jewess of Cairo" remind us, the Jewess is a charged figure in the Gentile imagination both because of her excessive passion, and because of the way she represents a form of racial difference. In some cases—perhaps to distance her from her father—the Jewess is marked as excessively white. As Shapiro points out, this is in keeping with the way in which Jessica is represented in *The Merchant of Venice*. Consider Lorenzo's description of Jessica's handwriting: "I know the hand; in faith, 'tis a fair hand, / And whiter than the paper it writ on / Is the fair hand that writ" (2.4.12–14). Later on in the play, in response to Shylock's insistence that he and Jessica are of the same blood, Soliano remarks on a difference that he casts in terms of skin color: "There is more difference between thy flesh and hers than between jet and ivory," he says (3.1.39). But, and as Shapiro suggests, this form of whiteness also opens up a whole set of interpretive dilemmas: "[P]aradoxically, the whitening of Jessica will only exacerbate the problem—like the Jewish people as a whole she is both recognizably different and somehow capable of passing, neither black nor white, except relatively so. Because her Jewish difference—unlike that of her circumcised father and brethren—is not physically inscribed in her flesh, Jessica's Jewishness remains invisible and therefore all the more difficult to identify and eradicate" ("Jew's Daughter"). The issues Shapiro outlines are especially pertinent to the racially charged setting of antebellum America, where the boundary line between white and black was of course increasingly porous and unstable. To marry the Jessica figure, that is to say, allowed for access to tabooed forms of pleasure, but such a move also carried the hint, often horrific, of miscegenation.

This disturbing possibility may help explain a remarkable 1856 passage from Nathaniel Hawthorne's *English Notebooks*. Here Hawthorne describes a woman sitting across from him at a dinner held at the home of the lord mayor of London, David Salomons. "My eyes were mostly drawn to a young lady who sat nearly opposite me, across the table," he writes. "She was, I suppose, dark, and yet not dark, but rather seemed to be of pure white marble, yet not white; but of the purest and finest complexion, (without a shade of color in it, yet anything but sallow or sickly) that I ever beheld. Her hair was a wonderful deep, raven black, black as night, black as death . . . [it was] wonderful hair, Jewish hair" (321).[19] Vacillating between categories such as "white" and "not white," "dark" and "not dark," Hawthorne depicts a version of Jewish difference that blurs the distinction between blackness and whiteness. Her skin is "without a shade of color," yet it betrays signs of racial difference nevertheless, a fact that makes the woman a figure of some confusion, even anxiety. And to be sure, Hawthorne seems unsettled by this woman, something especially clear in his closing lines of the passage: "I should never have thought of touching her, or desiring to touch her; for, whether owing to distinctness of race, my sense that she was Jewish, or whatever else, I felt a sort of repugnance, simultaneously with my perception that she was an admirable creature" (321). Hawthorne's "repugnance" is clearly linked to his sense that, as a Jew, this woman is racially inferior, but his excessive protestations ("I should never have thought of touching her," etc.) suggest that his distaste is also the result of a fairly strong sexual attraction to her. He is, that is to say, disgusted by the very form of Otherness he finds himself desiring, something that shows through in virtually every line of this powerful passage. And indeed, it's worth adding here that Hawthorne expresses a strange form of relief at the woman's "Shylock" companion, who, he explains, "justified me in the repugnance I have always felt toward his race" (321).

Michael Rogin suggests that for early-twentieth-century immigrant Jews, blackface performance (such as that performed by Al Jolson) provided the means of assimilation into American culture. For the antebellum Jew, however, blackness was less something that could be put on and taken off than it was a spectrelike double that often informed the very nature of Jewishness for a racist American culture: in some respects the antebellum Jew wears a kind of whiteface, one that masks, often with little success, a darker form of racial difference. Consider in this context Theodore Winthrop's best-selling novel, *Cecil Dreeme* (1861), seventeen editions of which were published by 1864. The majority of this novel revolves around the efforts of a young professional named Robert Byng to resist the powerfully felt temptations of a "Hebrew-ish" financier named Densdeth. He is a "Midas with the gold touch," we are told (64), and he offers Byng a decadent lifestyle of "luxury" and "perfect enjoyment" (63) if only he will give himself over to

Densdeth's control. "I saw . . . that you were worth buying, worth pervert-
ing," Densdeth says to him. "Are you a cheap commodity? Or must I give
time and pains and study to make you mine?" (64). But, and tellingly, there
are moments when Byng's efforts to evade Densdeth's Svengali-like powers
involve recourse to the language of race—in particular the more radical
form of racial difference found in blacknesss. As Byng explains at a crucial
moment when Densdeth spots Byng at a restaurant and sends a glass of
burgundy to his table, "Densdeth's servant had deposited the wine at my
right. He was an Afreet creature, this servant, black, ugly, brutal as the real
Mumbo Jumbo. Yet sometimes, as he stood by his master, I could not avoid
perceiving a resemblance, and fancying him a misbegotten repetition of
the other. And at the moments when I mistrusted Densdeth, I felt that the
Afreet's repulsive appearance more fitly interpreted his master's soul than
the body by which it acted" (64). This strategy, in which the Jew is linked
to blackness, suggests that the Gentile Byng, like much of his culture in this
period, is seeking to have it both ways. On one level, he desires—longs for—
the pleasure and enjoyment he locates in Densdeth-as-Jew (at one point he
describes himself as "a youth . . . dragged along by an irresistible attraction"
[180]). On another level, though, he seeks to distance himself from the sensational Jew by imagining the Jew's interior selfhood (his "soul") as marked
by a "repulsive" blackness that belies the deceptive whiteness of his white
skin.[20]

   This conflation of Jewishness and blackness is more fully played out in
Henry Ruffner's novella, *Judith Bensaddi,* which I cite above in discussing
the intense feelings of disgust the narrator ends up having for his lover,
the Jewess Judith Bensaddi. One of the more elaborate of the period's conversion romances, this text suggests that it is the fear of racial miscegenation—in particular as it revolves around the category of blackness—that acts
as a useful failsafe for the Gentile male in his efforts to distance himself from
the powerful allure of the Jewess. But what Ruffner also shows is the way
in which this problem can be solved, so that the Jewess and her considerable fortune might be converted and assimilated into Gentile culture, and a
disempowered Christian manhood reasserted. Perhaps not surprisingly, this
solution has to do with the discovery of gold, an event that Ruffner seems to
include as a means of balancing accounts, and providing the Gentile male
the sorts of resources he requires in negotiating his relationship to the Jessica figure.

   The novel's narrator, Mr. Garame, first meets Judith when he shares a
car with her and her brother on a train heading south toward Charleston,
South Carolina. She is, he explains, "the most beautiful gem of humanity
I have ever seen. . . . [T]he ebony black of her flowing hair, and the mild

black of her lustrous eyes, contrasted so strongly with the delicate hue of her complexion, that I pronounced her so fair, as to be only not florid" (42). Like both Jessica and the Jewess of Hawthorne's *English Notebooks,* Judith is represented here as intensely white, an attribute that is contrasted by her luxurious "ebony"-shaded black hair and large black eyes. But even as Garame praises Judith's whiteness, he is uncertain as to how to categorize her. "They spoke English with the perfect ease and idiom of well-educated natives of England and America," he says in reference to Judith and her brother, "but in their persons differed from my notion of the Anglo-Saxon race" (43). Garame eventually determines that the name Bensaddi must be Italian. As he puts it, "I shrewdly conjectured that their dark eyes and hair, with their brunettish complexion, were due to the influence of an Italian . . . sun upon their ancestors" (43). But even early on it is clear that Ruffner's Jessica figure is being marked as both intensely white and racially distinct from the category of whiteness.

This issue is complicated when the reader learns that Judith and her brother are actually traveling in America in order to observe the conditions of slaves in the South. Their father, Judith explains, has "some business with a planter in the West Indies," and they have accompanied him that they might "see the curiosities of nature in the torrid zone, and the black man in the miseries of West Indian bondage, and the white man in the highest state of freedom, as he is in your happy country" (44). For the most part, the brother and sister are remarkably blind to the suffering of the slaves they observe. "The slaves, in general, seem to be as contented and merry a set of beings as any in the world," Judith's brother blithely remarks. "They laugh, and sing, and dance, not to 'drive the dull care away,' for dull care never seems to visit them" (44). In keeping with his Southern mindset (he is from Virginia) Garame concurs with this sentiment, remarking that "Born to slavery, they grow up with minds conformable to their condition" (44).

Such racism might work to distance Judith and her brother from the taint of blackness, yet it is Judith's emotional response to a series of slave songs she hears that complicates the question of race. "A party of slaves were coming in from the field," Garame explains, "and as often happens, they began to sing with a full voice one of the melodious airs that they have among them. Judith listened with breathless attention as if the strain were new to her. I had heard it before. The same air was repeated to a succession of stanzas destitute of merit, but deriving pathos from the chorus or burden, 'Long time ago,' which sounded delightful because it was uttered with enthusiasm by many voices joining in symphony from different parts of the neighborhood" (71). Later on, the narrator overhears Judith composing music at the piano, and realizes that she is attempting to recreate the songs she found so affecting when listening to the singing of the local slaves. "She had arranged the notes on a blank page of the music book before her, which I found to be her own," we are told. "When she discovered that we were in the room, she rose with a blush to leave the instrument, saying that we had caught her attempting to learn the Negro's melody" (102). Judith's shame here surprises Garame, but some time later, once Judith reveals her secret to him ("will you not shudder at the thought of marrying a Jewess?" she asks [102]), the reader is led to understand the implicit link that Ruffner intends between Judith and the black slaves with whom she seems so affectively connected. It is as though her Jewishness provides a sympathetic link to the exceptional pathos of the slave songs, a link that, despite her shame, she feels compelled to explore by putting the songs to music on her piano. And indeed, it turns out that Judith's own emotionality is perhaps the central facet of her personality. As Judith's cousin, Mr. Von Caleb, puts it in listing what he describes as her faults, "[T]hey call her an enthusiast because, I suppose, she takes fits of high feeling sometimes and talks a little wildly, like a prophetess. I have heard her two or three times in these fits; I thought she talked very beautifully if she did go out of the common way" (111). While on the one hand Judith's "fits of high feeling" might be markers of a refined sensibility, they are on the other suggestive of an inability to rein in her passions. This quality seems to stem from her Jewish or "Hebrew" blood, but, given the many stereotypes circulating during the period about the overly passionate and emotionally immature nature of black men and women, it might also provide a not-so-subtle link to the slaves whose music Judith finds so alluring.[21]

Tellingly, Garame's fears about Judith's Jewishness cannot be overcome even by the news that Judith's father is in fact quite rich. As a Jewish friend of the Bensaddi family, Mr. Levi, puts it, "Is Nathan Bensaddi a banker, do you ask? Why, yes, sure he is. . . . Ah, he has the monies—sure; yes, money, money. Oh, so much money!" (108). Nor is he moved when, in a surprising twist to the Jessica narrative, Judith informs Garame that her father has actually expressed willingness to approve of a marriage between his daughter and a Christian man. "My father has told me," she says, "that if I should meet with a Christian whose temper and character were suitable to mine, he would not refuse to own him for a son-in-law" (103). (We also learn that Judith's sister, Rachel, has married a Gentile [109].) Indeed, rather than seize the opportunity to gain access to the Jew's fortune (much of which he learns is tied to the Caribbean slave trade [109]), Garame finds himself shamed by his own meager finances, or what he terms his "empty purse" (113). As he explains at one point, "She had put her purse into my hands at Norfolk and requested me to defray all our expenses out of it, but I told her that I would not consent to defray more than her own. . . . I returned the purse, telling her that she had better keep it now until we left the hotel. So I had given her no sign that my funds were low" (113). Judith's "purse" seems here to be a floating signifier not just for financial empowerment but for sexual empowerment as well. It is, that is to say, a kind of replacement for the phallus, which in his relative poverty Garame seems unable to wield with any real authority. Instead, it is Judith who possesses the agency in their relationship, both because of her financial superiority, and because of her frighteningly passionate Jewishness (in this she seems quite unlike Esther in Lee's "Aaron's Rod; or the Young Jewess," whose gift of gold coins reinvigorates the story's protagonist). Indeed, Garame's disempowerment extends to his very body, for what we see is that, just as he is initiating a more serious relationship with Judith, he is badly injured when he falls off a moving coach. "Mr. Garame, you are *seriously* hurt," Judith says, a diagnosis that proves correct when it turns out that his hip is severely bruised and his ankle badly sprained (90). Thus incapacitated, Garame is placed in a tellingly passive position as he and Judith develop their feelings for one another, and as he watches her dramatic mood swings from one day to the next. Indeed, only when Judith's departure is imminent is Garame able to walk on his lame leg without a crutch. "I had risen and was standing about the middle of the floor without my crutch, which I no longer needed," he explains of their final conversation. "I turned and met her eyes with mine" (114). Apparently, for Garame it is only the absence of his beloved Judith that will grant him the status of masculine self-possession and empowerment.

Garame thus finds himself increasingly unable—or unwilling—to act on his promise to contact Judith during their separation and confirm their engagement. "Write to me then," she says to him. "If you confirm our engagement, I shall rejoice as much as gratified love can make me" (106). Instead, as weeks and months pass, he wages an internal battle in which his love for Judith is matched against his deep-seated anti-Semitism and racial prejudice. As he puts it at one point, "Whilst I would be musing on my lovely Judith and seeing her with fancy's eye arrayed in all her charms, that troublesome word 'Jewess' would come with some ugly thought behind it and dissipate, as with a wizard's spell, the fascinating colors of the vision. . . . Oh, why was so beautiful, so amiable a creature born of the accursed race? The miserly knavish race!" (124; 126). Eventually, Garame ends up delaying contact with Judith for over a year, long enough that she finally writes and informs him that she has married someone else, and that she has converted to Christianity. It is only then that Garame begins to lament his loss: "Self-reproach for my unjust suspicions and my fatal procrastination wrung my heart," he says in the novel's concluding lines. "I am wedded to remembered beauty," he says. (145). This melodramatic posture provides him a convenient escape clause: longing for the Jewess only after she is no longer available, Garame allows himself proximity to a form of desire that is, for him, simply too frightening and overwhelming to be indulged in with any felt sense of safety or security.

The narrative doesn't end here, however. Instead, as a result of the popularity of *Judith Bensaddi,* Ruffner produced a sequel to his story entitled *Seclusaval* in 1843. Here we see Judith and Garame reunited and eventually married, this after Garame discovers Judith once more on American soil, working as a governess for a British family in order to support herself. For it turns out that Judith has met with ill fortune, first when her fiancé dies before their marriage was consummated, and second when her father's business is bankrupted and she "nobly surrender[s] her own large fortune to pay her father's debts" (*Seclusaval* 201). But the telling aspect of this text is that Ruffner imagines a marriage between the two only once Judith has converted to Christianity, and, perhaps more importantly, once Garame has made a large fortune of his own after discovering not one but two immense deposits of gold. As he explains in referring to the first discovery, "It was the most productive mine yet discovered in the country. Besides the fine grains usually met with, lumps of gold weighing often an ounce and sometimes a pound were picked out of the gravel. My clear profits from this source amounted to about a thousand dollars a month" (153).

Garame's discoveries are particularly remarkable, of course, in that they offer an imagined counter to the nation's consistent anxieties about the lack of gold bullion circulating in the economy. (Notably, the first mine is discovered on land purchased from a man desperate for funds after having been "defrauded by a speculator," and the second on a tract bought from a man "disgusted with mining speculations" [*Seclusaval* 153; 154].) It is as though this gold, extracted straight out of the ground as an almost premarket form of treasure, represents a pure form of economic stability, one that Garame can thus cash in, as it were, in his relationship with Judith. We might in this sense understand Ruffner as having used his sequel to shift the site of economic plenitude away from the anxious-making figure of the sensational Jewess (who wields the "purse" that Garame rejected) and over to the more stable site of a Gentile male—one who, significantly, is untainted by greed. "Avarice was not my passion," Garame tells us at one point in reference to his gold-mining (153), a comment he follows up on when explaining why he quickly sells off his mines after his initial profit. "I resolved to quit the pursuit at once before the spirit of adventure should grow into a habit and lead me, as it leads most of its slaves, to misfortune, debt, and imprisonment" (155). Garame thus gains money while avoiding slavery to market passion.

Equally important, he gains access to an already converted Jessica figure, this while avoiding a similar servitude to the Jewess as monied, overly passionate, and potentially emasculating. Indeed, it is in this context that we should interpret the absolute absence of any reference in this follow-up text to Judith as racially distinct from Garame. Apparently, once she is detached from the qualities that made her a figure of anxiety, her possible connection to blackness simply isn't useful to Garame in negotiating his relationship to her. In some respects, this looks like enjoyment drained of its most alluring and desirable qualities, for what we see is a Jessica figure who bears only slight resemblance to her literary forebearer, or even to the title character of *Judith Bensaddi*. But in this awkward sequel, it is fantasy resolution of the best sort, precisely because it provides safe access to the very forms of enjoyment that Garame, like so many other men within capitalist America, has projected onto the figure of the sensational Jewess.

CONCLUSION: THE DAUGHTER'S EXPENDITURE

Ruffner's narrative reliance on the figure of the alluring Jewess is thus very much of a piece with the material I have been describing throughout this chapter. Like various other writers of sensational fiction at mid-century, he seems to have been negotiating the vexed terrain of finance and gender by recourse to the mythos about Jews perpetuated by the many American incarnations of Shakespeare's *The Merchant of Venice*. Whether focusing solely on the Shylock figure and his money, or opening out to a more dynamic consideration of the Jessica narrative, these writers clearly saw Jewishness as a malleable, fungible category for imagining the status of desire and enjoyment for the antebellum professional male. Responding to the scarcity of hard money in circulation during this period (or the fear of such scarcity), antebellum sensationalism invented a version of the Jew who had stolen the nation's missing gold bullion, as well as the more abstract forms of enjoyment that were thought to go along with fiscal security. As we have seen, however, a range of antebellum writers saw in the Jessica character a way to imagine the transfer of both money and enjoyment away from the Jew's control and back over to the Gentile male. And the key to this transaction is that the Jessica figure allowed for the assimilation of the very excess passions of capitalism itself—passions that had been projected onto the Jewess, but which, via the magical alchemy of the conversion narrative, were returned in safely altered form.

I want to close this chapter with a brief reference to Jessica's own expenditures once she has escaped from Shylock's household. This is described in the quote I provide at the outset of this chapter: "Your daughter spent in Genoa, as I heard, one night fourscore ducats," Shylock is told after Jessica absconds with his cash and jewels (3.1.95–96). The news enrages Shylock, who bemoans his lost gold. But, and importantly, Jessica's spending spree also stages the return of Shylock's money to circulation within the general economy. Repeatedly imagined within antebellum sensationalism, such moments imagine an American economy reinvigorated, and with it, an American manhood revitalized and restored to a kind of gold-backed form of self-possession. This may not have been the exact solution a goldbug such as Jackson envisioned when he launched his attack on the paper economy. But if, like Bassanio, America has been "too prodigal" and has "great debts" to pay (1.1.128; 127), it was certainly better than borrowing from a speculator such as Antonio, or—worse—a usurer such as Shylock.

BANKING ON EMOTION

DEBT AND MALE SUBMISSION
IN THE URBAN GOTHIC

"[I]t is notorious that he was a very exacting man with regard to his dues—that he had a sort of mania for making his debtors do just right."

— *The Extraordinary Confession of Dr. John White Webster,*
of the Murder of Dr. George Parkman (1850)

———◆———

MALE PANIC: A STRUCTURE OF FEELING

In a popular antebellum murder pamphlet titled *The Extraordinary Confession of Dr. John White Webster, of the Murder of Dr. George Parkman,* an apparently repentant John White Webster explains that his crime—the murder of his colleague at Harvard University, George Parkman—was motivated by his status as much-persecuted debtor. "He had become of late very importunate for his pay," Webster writes. "He had threatened me with a suit, to put an officer into my house, and to drive me from my professorship if I did not pay him. I cannot tell how long the torrent of threats and invectives continued, and I can now recall to memory but a small portion of what he said. At first I kept interposing, trying to pacify him. . . . But I could not stop him, and soon my own temper was up. . . . I was excited to the highest degree of passion" (*Confession* 6).[1] In what follows Webster relates his gruesome efforts to dispose of Parkman's body and conceal the crime, details that included dismembering Parkman's body and dissolving portions of it in buckets of acid (Webster and Parkman were professors of chemistry). The narrative both shocked and gripped a readership not yet saturated with the lurid aesthetics of the true-crime, tabloid gothic. Yet what predominates in this text—and antebellum readers seem to have been quite responsive to this as well—are the politics of masculine sensibility. Thus at his sentencing,

Webster—described in one newspaper as frequently suffering from a "frantic excitement" and "paroxysm of sudden frenzy" brought on by financial embarrassment—was able to bring judge and jury to tears of sympathy with accounts of the persecution he and his family endured because of his debt to Parkman (New York *Tribune* 12-3-1849). Similarly, several petitions—one with 1,700 signatures and another with almost 1,000—were sent to the governor of Massachusetts, requesting that Webster's life be spared (*Boston Evening Transcript* 7-1-1850). The day of Webster's sentencing, the streets outside the courtroom were so filled with Webster supporters that local residents rented out standing space on their balconies and rooftops (New York *Tribune* 6-28-1850).

How was Webster able to garner such sympathy? One answer is that in his published *Confession* Webster positioned himself as the unfortunate victim of a sensibility too highly refined for the world of commerce, an image that had the paradoxical effect of transforming his status as self-indulgent and transgressive debtor into a form of subjectivity at once deeply feeling and irrevocably middle class. "I was an only child, much indulged," Webster explains, "and I have never acquired the control over my passions that I ought to have acquired early—and the consequence is—all this" (*Confession* 8). Webster's attorney concurred, suggesting that his client's great fault was his tendency to sympathize "to rather an unusual degree, in the tastes and recreations of a domestic circle exclusively feminine" (10). Webster's daughter, meanwhile, described him in a public letter as "timid, yet irritable, hasty, and sometimes passionate" (*Manchester Messenger* 4-14-1850). Local newspapers built on this logic, in particular by casting Parkman as a greedy oppressor who deserved his gruesome fate. In March, for example, the New York *Herald* suggested that "the character of Parkman . . . his association as a money-lender, his intimacy with tenants of every grade, high and low, render it possible that something may be revealed . . . which may exonerate Professor Webster" (*NYH* 3-21-50). Similarly, following Webster's conviction in April, the New York *Sun* denounced Parkman, stating, "[W]e want no other evidence than that afforded in Dr. Webster's trial, to prove that Dr. Parkman was a money-lover; that he worshipped wealth for its own sake, that he was selfish, grasping, and . . . not capable of judging kindly an unfortunate debtor." Had Parkman been more generous, the *Sun* concluded, "he would be alive at this moment, and the wretched murderer, who may expiate on a scaffold for the crime of his murder, might be in the midst of his innocent wife and daughter" (*NYS* 4-1-1850).[2]

Thus despite—or perhaps because of—his guilt, Webster provides what I will be arguing here is an exemplary form of male victimage, one constructed around the sentimental rhetoric of domestic innocence and vulnerability. Indeed, for anyone refusing the stance of debtor passivity assumed by the likes of Webster, the consequences could be dire. For example, in the equally well-publicized 1842 trial of clerk and textbook author John Colt for the murder of Samuel Adams, a printer to whom he owed money (Colt gained fame for hiding his victim's body in a printer's crate and mailing it to St. Louis via New Orleans), Colt *refused* to admit that he had been truly vulnerable, either economically or physically. "I could have paid his two-penny debt any day of the week," the adamantly self-reliant Colt proclaimed in one of a series of letters he published from prison before committing suicide the morning of his planned execution (*Trial* 18).[3] The irony here is that Colt was forced to publish these letters himself because none of the tabloid editors would write up his side of the story, a fact that seems to have turned public sentiment away from him, and that may have helped to seal his fate. Unlike Webster, Colt the struggling professional did not understand the value of marketing oneself as vulnerable, both physically and economically.

Tabloid figures such as Webster and Colt are but two of countless examples of the indebted professional male as staged within the sensational public sphere. Whether weeping and prostrate with guilt, or fleeing, eyes bulging and hair standing on end, from the persecutions of a malevolent creditor, this figure is a mainstay of the seemingly limitless production during this period of pulpy newspaper, pamphlet, and novel-length narratives that revolve around financial hardship and betrayal. But while easily dismissed as the debased and silly product of an incipient mass culture, this ubiquitous presence and the narratives of submission and terror to which it is linked should in fact be understood as signaling a profound response to the period's perilously unstable economy. Indeed, while sensational narratives of financial failure became increasingly common in the years following the devastating Panic of 1837, perhaps none registered so fully the social trauma brought about by the boom-and-bust economy as those depicting masculine crises of debt. The most famous of these scenes is perhaps the encounter between the slave trader Haley and Mr. Shelby in Stowe's 1852 *Uncle Tom's Cabin.* "So much for being in debt,—heigho!" Mr. Shelby says after selling Uncle Tom to pay off the notes of credit held against him by the slave trader Haley. "The fellow sees his advantage and means to push it" (50). But there are dozens of other such examples in urban stage melodramas and urban sensation novels, all of them depicting panicked debtors and persecutory creditors, and all of them reflecting the emergence of a new form of professional masculinity, one increasingly enmeshed within a bewildering chain of random and often anonymous economic relations. As Mihm puts it in characterizing the contingent nature of economic security during this period, "Each person's fate was increasingly tied to individuals and institutions that he or she did not know and could not comprehend. New paper instruments—bills of exchange and bills of credit—function as proxies for distant financial forces" (*Counterfeiters* 11). Karen Sánchez-Eppler provides a similar perspective in her discussion of Ralph Waldo Emerson's debtor insecurities. "What the boom and bust cycles of the 1830s amply illustrate," she writes, "is the insecurity of possession: how easily beautiful estates may be lost; how—in the figure of the debtor whose bankruptcy incurs losses for others—possession is not singular but rather forges flexible and multiple links" ("Clutch Hardest" 79).[4]

This insecurity saturates the popular subgenre of the "Wall Street" novel, a form that was overt in staging masculine economic crisis and anxiety. Thus in Frederick Jackson's *The Victim of Chancery: or a Debtor's Experience* (1841), a debtor named Mr. Adams, described as "one among the great number who in the year 1837 were fated, by means not within their control, to meet a reverse in their worldly circumstances" (30), is thrown into debtors' prison for money owed to a network of often unknown creditors, including the aptly named Mr. Gouge and Mr. Heartless.[5] Similarly, in Timothy Shay Arthur's *Debtor and Creditor; A Tale of the Times* (1847), the scheming financier Turner buys up the debts that the honest Coleman owes to a creditor named Everton, and thus obtains the legal right to persecute him and his family mercilessly. As Arthur's narrator puts it at one point, "When a man is in debt beyond his ability to pay, he no longer possesses, of right, a free control to what he calls his own." Instead, he explains, the creditor has "carte-blanche . . . for all manner of indignity and insult" (60; 36). Popular writer Catherine Sedgwick offers a related narrative in "Wilton Harvey," a long story serialized in *Godey's Lady's Book* in 1842. Here Sedgwick provides sentimental gloss on the sensational and widely publicized true-crime story of Peter Robinson, a debtor who, much like Webster, murdered his creditor and sought unsuccessfully to hide his crime by burying his victim in his basement.[6] "I thought this wa'nt fair play," writes the repentant Robinson character in a deathbed confession to the murdered man's son. "I saw your father making money, hand over hand, his very words turned into gold. . . . I thought it had all been a plan of his from the beginning to snarl me up in that mortgage, and heap interest on interest, and so to take away my little to pour into his cup that was already running over" ("Harvey" 243). Sedgwick extends the thematic of masculine failure by following the career of the title character Harvey, who loses everything in the 1837 Panic, and who—as a sign of his poor judgment—finds himself hoping that his daughter will marry the greedy son of the guilty Robinson. "[H]e has been inveigled into joint-stock companies," we are told, "deluded into buying stock here and there, and lots everywhere, in city, forest, and morass. . . . He dwells continually on his folly and madness, and on the risks and losses in which he has involved others" (326).

Such narratives were so commonplace that a novel such as J. B. Jones's *The City Merchant; or, The Mysterious Failure* (1851) seems intended to provide corrective commentary on tales of masculine disempowerment. Opening on the eve of the 1837 Panic, the narrative tells the story of a businessman named Edgar Saxon savvy enough to outsmart his creditors—in particular a "cunning Jew" named Abraham Ulmar who has purchased a note held against him at a large discount (66)—by selling all of his shares in the U.S. Bank and refusing to deal in any currency other than specie. Ignoring even the entreaties of Bank president Biddle to repurchase his Bank stock, Saxon endures rumors of his "mysterious failure" in order to achieve a rare escape from the trammels of debtor dependency—an escape perhaps available only in a retrospective narrative such as Jones's.

The vexed gender formation I am describing—which I will term here a "debtor masculinity"—began taking shape during the financial revolutions of the 1790s, and cohered in the interval between the 1837 Panic and the 1857 Panic. Characterized chiefly by excessive affective states of panic and hysteria and by postures of submission and humiliation, the debtor male embodied anxieties over an economy based increasingly on the ephemeral foundation of credit, speculation, and paper money. More specifically, much like the "corrupt new men of paper and place" Smith-Rosenberg describes, the debtor male threatened to undermine the stable forms of self-possession and embodiment so crucial to ideologies of individualism and middle-class manhood emerging during this period. The inverse of Melville's infamous Bartleby, whose mantra of "I would prefer not to" seems to reflect a radical form of market renunciation, this emergent gender category came to represent, for many, an insatiable form of market desire that threatened to render the private sphere of domestic enclosure vulnerable to the vitiating effects of the paper economy. According to Timothy Shay Arthur in *Advice to young men* (1848), for example, "The habit of spending money too freely in the gratification of a host of imaginary wants, is one into which young men of generous minds are too apt to fall. . . . The young man who spends his salary of four or five hundred dollars, is almost sure to run through every thing he receives when that salary is doubled. The gratification of one desire only makes way for another still more exacting" (31). The victim of his ever-increasing desire (a condition Henry Ward Beecher describes in a similar advice manual as a "rigorous servitude" [*Lectures* 58]), the debtor male depicted by Arthur poses a threat to the social fabric, but he is also, tellingly, held in a kind of bondage by market forces far beyond his own control.[7] The infamous John White Webster quoted in the above passages might thus be thought of less as an aberration than as a representative of this new masculine sensibility. For while Webster's actions—in particular the gothic efforts to dispose of Parkman's corpse—certainly had to do with fear of detection and public exposure, they can also be understood as the hysterical attempt to repress the humiliating and uncanny mirror image of his own failed financial self, one split by the very dispossession he has suffered at the hands of the economic market.

The debtor male of antebellum sensationalism might thus seem to offer a fairly direct example of an anti-Bank form of class critique. But these stories also reflect the way in which this new gender formation acted as a kind of compensatory rebound ideology. Indeed, the scenarios of masculine panic and disempowerment so central to sensationalism are frequently part of a paradoxical logic whereby the self-possession of the professional male is achieved *through* the loss of affective and bodily control brought about by debt and financial humiliation. Far from being the crisis that renders the professional male an excessive threat to the social order, in other words, debt is within the antebellum urban gothic *productive,* precisely because it places the debtor male in possession of a highly emotional, feeling body.

Joseph Fichtelberg describes a similar process in his reading of antebellum sentimentalism. Describing a "sentimental commerce immune to economic change," Fichtelberg argues that sentimentality was "engaged in a complex cultural dialectic, the goal of which was to humanize economic crisis and make it manageable" (*Critical* 9). As he puts it, "Sentimental narratives groped toward a morally satisfying solution to this problem [of economic crisis] by reimagining the excesses of the market through limitless feeling and by making sentimental heroines and heroes the only figures who could regulate its excesses. The boundless ability to circulate, negotiate, and sympathize became the mark of a new, more supple morality. . . . The new model individual would need to be as supple and fluid as the market itself" (9). Echoing a similar argument by James Thompson, who suggests that British novels such as Fanny Burney's *Camilla* (1796) stage the regulation of female affect as the solution to the wider crisis of an unstable economy (*Models* 156–84), Fichtelberg reads sentimentalism as a way to balance accounts, as it were, in particular by imagining a middle-class subject whose emotional life can be regulated and contained. Thus, in a provocative reading of Ralph Waldo Emerson's anxieties about debt in the years following the 1837 Panic, he contends that the affective expressions of the debtor male, Emerson's in particular, reflect an effort to "redeem[]" indebtedness through "an imagery of sympathy and sincerity" (*Critical* 118). Emerson, he explains, "aspired to be a transparent medium, an affectionate general equivalent like money itself, trading on feeling. It was a capacity, he insisted, that he shared with all true souls. All could rise above contingency in a sincere exchange rooted in the behavior of the marketplace" (118).

I will argue something similar but different here about the exchange value of male affect. For while the postures of debtor masculinity did seem to rely on the inclusive relays of sympathy, this alternate form of male affect was also characterized both by an interior space of affective development, and—crucially—by postures of submission and disempowerment. I thus want to demonstrate how sensational narratives of the sort I am describing operate according to a logic whereby the hystericization and humiliation of the indebted male acts as the means by which to reconceive professional manhood under the sign of a radically unstable economy. The frantic excitement described by Webster should thus *also* be read as one instance in a "structure of feeling" taking shape in the first half of the nineteenth century, the specific task of which was to provide an adaptive—and compensatory— response to the panic-oriented climate of financial instability.[8] Trading in traditional models of Jacksonian self-possession and self-reliance for the more intangible qualities of deep-feeling sensibility modeled by the panicked and dispossessed debtor John White Webster, the debtor masculinity of antebellum sensationalism provides the outline of a new form of manhood emerging in the first half of the nineteenth century, one that—and again, paradoxically—ends up embracing and utilizing the very submission and disempowerment by which it is threatened.[9]

The masculine disempowerment depicted within the period's sensationalism found especially complex expression within the various antebellum forms of urban gothic sensationalism. Usually involving elaborate plots centered around confidence men and forged banknotes, disputes over property and inheritance, and violent (often ghostly) encounters between persecutory creditors and paranoid debtors, the urban gothic emphasizes a world given over to the radical immateriality of the paper economy. Simultaneously, it offers as the embodiment of these issues a male subject who, seeking emotional stability and self-possession in fiscal security (a kind of personal gold standard), instead finds himself dispossessed and haunted by the uncanny spectral world of the Jacksonian marketplace. This gothic masculinity is captured usefully in an anti-Jackson lithograph produced by Edward Clay in 1837, in which commerce itself is represented as a ghostly return of the repressed (figure 14). Ironically titled *New Edition of Macbeth. Bank-Oh's! Ghost,* the image suggests that although Jackson managed to slay the Bank, his notorious decision to issue the so-called Specie Circular (which attempted to halt a rash of speculation on government-owned western land by requiring that only gold and silver specie be accepted as

Figure 14 *New Edition of Macbeth. Bank-Ohs! Ghost.* 1837 by Edward Williams Clay. Printed and published by H. R. Robinson. Lithograph on wove paper; 25.2 x 41.5 cm. Reproduced with permission of the American Antiquarian Society.

payment for these properties) continues to haunt him and his horrified successor, Martin Van Buren, in the spectral form of inflation, speculation, and debt.[10] The lithograph also captures the ways in which such sensational commentaries on the economy almost inevitably rely on registers of masculinity and male panic. Depicting Jackson in drag as a kind of ironic "Lady Liberty" and Van Buren in the classic male posture of the antebellum gothic—horrified self-defense, with arms thrown up and eyes wide in terror—the lithograph offers a tableau of masculine disempowerment, one which by extension suggests an entire nation emasculated by the spectral presence of a debtor economy. Indeed, the dynamic here closely echoes the image Irving provides in his 1819 depiction of the encounter between Ichabod Crane and the Headless Horseman in "The Legend of Sleepy Hollow," which I discuss in chapter 2. In each case, the professional male is haunted by an apparitional figure that embodies the spectral economy, and which thus acts as a return of repressed fears about masculine self-possession and potency.

The emphasis within these narratives on male panic and humiliation suggests that we read them through the lens of the rapidly growing body of criticism devoted to emphasizing the importance of masculine affect in the formation of liberal subjectivity. Focusing primarily on sentimentalism and the emotional politics of sympathy, critics have begun to revise the standard gendering of affect whereby deep-feeling sensibility is associated with femininity, privacy, and domesticity, while a rational and disembodied public sphere is coded masculine. More importantly, these critics have emphasized the rhetorical and political uses of male affect, making it clear that the performance and manipulation of masculine emotion within the period's sensationalism is itself bound up with complex negotiations not only of gender but also of class, race, and sexuality. For example, describing the "early cultural prestige of masculine tenderheartedness," Julie Ellison argues that "[t]he deep-feeling, fragile man of sensibility is thoroughly masculine, for his emotional nature is crucial to the drama of homosocial friendships. The style of his masculinity forces us to rewrite the history of gender" (*Cato's* 9; 20). Similarly, in an overview of male sentimentalism in nineteenth-century U.S. culture, Mary Chapman and Glenn Hendler suggest that "Rather than see American 'men of feeling' as somehow oxymorons—exceptions to the hard and fast gender rules of sentimental culture—we consider them as exemplary of the competing definitions of masculinity available in the pre-twentieth-century United States" (*Sentimental Men* 8–9). In this chapter I want to outline a "history of gender" that helps explain how the twin rhetorics of male panic and male submission represent a new mode of masculine self-fashioning. For the debtor male of antebellum sensationalism was himself "thoroughly masculine," but in a way that reflects an apparently broadly felt need to instantiate an adaptive response to the culture of male panic inherent in an economic system increasingly predicated on the logic of indebtedness, failure, and dependency.

The period's sensationalism thus represents an attempt to rewrite the affective energies of the debtor male into a structure of feeling that might help manage the frightening instability of the speculative paper economy. This kind of compensatory logic, wherein sensationalism works to transform political anxieties into other, more manageable fears and concerns, is a process Ann Cvetkovich highlights in examining the vogue for British sensationalism in the later nineteenth century. As she explains, "[T]he sensation novel performs the cultural work of representing social problems as affective problems and hence confirming the importance of emotional expression to private life. The middle-class subject . . . is constructed as a feeling subject" (*Mixed* 7). For Cvetkovich, in other words, a sensational genre such as the antebellum gothic reflects the way in which new modes of emotional expression (such as male panic) are themselves discursive constructions that emerge in response to dramatic social and economic upheavals (such as the economic crises of the early and middle nineteenth century). Further, such narratives and the extreme modes of affect they rely on often act in the service of imperiled categories of class and gender, rather than as somehow radical agents of transgression and change.

Much of the recent work on the representation of male affect in antebellum fiction follows a similar line of thinking. For example, in a reading of "male emotionality" within 1840s temperance narratives such as Walt Whitman's *Franklin Evans* (1842), Hendler claims that the intensive embodiment that accompanied the lachrymal scenes of abjection and sympathy so central to these narratives was ultimately a source of great anxiety; accordingly, he suggests that male sentimentality operates through a logic of "identification and disavowal," wherein affective and bodily excess are generated for the express purpose of taking these qualities away (*Public* 15; 52). Similarly, in a discussion of Winthrop's popular *Cecil Dreeme,* Michael Millner argues that the often excessive sentimentality that informs male friendship in the text is counterbalanced by the felt panic over the sodomitical persecutions of the Jewish financier Densdeth ("Fear" 19–52). The result, Millner suggests, is that the threatened transgressions of the antebellum urban gothic are crucial to the maintenance of a more normative and privatized form of liberal masculinity. "The protagonist's and the reader's bodies become first penetrated but then purged of gothic sensation and sympathetic affect," Millner explains. "In this sense, the novel is a peculiar amalgam of old-world propriety and hemorrhaging urban anxiety" ("Fear" 24). Millner's discussion is especially useful in its emphasis on the way affect is deployed and manipulated in sensational texts to delineate the boundaries defining specific masculine categories of class, gender, and race.

Such analyses help us understand that while the debtor male seemed on the one hand to embody a threatening form of desire and transgression, he was in fact being refashioned into a submissive subject, one who *inter alia* ends up more fully incorporated within the spheres of a genteel and often feminized form of middle-class masculinity. Thus while narratives of male panic produced in relation to the issue of debt frequently involve disciplinary agents (persecutory creditors, debtors' prison, and various officers of the law), the real "policing" that takes place has to do with masculine categories of class and sensibility. Fears of debt and financial retribution might thus be thought of as undergoing a subtle but significant shift within the antebellum gothic, such that the new and more powerful mode of feeling is a form of panic that is itself the curious but necessary pathway to cultural distinction and advancement.

"*KON*-SIDERABLE BETTER THAN 'NITED STATES BANK STOCK!": POLICING CLASS AND MANHOOD IN *THE QUAKER CITY*

The text most thoroughly informed by the submissive postures of the anxious professional male post-1837 is George Lippard's *The Quaker City*.[11] As critics have shown, Lippard was a committed supporter of labor and anti-Bank policies in general, and sought in his fiction to provide a sensationalized exposé of the financial corruption plaguing Philadelphia, the "Quaker City."[12] In *The Quaker City,* this is accomplished by organizing the action around the notorious Monk Hall, a criminal's den for the most corrupted of the city's professional men. A three-story structure located on the city's margins, the building itself is replete with gothic claptrap such as two-way mirrors, trapdoors, and a dungeonlike basement where various unwitting victims are buried—several of them by its deformed and murderous proprietor, Devil-Bug, while they are still alive.

The general state of financial and moral collapse Lippard outlines is suggested midway through the novel in an exchange between Job Joneson, President of "* * * * Bank," and a mechanic named John Davis, who has lost his life savings after Joneson's bank has failed (406). Davis has broken into Joneson's mansion to say that because of the bank failure his wife has died, his daughter is starving, and he is unable to find work. Joneson, "jingling the silver in his pocket with gouty hands," responds by asking, "Well then, where's your credit?" Davis's reply is telling: "There is no imprisonment for debt," he says. "No poor man gets 'trust' now-a-days" (407). Sounding much like a prolabor writer such as Theophilus Fisk, Davis is pointing to the paradoxical situation whereby in the absence of the threat of debtors' prison, he is *unable* to go into debt as a means of giving his family adequate support. The implication, both for Davis and for the novel as a whole, is a crisis of capital. In the world of *The Quaker City,* it seems, there is no money anywhere—a fact that leaves men such as Davis in various states of humiliation and disempowerment.

Dana Nelson suggests that *The Quaker City* provides "a cultural thematic of middle-class (or professional) male identity" in early formation (*National* 142).[13] I would suggest as well that this nascent manhood is represented in terms of a revised model of masculine selfhood, one that has exchanged a labor-based model of self-possession (signaled here by the unfortunate John Davis) for less material notions of sensibility (such as those modeled by Webster). Lippard's novel, that is to say, enacts a form of affective exchange in which gothic modes of masculine affect such as panic and hysteria are bartered for emotional categories that have the texture and, ultimately, the "cultural prestige" of something resembling a sentimentalized and recognizably middle-class manhood. This movement from gothic to sentimental is also enacted in more canonical gothic narratives from the period, most notably Nathaniel Hawthorne's *The House of the Seven Gables* (1851). Here, as critics have observed, the potentially radical working-class male Holgrave ends up marrying the aristocratic Phoebe Pyncheon and establishing what looks very much like a depoliticized and markedly sentimental middle-class future.[14] In pulpier, sensational texts such as *The Quaker City,* though, such movement is predicated much more overtly on new postures of panic and submission for upwardly aspiring men—postures that signal a compromise with an economic system threatening to leave men such as Holgrave and John Davis far behind.

A paradigmatic example of the affective male display in which Lippard specializes (and which eventually intertwines with John Davis's debtor humiliation) is offered a short way into *The Quaker City,* when a libertine named Byrnewood Arlington makes the unhappy discovery that his bet with fellow rake Gus Lorrimer about the seduction and rape of a young girl in Monk Hall actually involves his sister, Mary Arlington. Here is the description of Arlington's shocking discovery: "Over his entire countenance flashed a mingled expression of surprise, and horror, and woe, that convulsed every feature with a spasmodic movement, and forced his large black eyes from their very sockets. For a moment he looked as if about to fall lifeless on the floor, and then it was evident that he exerted all his energies to control this most fearful agitation. He pressed both hands nervously against his forehead, as though his brain was tortured by internal flame" (74). Though excessive in its sensational hyperbole, the description of Arlington's emotional state says much about the politics of masculine humiliation within the period's gothic sensationalism. On the one hand, such scenes remind us that this material frequently operates according to a logic whereby, as Streeby puts it, "exploited men imaginatively experience the threat of violation by . . . rely[ing] on a set of analogies between imperiled women and oppressed men" ("Story Paper" 202).[15] And to be sure, we find that Arlington's real predicament is that he is *himself* Lorrimer's captive. Bound and gagged by the villainous Devil-Bug (Lorrimer's henchman), Arlington can only sit in silent horror while his sister is raped in a nearby room—a humiliation Lorrimer underscores emphatically. "Sir," he says, "you are my prisoner" (102).

But while Arlington's anxiety might be understood as arising from the possibility that he is moving from gothic villain to gothic maiden, the most notable feature of this crisis is the transformative effect it has on his libertine lifestyle. After escaping from Monk Hall, Arlington is found unconscious in the street by two Irish policemen (tellingly, they are engaged in a debate about the effects of Jackson's removal of the deposits from "the Nasshunal Bank" [401]). Upon reviving, he springs to his feet, shouting, "Mary, I will save you, save you yet" (402), and runs off into the night. But in one of the novel's many melodramatic coincidences, Arlington ends up responding to pleas for help from a friend of the debtor John Davis and his family. Arlington goes to Davis's home, only to find that Davis's daughter, Annie, has died of illness and starvation, and that Davis himself has committed suicide. Even worse, at least for Arlington, he discovers that Annie has died just three weeks after giving birth to a child—and that he is himself the child's father. Linked now both materially and affectively with the fiscally disempowered Davis, Arlington experiences another scene of emotional overload: "Again that wild cry burst from his heaving chest," we are told. "[H]is hands were pressed madly against his forehead" (410). This time, however, Arlington's mode of affect is both sentimental and recuperative in form, something Lippard makes clear. Describing Arlington's "terrible remorse," Lippard explains that "the better soul of Brynewood awoke within him and plead [*sic*] for the woman he had wronged" (416; 417).

Such moments are ubiquitous throughout *The Quaker City*, making it clear that humiliation and disempowerment are the linchpins of affective transformation for the male homosocial community of Lippard's urban world. Here, though, I want to focus on how postures of male submission and panic intersect with and, indeed, are directly organized by the climate of financial panic Lippard criticizes in his text. This is particularly true of the narrative involving a con artist calling himself Colonel Fitz-Cowles. Fitz-Cowles is a distant relative of libertine-speculators from early republican fiction such as Thomas Welbeck in Brockden Brown's *Arthur Mervyn* (1799–1800) and Dorval in Sara Wood's *Dorval; or The speculator. A novel founded on recent facts* (1801). But he is also the fictional embodiment of real-life counterfeiters such as Stephen Burroughs, Ebenezer Gleason, and Lyman Parkes, whose incredible success highlighted the fraught nature of the paper money system.[16] For again, many—especially Jacksonians—viewed paper money as itself a false representation of value. As Mihm puts it in his study of early-nineteenth-century counterfeiters, "What was the difference between a capitalist banker and a criminal counterfeiter? There were differences, to be sure, but not to the extent that many people would have preferred. Both trafficked in confidence, [and both] captured the ambiguities of an economy based on very little in the way of 'real' money" (*Counterfeiters* 51).

Lippard's Fitz-Cowles captures this ambiguity. Joining forces with the "Jewish dwarf" Gabriel Von Gelt, he manages to procure over $100,000 by forging banknotes up and down the east coast. The trouble for Fitz-Cowles is that although he has managed to convince various businesses to forward him large sums of money, he is unable to spend it for fear of attracting notice. This problem is exacerbated by the fact that he owes money to a large number of creditors: "In debt up to my ears, forced to leave the United States Hotel only a day since, in order to avoid my creditors . . . [A]nd why? Because I can't use the solid stuff, locked up in that old hair trunk. *Can't* use it. Somebody might find out something if I did. Curse the thing but I think the old trunk's laughing at me—. . . . Half in sovereigns—half in notes! . . . [W]hy couldn't [I] get it all in American gold? (154). Fitz-Cowles's notion of his trunkload of money laughing at him is telling. Like the United States itself in the years leading up to and following the 1837 Panic, Fitz-Cowles discovers that the "notes" he has obtained are worthless and that only "American gold" offers a viable form of currency. (It's worth adding that Lippard may be referring to an 1827 case in which officers working for the U.S. Bank found a trunk containing $100,000 worth of counterfeit notes on the U.S. Bank in a raid on the home of a counterfeit gang connected to the notorious Parkes.[17]) The other hoard of accumulated capital in *The Quaker City*, the chest of gold coins and doubloons maintained by the "Widow Becky Smolby" (herself a key player later in the novel), is described in related terms. "How Becky made all her money was a mystery," we are told. "[E]ven the grand question, 'what ever became of the funds of the United States Bank,' [was] nothing to it" (200). Mysteriously acquired, the Widow's gold represents the accumulation and saving of specie otherwise absent from America during this period. This is also suggested a short time earlier, when Devil-Bug comments that a robbery of the Widow's home is a near sure bet, one "*kon*-siderable better than 'Nited States Bank stock!" (231).

The result of such financial problems for Fitz-Cowles is what he experiences alternately as a form of bodily retention and bodily vulnerability. Either way, the notorious forger finds that, unable to spend his currency, he is similarly disadvantaged when it comes to his sense of masculine self-possession and embodiment. And to be sure, Fitz-Cowles's physical problems are reflected by the fact that he has been forging more than banknotes. As the description of him early in the novel preparing for a meeting with his many angry creditors makes clear, the image of masculine prowess he presents to the world is quite literally a performance, one aided by the various pieces of padding that his black servant, Dim, attaches to his body each morning in an elaborate dressing ceremony: "Which hip you want, Massa?" Dim asks. "Big hip or little hip?" (156). Beneath the handsome and confident exterior of the dandyish aristocrat, in other words, Fitz-Cowles is actually a skinny and effeminate wimp. In this Fitz-Cowles is similar to the image of U.S. Bank president Nicholas Biddle provided in William Whiting's mock-epic on the bank wars, *The Age of Paper; or, the Bank Contest* (1838). Described as "Cased in paper armor well put on" (4), Biddle is, like the Fitz-Cowles of Lippard's novel, true to the stereotype of "paper money men": all exterior and no substance.

The implication of gender trouble attached to Fitz-Cowles is why the narrative of pursuit involving Fitz-Cowles and an investigator named Luke Harvey is so important. Though Harvey is a white-collar merchant-in-training, his private passion is to right the wrongs of the legal system, which he (along with Lippard) sees as a mockery. "Justice in the Quaker City!" Harvey exclaims sarcastically. "One moment it unlocks the doors of the prison, and bids the Bank-Director . . . go forth! The next moment it bolts and seals those very prison doors, upon the poor devil, who has stolen a loaf of bread to save himself from starvation!" (205). Harvey the amateur detective is thus directly linked to a broader fantasy about policing the runaway paper economy—a fantasy about which Fitz-Cowles himself is nervously aware. As he puts it at one point, "[T]o feel an officer's finger on my shoulder, 'you are my prisoner, Sir'—ugh! I have not seen Harvey to-day—this silence annoys me!" (459). Nor is Harvey the only figure through whom such fantasies are voiced. For example, in Boucicault's *The Poor of New York*, the previously corrupt bank clerk Badger ends up a sheriff's deputy, a transition he celebrates by arresting his former employer, the banker Bloodgood, for embezzling funds from his bank during the Panic of 1837. "Congratulate me," Badger says in a moment of triumph. "I have been appointed to the police. The commissioner wanted a special service to lay on to Wall Street's savagery" (163). For both of these very popular writers, the fiscally transgressive Jacksonian male is sometimes mirrored by an opposing, disciplinary self, one manifested as a literal agent of the law.

The policing operation staged within *The Quaker City* involves a complicated mix of gothic-style gender persecution and sentimentalized romantic intrigue. For it turns out that Harvey himself was once romantically involved with Fitz-Cowles's lover, Dora Livingstone (with whom Fitz-Cowles plans to flee the country), and is in fact still in love with her. To complicate matters, Dora happens to be the wife of Harvey's boss at work, a wealthy and corrupt financier named Albert Livingstone. One of the novel's central narratives thus revolves around the game of cat-and-mouse between Harvey and Fitz-Cowles, in which Harvey seeks to prove that Fitz-Cowles is in fact the paper money forger he suspects him to be. The key move in this game is the decision by Fitz-Cowles and Dora to hire the notorious Devil-Bug to kill Harvey, and thus save themselves from detection. As proof of his success, Dora tells Devil-Bug that he must retrieve a gold ring that Harvey always wears on the third finger of his left hand. "This ring was given him by his ladye-love long, long ago," she tells Devil-Bug. "[H]e values it, as his life, and will not part with it save with his life" (280). Needless perhaps to say, the ring was given to Harvey by Dora, and it continues to represent his undying love for her.

Harvey's gold ring represents his refusal to let go of his love for Dora, but it also suggests a more general desire for control and retention at the level of economic self-possession—exactly what the prolabor Harvey has had threatened in losing Dora to paper money men such as Livingstone and Fitz-Cowles. As Harvey complains bitterly to Dora at one point, "One night you kissed me so sweetly, Dora, so lovingly. . . . The next day you picked a delightful quarrel with me, and forbade your 'plighted love,' the house. Why? Because the *rich* merchant, Livingstone, had called at your mother's dwelling. . . . The *poor* clerk was eclipsed!" (254). Harvey's ring thus represents an anxious site of potential vulnerability, an anxiety Lippard exploits in a violent confrontation between Harvey and Devil-Bug that takes place in the basement of Monk Hall. Rendered in the seriocomic hyperbole typical of Lippard's gothic sensationalism, the fight begins when Harvey surprises Devil-Bug as he is in the process of burying a semiconscious Byrnewood Arlington after his earlier encounter with the libertine Gus Lorrimer. Thus startled, Devil-Bug accidentally falls into the grave he has dug, whereupon Harvey seizes the moment and strikes him on the head with a shovel. Tempted by Devil-Bug's vulnerability, Harvey then begins to bury *him*: "[T]he spade rose and fell in his active grasp," Lippard tells us, "and his face warmed with excitement" (313). Unfortunately for Harvey, his excitement prevents him from noticing as Devil-Bug crawls to the edge of the grave, grabs Harvey by the ankle, and pulls him into the grave. In a moment, Devil-Bug is above ground, Harvey has been pummeled into unconsciousness, and his "ring" is free for the taking. "Now for the ring!" Devil-Bug cries out. "Ah-ha! Here it is; on the third finger, and a werry purty ring it is! He wouldn't part with it except with his life—ha, ha! I reether guess that he'll part with the ring and his life at wonst!" (314). Devil-Bug then attempts to choke Harvey to death: "Bending over the unconscious form of Luke, he extended his hands and fastened the talon-like fingers around his throat, with the grasp of a vice" (314). Before he can finish the job of killing Harvey, however, Devil-Bug is called away, and leaves Harvey unconscious in the grave.

Trading one ring for another (Harvey's "purty" prize for his own "grasp of a vice"), Devil-Bug wages battle at exactly the level most disturbing to his opponent. For in Lippard's overwrought narrative, the men's struggle over Harvey's ring might be read in terms of the rhetoric of anality. In her discussion of the homosocial violence structuring gothic masculinity, Eve Sedgwick suggests that anal control and its loss is often represented by objects such as rings, vices, and clamps, and that the relative retention and release signaled by such objects parallels a like status of control and self-possession based on class and gender (*Between* 169–71). Michael Moon offers a similar reading of the masculine politics of Horatio Alger's many urban narratives about the upward mobility of "ragged" young. For example, Moon suggests that in *Paul the Peddler* (1868), this dynamic is figured by a ring Paul attempts to sell to an older man who then drugs Paul and steals the ring from the unconscious and helpless boy. According to Moon, such moments represent the major cultural work of the Alger narratives, and vulnerable (and highly sexualized) postures such as Paul's act as part of the bargain in the "boost" up the homosocial class ladder ("Gentle Boy" 103–5). This vulnerability is exactly the threat faced by Harvey, who experiences the possible loss of his own ring as a form of humiliation and disempowerment in which class and sex are seen as collapsing into a horrific mode of anal submission.

Harvey's vulnerability, echoing the threat of sexual violation faced by the terrified Ichabod Crane in his flight from Brom Bones–as–Headless Horseman ("he had much ado to maintain his seat," we are told as the Horseman closes in from behind [294]), is especially disturbing because it is directly connected to the "eclipse" he suffered when Dora jilted him for Harvey's employer, the "rich merchant" Livingstone. In attempting to bury Devil-Bug—the hired assassin of Dora and Fitz-Cowles—Harvey has been seeking to wipe out his humiliation, which is felt so keenly by "the *poor* clerk" at the levels of class and gender. In fact, much the same might be said of the gothic attempts by Webster and Colt to dispose of the bodies of their victims. In each case, the motive for concealing the corpse had to do with fear of detection, but, more important, with shame over financial failure and the gender-panic that is its almost inevitable result. In erasing the persecutory Other, all three men seek to conceal the humiliating and uncanny mirror image of their own failed financial selves—a failure that in Harvey's case is underscored by the rhetoric of anal submission.

But if in losing his "ring" Harvey seems to have been the victim of a sexualized violation similar to that suffered by the hapless Ichabod Crane, it is notable that Lippard acts quickly to prevent this from being a permanent state of affairs. For the reprieve Harvey receives when Devil-Bug releases his choke hold gives him the opportunity to escape the Monk Hall basement and ambush Devil-Bug, who is about to rape Dora Livingstone as extorted payment for the ring he has brought her. More important than another conflict between Devil-Bug and Harvey, however, is the fact that Harvey ends up helping Dora escape from Monk Hall despite her attempts to have him killed. His gesture has a restorative effect: standing "[t]all and erect" (363), Harvey tells Dora that he forgives her for her crimes against both him and her husband; further, he urges her to ditch Fitz-Cowles, return to Livingstone, and live a virtuous life as his wife. The result is a repentant Dora, who suddenly feels "the modesty of a wife once more" (365). More telling still, she returns to him the ring she believed she had purchased with his blood: "Dora was silent. She bowed her face on her bosom as she knelt at his feet . . . and veiled her eyes with her hands. The ring dropped from her finger. Luke knelt silently by her side. He took the ring from the floor" (364).

"Tall and erect" and in possession once more of his "ring," Harvey is transformed from abject gothic male to self-possessed and recognizably sentimental masculine subject. That this transformation is accomplished despite his failure to regain Dora is not a contradiction so much as a fitting illustration of the debtor masculinity I am describing. For what Harvey achieves is a moral superiority, which is the intangible form of self-possession that lifts him above men more fully linked to the paper economy, such as Fitz-Cowles and Livingstone. As Harvey puts it to Dora before his Monk Hall encounter with Devil-Bug, when she attempts to seduce him into abandoning his investigation of Fitz-Cowles: "I have still the *moral* self-denial, ha, ha, ha! to scorn the embraces of an—*Adulteress!*" (259). Manifested a second time, after the loss and subsequent retrieval of his ring, Harvey's "moral self-denial" is even more impressive: he truly seems to advocate her return to a life of domestic sanctity with her husband. Thus, in ways that say much about the masculine class politics of the period's gothic sensa-tionalism, the police work Harvey conducts is accomplished by losing his ring—temporarily—and getting it back again.

Lippard's apparent interest in a recuperative form of sentimentalized domesticity and upward mobility is even further underscored by the mar-riage of Harvey to Livingstone's (supposed) daughter, Mabel. In a convenient shuffling of financial resources, Mabel becomes wealthy when it is discov-ered that the Widow Becky Smolby is Mabel's grandmother, and that she has willed to Mabel her hoard of gold specie (476); Mabel's fortune increases further when Livingstone kills Dora in a fit of jealous rage over her affair with Fitz-Cowles and then fakes his own suicide, leaving Mabel as his sole heir (501; 571). The marriage between Harvey and Mabel thus almost seam-lessly combines the "police" with a vision of financially solvent (and notably specie-based) domestic bliss.

But while the marriage between Harvey and Mabel might seem to signal a sentimental form of middle-class closure very much like that offered in the marriage between Holgrave and Phoebe Pyncheon in *The House of the Seven Gables,* it is important to note that Lippard complicates—and seems resistant to—an unproblematized notion of middle-class security. This posi-tion is signaled first in a melodramatic twist that reveals Mabel as the daugh-ter of Devil-Bug, who we learn has decided to hide his parentage to allow the girl to grow up in the spheres of genteel domesticity so different from the radically antidomestic world of Monk Hall. As Devil-Bug explains, "I'll skulk along the street, and see her ridin' in her carriage; I'll watch in the cold winter nights and see her—all shinin' with goold and jewels—as she goes into the theatre, with the big folks around her, and the rich merchant by her side. . . . *There,* I'll cry to myself—there is old Devil-Bug's darter among the grandees o' the Quaker City!" (338). On the one hand, Devil-Bug's explana-tion suggests a certain reciprocity between the corrupted world of finance, which he represents, and the cordoned-off space of upper-class enclosure. Taking a servile and highly affective pride in his ability to access the upper classes vicariously (we are told that he is charged with "superhuman emo-tion!" [333]), Devil-Bug might seem to be modeling a sentimentalized form of class desire that involves abdicating his own form of masculine agency to the "rich merchant" Livingstone—and after Livingstone's suicide, to the white-collar Luke Harvey. But on the other hand, the insertion of Devil-Bug's "blood" into the middle classes suggests that sentimental narratives of middle-class stability and purity are themselves a fiction, one especially difficult to maintain in an era when financial panic meant that lines of class and superiority were under almost constant threat of dissolution. In this sense, the affect displayed by Harvey, Devil-Bug, and other financially strapped men in antebellum sensationalism performs crucial cultural work: standing in for a lost sense of fiscal security or class stability, this form of emotional expression becomes an immaterial form of social capital that works to reinvent the postures of masculine humiliation and disempowerment so endemic to the Jacksonian period.

Perhaps this is what is meant by the fact that Luke Harvey's efforts to capture and imprison Fitz-Cowles are ultimately unsuccessful. Near novel's end, Fitz-Cowles is arrested by Harvey and the police, an event that provides Harvey with an initial moment of excitement. "Do your dapper limbs already feel the cheering warmth of the convicts [sic] dress—and then the manacles, and the lash!" he asks Fitz-Cowles mockingly (490). But the elusive, paper money man of this novel is able almost immediately to buy his freedom from "Easy Larkspur," one of the arresting officers. "In less than a month," we are told, "Fitz-Cowles walked the streets a free man. The mysteries of the forgery, the hooks and crooks, by which that pliable old gentleman THE LAW was evaded and conciliated, are they not written in the Chronicles of the Courts?" (553). Unlike the libertine-speculator of early republic fiction, then, Fitz-Cowles is not ultimately contained within the walls of a prison. (In both *Arthur Mervyn* and *Dorval,* the libertine villains die in debtors' prison; in Hannah Foster's *The Coquette,* the libertine Major Sanford is placed under house arrest pending payment of his debts.) In fact, Fitz-Cowles's escape suggests that the crisis of debt and financial panic plaguing the country will continue for some time.

Thus the marriage between Harvey and Mabel is not ultimately a guarantee that the postures of disempowerment assumed by the likes of Harvey, Webster, and so many others are no longer necessary in the continuing efforts to establish a stable mode of middle-class masculine self-possession. Quite the contrary, the lurking presence of Fitz-Cowles suggests that such postures are a long-term, perhaps even permanent, component of upwardly mobile masculine selfhood. For while the sensational aesthetics of male panic and debtor masculinity offer an adaptive, and in many ways compensatory, response to the vicissitudes of financial instability and homosocial rivalry, they are not, finally, the same as bank vaults (or personal bank accounts) filled with actual gold specie. What they do offer, smuggled in with the perverse and often silly pleasures of antebellum sensationalism, is a way to make sense of an increasingly common form of cultural disempowerment and embarrassment. This, it seems to me, is the fantasy bribe offered by such texts. Rather than straightforward Jacksonian-versus-Whig narratives of political complaint or class conflict, sensationalist narratives such as *The Quaker City* and *The Extraordinary Confession of Dr. John White Webster* provide compensation to a financially anxious and disempowered readership by instantiating a language of sensibility that works to recode the gap left by the movement from labor-based to paper-based forms of value. Indeed, it is the very shift to the new economy that lays the groundwork for this mode of masculine affect—this structure of feeling—as it emerged within the period's sensationalism.

In the sensational category of debtor masculinity, then, we can see the outlines of a culture's anxious attempt to deal with the trauma of a perceived fall away from the supposed wholeness of a reliable and fixed gold standard. The movement from wide-eyed male hysteria to weeping and abject manhood that frequently marks both sensationalism and this gender category—the movement, that is, from gothic horror to domestic sentimentality and emotional interiority—is thus deeply ideological; it is one instance of the gradual but powerful drift into middle-class hegemony. This is the image of "the police" according to antebellum sensationalism, one much more effective than that which Luke Harvey, Easy Larkspur, or even the jury in the Webster trial could provide. We might therefore think of debtor masculinity as offering the next best thing to a gold standard. To "invest" in this emergent mode of manhood and sensibility did not promise a material form of fiscal security or self-possession. But, to quote from the villain Devil-Bug, this form of affective investment was "*kon*-siderable better" than banking on the illusory profits of paper money or "'Nited States Bank stock."

TABLOID MANHOOD,
SPECULATIVE FEMININITY

Now here is an example worthy of the notice of banks. Public credit—paper credit—like the beautiful Helen Jewett on the green banks of the Penobscot, before her fall, was in youth, beautiful, fair, engaging, virtuous. . . . At last, falling into the hands of several young speculators, who, like Robinson, appeared covered with youth, beauty, and innocence, she became a prey to folly, launched into extravagance, and was soon hurried into the loss of all decency, and all virtue. Like Helen Jewett, running with a love letter in her zone, over Wall street, and up and down Broadway, paper money, arrayed in gaudy habiliments, fine engravings, and beautiful vignettes, has flooded the land till she is a trouble and an annoyance to those who have brought her upon the country.

—The New York *Herald,* May 9, 1837

"[U]NDER THE PALE MOON BEAMS":
TABLOID SENSATIONALISM AND POLITICAL ECONOMY

On April 11, 1836, an enterprising newspaperman named James Gordon Bennett Jr. printed the first of many accounts of the murder of a twenty-three-year-old prostitute named Helen Jewett in his upstart tabloid, the New York *Herald.*[1] Describing "a sensation in this city never before felt or known," Bennett explained that early that morning Jewett had been bludgeoned to death with a small hatchet while in a room she occupied in the City Hotel brothel at 41 Thomas Street, New York, and that, in an attempt to conceal the crime, her assailant had set fire to the bed in which she lay (*NYH* 4-11-1836).[2] Soon, however, the smoke was detected; Jewett's partially burned body was discovered, and a search was begun for a nineteen-year-old office clerk named Richard P. Robinson, whom witnesses claimed had visited Jewett that night, and whose cloak was found behind the fence at the rear of the brothel. But as Bennett also explained, upon his arrest the next morning, Robinson, while admitting to frequent visits to Jewett's, claimed he had not been to see her the previous evening, and that the cloak did not belong to him. Further, Robinson contended that a blood-stained hatchet found in the brothel's backyard, identified as stolen from the office where he worked, was unknown to him, and that the whitewash found on his pants, which matched that of the fence behind the brothel, was paint from the store where he worked.

For Bennett, the murder represented an especially opportune chance to generate sensational copy for the *Herald*. The son of an upstanding Connecticut family and the employee of a reputable merchant named Joseph Hoxie, Robinson was not only well connected but handsome and charming; his alleged involvement in the case captivated readers, especially those who saw him as an example of the new breed of young men whose licentious, antidomestic lifestyle had begun to pose a troubling challenge to the city's middle class—especially by encouraging the growth of the city's prostitution industry.[3] Jewett was a figure of extraordinary fascination as well. The daughter of a poor shoemaker in Maine, Jewett had worked as a servant for the family of a powerful judge there, and was eventually educated at a female academy along with the judge's daughters. Somewhere along the line, however, Jewett had either rejected or had been unable to maintain the privileges of class and culture, and worked instead as a prostitute in various cities before ending up in New York in 1833, at the age of twenty. Like Robinson, Jewett was thus intriguing to the public for her ability to challenge middle-class definitions of gender and sexuality.

No one seems to have been more aware of this than Bennett, who, having gained entrance to the City Hotel before Jewett's body was removed from her bedroom, began providing lurid details of the crime scene in the days following the murder. Representing the slain Jewett in Poe-esque fashion as a mix of deathly erotics and aesthetic beauty, Bennett offered Jewett as a figure in whom a variety of fantasies could be exercised by a reading public. Describing her "beautiful female corpse" as a "passionless" object that "surpassed the finest statue in antiquity" (*NYH* 4-11-1836), Bennett seemed to be negotiating between illicit sexual desire and the forms of class and culture by which such desire might be mediated. This was a strategy he would use repeatedly in the days and weeks to follow. Again and again Bennett provided scenarios in which Jewett's "beautiful" corpse was the central figure. In a story printed several days after the murder, for example, the paper claimed (falsely) that shortly after her burial a team of coroners had exhumed Jewett's body in order to perform what was presumably a second, more exacting, autopsy: "We learn that no sooner than Jewett was committed to the earth, several medical goths shouldered spade and pick axe—went to her grave under the pale moon beams—dug up her beautiful body—put it unceremoniously into a bag—and carried it to a certain place, where, after the measure of her lovely lineaments had been accurately taken, it underwent the process of dissection" (*NYH* 4-16-1836). Again echoing the gothic fascination with the female corpse expressed by Poe, Hawthorne, and others during this period, the passage displays the same ambivalence about how to negotiate between an illicit erotics and aesthetic containment as Bennett's earlier description of the murder scene.[4] "Beautiful" and "lovely" even fresh from the earth, Jewett seems nevertheless to require further investigation. According to Bennett, even the grave is suspected of keeping secrets.

Bennett was not alone in his interest in the case. In the ensuing three months the murder was covered relentlessly by the media, eventually becoming one of the most publicized in history. Newspapers from all over the country carried the story on a regular basis, while many of New York's major papers provided complete transcripts from the five-day trial in early June.[5] No fewer than six pamphlets devoted to the crime were published in the months following the murder, each attempting to suggest why a woman such as Jewett had chosen a life of prostitution over the available security of domesticity (figure 15).[6] In addition, local artists circulated various images of Jewett and Robinson throughout the city, most depicting the murdered Jewett on her bed in various states of undress, and Robinson fleeing her room, hatchet in hand.

Such publicity seems to have incited considerable public response. For months after the murder reported sightings of Jewett's ghost were apparently frequent, and local papers reported on crowds gathering outside the City Hotel and elsewhere after her spectral image had been seen by incredulous witnesses.[7] More materially, on May 18 *The Illuminator* reported that a crowd of young women—possibly fellow prostitutes—had gathered to take away the burnt remains of Jewett's bed frame after it was set outside the brothel as trash (*Illuminator* 5-18-1836; quoted in Cohen, "The Helen Jewett Murder" 376). Similarly, prior to a sale of the furniture from the City Hotel (which Rosina Townsend, the brothel's madam, decided to close just after the murder), a group of clerks supposedly entered Jewett's room and cut small pieces of wood off of her furniture, either as souvenirs or, as Bennett put it ironically, as "relics" of the deceased woman's life (*NYH* 4-14-1836). In addition, various groups in the city began taking sides in the case according to allegiances of class and politics: one working-class gang took to wearing a type of white fur hat with black crepe ribbons called the "Helen Jewett mourner," apparently in opposition to the white-collar clerk class represented by Robinson.[8] Conversely, in the months before the trial large numbers of the city's clerks could be seen sporting "Robinson cloaks" and "Robinson caps" in support of the accused clerk.

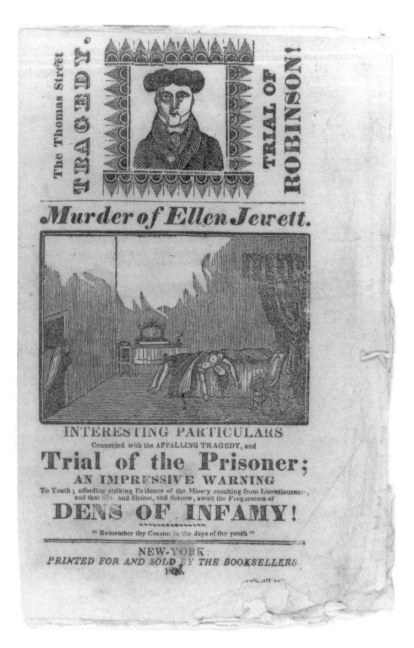

Figure 15 Cover of *The Thomas Street Tragedy. Murder of Ellen Jewett. Trial of Robinson!* 1836. Reproduced with permission of Clements Library, University of Michigan.

What then to make of the considerable interest and anxiety the case generated? I want to suggest that while descriptions such as Bennett's were certainly sensationalist attempts to increase circulation, they also reflect the emergence within the sensational public sphere of the sort of paper money manhood I have been describing. Indeed, as I will discuss, the Jewett case is in many respects the birthplace of the sensational public sphere; it is Bennett's sensational aesthetic of somewhat campy horror that writers such as Poe, Lippard, Thompson, and many others came to emulate in the early 1840s, and which writers such as Hawthorne and Melville tapped into in more distanced ways in the early 1850s. And this comparison works in reverse historical order as well: we might think of the sensational public sphere as composed almost entirely of moments such as Ichabod Crane's pursuit by the Headless Horseman, and all but entirely absent of the recognizably Federalist, even Burkean, conservatism reflected in portions of *The Sketchbook* such as "The Country Church" or "Roscoe."

But, occurring as it did on the eve of the 1837 Panic, the murder and ensuing trial were also caught up in the heated debates between Democrats and Whigs over the U.S. Bank and the paper economy. Accordingly, I want to show here how the tabloid coverage of the case became a long-running gothic melodrama set quite closely against the backdrop of the period's concerns over political economy. The quote from the *Herald* with which I begin this chapter is a useful example of what I am suggesting. Depicting Jewett as a figure for "paper money" and Robinson as a "young speculator" who has stolen the "virtue" of Jewett/public credit, the editorial captures, albeit playfully, the intersecting rhetoric of gender and political economy so central to the antebellum sensational public sphere. Here, of course, "falling into the hands of several young speculators," Jewett/paper money is represented as the victim of speculative excess and male passion, which is to say that the description relies on the image of the rapacious rake—Smith-Rosenberg's "corrupt new men of paper and place"—that we see in characters from Major Sanford in Hannah W. Foster's *The Coquette* up through Irving's more comic Ichabod Crane. In this Bennett seems to be offering what was by 1837 a somewhat standard critique of the paper economy and its excesses.

But it's important to note that this was a stance Bennett took up only in mid-1837, when the Panic itself was in full bloom, and when, perhaps more importantly, the *Herald* had become the nation's most successful newspaper. Prior to this, Bennett was a struggling and (often quite literally) embattled entrepreneur. And it was during *this* period that Bennett provided his extensive coverage of the Jewett murder and Robinson's trial. And what we find is a richer, more complicated narrative. For prior to the above denunciation of Robinson, Bennett had long insisted that Robinson was the victim of a setup by financier Whigs, whom he claimed had murdered Jewett. Bennett even suggested that the murder was part of a broad-based Bank conspiracy, and that Whig-oriented mercantile trade papers such as James Watson Webb's *Courier and Enquirer* were aiding in the cover-up. From *this* perspective, Jewett represented corrupt spheres of class and privilege that, inhabited largely by Whigs and speculators, had long excluded upwardly mobile men such as Bennett. Indeed, described at another point in the *Herald* as "the goddess of a large race of merchants, dealers, clerks and their instruments" (*NYH* 4-15-1836), and often visible on Wall Street in her trademark green dress and expensive jewelry, the Jewett that Bennett depicts in 1836 is a volatile, mysterious, and finally quite threatening form of femininity, one linked in a variety of ways with the corrupt economic and social world that Bennett, as a staunch Jacksonian Democrat, saw as linked to Nicholas Biddle and other members of the fiscal elite that had steered the economy toward ruin with its reliance on paper money fiscal policies.

Put another way, Jewett became in many ways a figure of sensational Otherness similar to the likes of Irving's Headless Horseman, the Shylock figure of so many antebellum narratives, or Colonel Fitz-Cowles, the paper money con man in Lippard's *The Quaker City*. She was, that is to say, a figure through whom the antebellum professional male—here Bennett and his proxy Robinson—sought to negotiate on a psychological level the desires and fantasies of the emergent paper economy. Indeed, Bennett's coverage of the Jewett case in the *Herald* is especially interesting because it provides a kind of "real time" narrative in which we see his story unfold in almost daily response to actual events. And what we see is a constant, and at times quite dramatic, effort on the part of Bennett to establish imagined control over the threat that Jewett seems to pose to aspiring professional men such as Robinson and himself. For Jewett is in Bennett's version of her a fascinating but disturbing figure of "theft" and symbolic castration; it is in her, one might say, that the anxieties over the paper economy are located. In this regard, the gothic search for Jewett's corpse offered in the *Herald* may have been imagined, but it was also significant: at least metaphorically, what the *Herald*'s "medical Goths" were seeking was a site of social and economic affirmation that, as the ghostly Jewett and the excitement surrounding her murder would suggest, did not exist.

But this, again, is something that Bennett struggles against. And in this sense I want to read his coverage of the Jewett affair as an attempt both to retrieve, somehow, the sense of lost potency that Jewett has "stolen" from him, and—simultaneously—to offer a series of compensatory postures in relation to the threat that Jewett poses. For, and as with the various debtor narratives of the 1840s and '50s that I discuss in chapter 3, Bennett's particular brand of sensationalism involves the staging of what we might think of as alternative forms of manhood. Here again, notions such as submission and humiliation are quite central to the formation of a sensational manhood. Indeed, it may be that Bennett provides the testing ground for the submissive debtor masculinity of the following decades. But the representational strategies that Bennett offers are also uneven, for certainly aggression and misogyny remain viable approaches to gender conflict even as Bennett experiments with a less self-possessed form of manhood. What we see in Bennett's tabloid narrative about Jewett and Robinson is thus an effort—sometimes lurid, sometimes absurd and comic, and occasionally poignant—to negotiate and ultimately to rewrite the growing sense of anxiety that the professional male was feeling in 1836. The irony here, of course, is that Bennett, much like Washington Irving, was able to cash in on the representation of male anxiety by creating and selling a form of sensationalism that proved incredibly popular. But this is perhaps the point. For inasmuch as these writers were offering fantasies for readers in which they might see their own concerns reflected and negotiated—and sometimes solved—they were telling a story that was much in demand.

Indeed, one measure of this demand can be found in a narrative that picks up on and extends many of the issues circulating in Bennett's coverage of the Jewett murder: Nathaniel Hawthorne's *The Blithdedale Romance* (1852). As I suggest in a short coda to this chapter, Hawthorne's novel provides a further exploration of a paper money masculinity that projected many of its anxieties onto figures of female mystery and empowerment. This is true both of the waiflike and ghostly (and at least symbolically prostituted) Pricilla, and the horrific figure of the female corpse that we see in Zenobia at book's end. In each case, we see depictions of female Otherness that, much like the mysterious Helen Jewett, force a male narrator (and in each case a male writer) to articulate and negotiate the shifting and unstable contours of professional manhood during this period.

PUBLICITY AND HUMILIATION:
BENNETT AND THE *HERALD*

The *Herald* was started by Bennett just under a year before Jewett's murder, on May 6, 1835, for approximately $500.[9] Before this date Bennett had worked as a staunchly Jacksonian "party editor" for a number of the city's newspapers, including the city's dominant mercantile trade paper, the *Courier and Enquirer,* and the *Pennsylvanian,* a pro-Jackson daily begun in Philadelphia in 1832. But, and as a result mainly of disputes over the role of the Bank of the United States, which he vehemently denounced, Bennett inevitably left these positions, usually with hard feelings on both sides. The founding of the *Herald* was Bennett's opportunity to assert his independence, both financially and in terms of editorial policy. Bennett's hope was to create a niche for the *Herald* in the penny press market carved out several years earlier by the New York *Sun* and the New York *Daily Transcript*.[10] And to this end he was fairly successful. With its pages devoted to feature materials such as murders, robberies, and advertisements for patent medicines and abortionists such as the notorious Madame Restell, the paper quickly gained a reputation as a sensationalist rag. Sold primarily in the city's downtown area on the "cash-and-carry" system by young "street urchin" newsboys, the paper went for a penny—one-sixth the cost of trade papers such as the *Courier*—and its four-page, five-column tabloid format was considered by many to be as "ugly" as its contents.[11] As former mayor Philip Hone noted disdainfully in his diary, the *Herald* was published by "an ill-looking, squinting man called Bennett," and was "one of the penny papers which are hawked about the streets by a gang of troublesome, ragged boys, and in which scandal is retailed to all who delight in it, at that moderate price" (*DPH* 193). Such denunciations of Bennett and his paper were not limited to private asides. Throughout the 1830s and early 1840s Bennett was subjected to a number of efforts either to censure him, or to put him out of business altogether. The most serious attempt came in 1840, in response to an editorial by Bennett challenging the American Catholic church to "come forth from the darkness, folly, and superstition of the tenth century" (*NYH* 5-10-1840). Following this, Bennett found himself the subject of a "Moral War" waged by a committee of many of the city's most powerful clergymen, news editors, politicians, and businessmen. This committee was often given voice by James Watson Webb in the pages of the *Courier and Enquirer*. For example, describing Bennett as, among other things, "a worthless vagabond" peddling "moral leprosy" (Webb, *CE* 6-3-1840), the group called for a general boycott of the *Herald* and any businesses that carried it.[12] The boycott was temporarily successful, but within a month the *Herald's* sales began to surge again, probably as a result of the publicity the "War" was generating. As Bennett was proving, sensationalism in whatever form sold newspapers.

But even in its early stages the *Herald* manifested aspirations for a rise to "credibility." Before starting the *Herald*, Bennett had often written on banking news and other financial matters for mercantile trade papers such as the *Courier and Enquirer*. Such work gave him an intimate knowledge of both local and national economic trends, knowledge he sought to make available to a more general readership. As Bennett was aware, many of those purchasing the paper were white-collar clerks who worked in the city's downtown area and (like himself) desired upward mobility. This is why the paper included, in addition to its coverage of more sensational events, a common-sense—and for a penny paper, unusual—"Wall Street" column that provided an easy-to-read update on daily stock prices and basic investment advice, as well as a series of mini-editorials about the evils of credit and speculation. As Bennett explained, "The spirit, pith, and philosophy of commercial affairs is [sic] what men of business want. Dull records of facts, without condensation, analysis, or deduction, are utterly useless. The philosophy of commerce is what we aim at, combined with accuracy, brevity, and spirit" (*NYH* 2-28-1838). Such efforts did not go unnoticed. The *Journal of Commerce*, for example, noted shortly after Bennett began his new feature that "The number of [*Herald*] readers is doubled . . . among those classes who have suffered greatly from their want of intelligence [on financial matters]" (*JC* August 1835; quoted in Crouthamel, *Webb* 70). Not surprisingly, this was something for which Bennett was willing to praise himself. "Our neighborhood is rapidly becoming a second Wall Street," Bennett claimed in one issue. "Our [financial] bulletin, which we always keep in fine trim, is drawing crowds to this part of the city. We are rapidly taking the wind out of the big-bellied sales of the *Courier and Enquirer* and the *Journal of Commerce,* that pair of unclean speculators and deceivers of public opinion" (*NYH* 4-21-1836). As usual, Bennett's main intent here is to generate interest in his product by stirring up public disputes with the city's other newspapers. But as newspaper historian James Crouthamel suggests, Bennett's confidence was well founded. As he puts it, "These economic columns, in their accuracy and acute analysis, surpassed anything in the mercantile sheets" (*Bennett's* 70). Along with sensationalist headlines, Bennett was also selling class mobility; apparently, he was doing a good job of it.

Bennett was also consistent in his political attacks on the city's other papers and editors, in particular those who expressed Whig sympathies. This was especially the case with the *Courier* and its editor, James Watson Webb. Bennett had been employed by Webb several years before starting the *Herald,* but the two had had a falling out during the 1832 Jackson reelection campaign when Webb abandoned his earlier opposition to the U.S. Bank and came out in favor of recharter. To Bennett, who abhorred the powers and protections the Bank had been granted by the government, and whose support of Jackson was based on the president's opposition to recharter, such a shift was heresy. Indeed, the *Herald* was one of New York's—if not the nation's—most vociferous anti-Bank voices of the mid-1830s. As he put it in a typical editorial, "Of late years, and particularly since Mr. Van Buren and Mr. Biddle came before the world as the Caesar and Pompey of the age, the banking system has departed from being a humble instrument of

commerce, to be the great element of political power, and of popular government" (*NYH* 1-30-37). An anonymous poem that Bennett ran on the
front page of the *Herald* in 1837—perhaps in imitation of Peacock's 1837
Paper Money Lyrics—makes his staunchly bullionist posture even clearer.
Warning that "Bank Notes are all deceitful trash / . . . Their faithless word,
a promise rash," the poem concludes with a sentiment that links the paper
economy with the spectral world of the gothic: "Poor, worthless dirty rags
avaunt! / And may destruction seize ye / Such 'ghosts of cash' I do not want
/ Nor shall ye more my pockets haunt— / There's nothing safe but specie"
(*NYH* 6-15-1837). Webb's reversal on the Bank issue thus smelled to Bennett
of the very corruption he feared would ensue from the Bank's control over
the nation's economy. As he put it in an 1836 reference to Webb, "The New
York *Herald* is entirely conducted on the *cash* system. We never had, and
never will have the slightest favor from any bank. We despise incorporated
banks and bankers. . . . The chartered banking system has woven this country in a web of credit. It has destroyed the liberty of the press and checked
the very thoughts of men" (*NYH* 9-20-1836). To Bennett the Jacksonian, the
"cash system" meant a form of defense against the oppression of Whig interests—interests to which Webb and the *Courier* seemed to have yielded.

The conflict between Webb and Bennett reached a boiling point in early
1836, when the *Herald* carried several pieces accusing Webb of a variety of
misdeeds, including accepting an illegal loan from the U.S. Bank. An editorial in March of 1836 was typically blunt. Titled "Queries to the editor of
the Courier and Enquirer," the piece poses a series of questions to Webb,
including the following: "Did you, or did you not, say that 'the U.S. Bank and
the Courier and Enquirer acting in concert, could always control the money
market?' and also—'I and Mr. Biddle can give a tone to the stock operations
of the country'? . . . Had you, or had you not, a very private conversation
with a distinguished broker, on the morning of the first Tuesday in March,
at No.— Wall street? If so—did you, or did you not, enter into new contracts
for certain other stocks as purchaser on time, under a belief that the Bank
and the Courier and Enquirer could still control the market? . . . Are not all
of your articles on the money market, in the C and E, written and concocted
with a view entirely to effect [*sic*] your own contracts on time?" (*NYH*, 3-19-
1836).

Webb's response to such accusations was to seek out Bennett as he was
canvassing Wall Street for his economic column, and beat him with his cane.
As Bennett described it following an earlier such event, in January of 1836,
"The assassin Webb, by coming up behind me, cut a slash in my head of
about one and one half inch in length, and through the integuments of the
skull. . . . He did not succeed, however, in rifling me of my ideas as he did

the United States Bank and the brokers" (*NYH* 1-25-1836). The metaphorics of class struggle could not have been clearer. Caught out on Wall Street, the territory of the city's more established money, Bennett met with resistance of an extremely violent sort. Wishing to keep Bennett down economically, Webb performed that act physically, with the specific intent of exposing Bennett to a public form of bodily humiliation.

Bennett is even more direct in linking Webb's assault to Bank politics in a piece he published a short time later. As he puts it, "Who has forgotten the cowardly attempts made upon us by the editor of the Courier and Enquirer, because we dared to tell the truth of certain base stock operations in which he was engaged? And even so mad had the mania become among the speculators, that it was at one time deliberately decided by a class of swindlers in Wall street, and another coterie of scoundrels in Ann street, to maim, break a limb, or so disable me personally that I should never be capable of writing another paragraph or another Wall street report. I knew of all these projects and plans, but never feared the dastardly cowards from the editor of the Courier down to the lowest vagabond" (*NYH* 4-13-1837). As such pieces suggest, physical violence was a central component of professional life for the men involved in the city's newspaper trade during this period. Throughout the 1830s and 1840s, many of the city's news editors confronted one another, as well as other political enemies, in street fights and even in actual pistol duels.[13] This was especially true of Bennett, who refused to remit in his attacks on Webb or various other editors. In May Bennett reported that Webb had deliberately published misleading market information so as to benefit from the stock fluctuations. The accusation brought about a grand jury investigation, but it also brought about two more Wall Street brawls between Webb and Bennett, one in early May and another in early July. Each time it was again Webb who came away the victor, once after having kicked Bennett down a flight of stone steps as a crowd of eager onlookers shouted their support for the two combatants. Following the second confrontation, in an item titled "Yet once more," the *Sun* ironically termed Bennett "Common flogging property," adding that "[u]pon calculating the number of public floggings which that miserable scribbler Bennett has received, we have pretty accurately ascertained that there is not a square inch of his body which has not been lacerated somewhere about fifteen times" (Day, *NYS* 5-5-1836). Nor were Bennett's brawls limited to those with Webb; as "common flogging property," Bennett and his one-penny *Herald* suffered assaults from a number of competitors. In addition to his confrontations with Webb, Bennett was also physically beaten by Peter Townsend of the Whig-based *Evening Star* in October of 1835, and by William Leggett of the staunchly Democratic New York *Evening Post* in December of the same year.[14]

Clearly, Bennett had entered into a struggle in which more was at stake simply than the $500 he had invested in the *Herald*. Having made himself a key player both in the rapidly expanding newspaper world of the mid-1830s and in the emergent world of financial reporting, he had involved himself in a dynamic in which the threats of bodily violence and humiliation—"caning," "rifling," "flogging," "slashing"—were tied to categories of public reputation and economic status. Public attacks upon one's "honor" (a term Webb often invoked) seem to have signified the need for equally public and often bodily retaliations against one's challenger. In these instances the public self being circulated in the city's papers was closely related to the private, bodily self one might inhabit or "possess" individually; the two were not autonomous.

Entrance into this world also seems to have meant intensive challenges to one's masculinity. As nearly all of the tabloid accounts of the encounters between these men suggest, to be beaten or humiliated in public was to be feminized, which in these cases meant being rendered both physically and economically vulnerable. This is perhaps why Bennett often responded to Webb's attacks with a show of bravado. Following his second attack, for example, Bennett claimed, "Neither Webb nor any other man shall or can intimidate me. . . . I may be attacked—I may be assailed . . . but I will never succumb" (*NYH* 5-10-1836). But this is also why, paradoxically, Bennett's descriptions of his beatings are such an odd mix of indignation and playfulness. In Bennett's account of Webb's January 1836 attack on him, for example, the metaphorics of penetration and submission are so brutal and excessive that they seem almost silly. In a similar story following Webb's second assault, Bennett gives considerable—one might even say "campy"—attention to Webb's "superior physical strength," stating finally that Webb was "altogether too powerful for me to contend with" (*NYH* 5-10-1836). My sense is that by overdetermining his role as victim Bennett was able to recuperate at least a portion of his losses—if not those to his person or his masculinity, then perhaps those to his pocketbook. For if nothing else, the beatings Bennett was taking made for good publicity, which meant increased sales and revenue for the *Herald*. In other words, by playing up his reputation as a sort of communal whipping boy, Bennett seems to have hit upon a means of competing with his oppressors where it may have hurt most: economically. In fact, one wonders whether Bennett didn't intentionally provoke some of these encounters, using himself as bait in order to cause a public sensation. Indeed, after Webb's first attack Bennett sometimes took to announcing in print when he would be appearing on Wall Street. As for example he put it following Webb's second attack, "Today it is said another attack will be made upon me in Wall st. I shall be there between one and two o'clock to see it"

(*NYH* 5-16-1836). Perhaps, like the prostitute Jewett, Bennett found himself forced to compete by whatever means necessary—namely, by selling his body for profit.

In this Bennett was offering a rhetoric of masculine submission that, as I suggest in chapter 3, was utilized by Lippard and a number of the male writers producing sensational fiction during the period. And, again, what this rhetoric suggests is that assuming an enfeebled, even masochistic posture was often useful as a means of negotiating the vicissitudes of self-possession and economic advancement. In an 1836 piece titled "Penny Literature versus Loafer Literature," Bennett lashes out at "trashy publications" such as the New York *Mirror* and the *Knickerbocker*, which he claims have "degenerated into vehicles of mere sickly sentimentalism, fit only for the kitchen or the laundry" (*NYH* 9-30-1836). The antidote to such sentimentality, he explains, can be found in "the daily press and the cheap periodicals," venues which, because they are "[c]onversant in matters of business," should be understood as "possess[ing] the only strength—the only nerve—the only real talent and genius" (*NYH* 9-30-1836). But what are we to make of Bennett's repeated— and apparently quite intentional—postures of humiliation? I would suggest that, in the highly competitive world of the penny presses—a world echoed in the fiction of Lippard, Poe, and others—violent class rivalry between men seems to have necessitated more fluid forms of gender identity, forms of selfhood in which the personal autonomy of more standard types of self-possessed, middle-class masculinity was undermined. In some cases this was simply because the privilege of being "on top" was not always available. For example, in the tales and poems of Poe (whose personal struggles for distinctions of class and culture were if anything more violent and humiliating than Bennett's), the infamous subservience of his male characters before hypersanctified or demonic women becomes the means by which masculinity and "self-possession" are reconfigured, thus allowing Poe to critique the landed aristocracy that so long excluded him.[15] In other cases, however, it seems that a rhetoric of physical disempowerment was utilized to affiliate oneself with more effete spheres of class distinction, the cultural capital of which was far more enabling than mere brute force. In eschewing the pose of masculine prowess, in other words, Bennett seems to have been seeking an alternative—and less embattled—form of manhood, one located somewhere between the gothic abjection of Ichabod Crane in his flight from the Headless Horseman, and the more overtly sentimental postures assumed by the infamous John White Webster in his *Confession of the Murder of Dr. George Parkman*. The question of how successful he would be with such a stance was of course an open one that (again paradoxically) he struggled to answer with sometimes alarming vehemence.

"CHEERINGS AND HUZZAS":
WHITE-COLLAR MANHOOD ON TRIAL

Though 1836 found Bennett a struggling and oft-abused newspaper entrepreneur, it was also the year in which, with his coverage of Jewett's murder,
his fortunes changed. What quickly became apparent was that the case provided Bennett an opportunity to champion the scandalous Robinson, and to
sell thereby an enormous number of newspapers. In his many editorials on
the case from April to June, Bennett suggested that the real killer could likely
be found amongst the ranks of the city's Whig-based "*soi-disant* fashionable
society" (*NYH* 4-15-1836), who needed Robinson as cover for their own
presence at 41 Thomas Street the night of the murder. These people, Bennett
claimed, had paid off Rosina Townsend, the brothel's madam, to maintain
silence. According to Bennett, "The affair is to be hushed up. Young Robinson is to be considered guilty. He is young and penniless. To make another
search after the murderer might unfrock some of the most respectable men
in New York, who were in the City Hotel on that very night. . . . The trial is
a juggle—the arrest was a juggle—the whole affair is a juggle. It is a juggle to
criminate Robinson, in order to save others, some of them worth $150,000,
who were in that house, from public exposure" (*NYH* 5-10-1836). In the
weeks to follow, Bennett elaborated on his conspiracy theory, suggesting
that the police were also involved in the cover-up, that competing tabloids
such as the *Sun* were in the pay of the city's Whig aristocracy, and that the
killer might have been Townsend herself, who he claimed owed Jewett a
large sum of money.[16]

Other papers, however, most vocally the *Sun* and the *Transcript*, saw
Robinson as the murderer and touted him as an example of the new breed
of young clerks so threatening to the city's class structure. Indeed, the *Sun*
eventually claimed that Robinson was guilty of murdering another woman,
Emma E. Chancellor, "whom he had seduced from the home of her friends,
to become the inmate of a brothel of this city" (*NYS* 6-14-1836).[17] According
to these papers, it was Bennett who was himself on the take from Robinson
and his supporters. Perhaps the clearest statement of this charge came after
the *Herald's* publication of an anonymous letter from someone claiming
to be the "real" murderer. Describing himself as a fellow clerk, the author
explained that a fallout with Robinson and a later rejection by Jewett ("[A]nd
for whom? why, for Robinson") had driven him to kill Jewett and frame
Robinson for the deed (*NYH* 4-15-1836). The next day the *Sun* denounced
Bennett for fabricating the story: "It is scarcely necessary to say that the letter which appeared in a certain loathsome print yesterday, purporting to be
written by some unknown person, who is made to confess that he and not

Robinson, was the murderer of Ellen Jewett, the unfortunate cortezan, was a diabolical forgery by James Gordon Bennett, the unprincipled editor. We know it to be a fact that this wretch actually received a bribe of $50 from the friends of the murderer Robinson, to create, by this infamous means, a public rumor of his innocence. . . . We have long known this man to be more unblushingly unprincipled than any other that pollutes the public press, but from so callous, unmanly, and heartless an extent of villainy as this, our charity had hitherto exempted him" (*NYS* 4-16-1836).

Representing Bennett as "unmanly" for his alleged willingness to sell his public support for cash, the *Sun*'s editors were tapping into the same issues of self-possession and gender at work in Bennett's running feud with Webb. According to the *Sun*, Bennett was nothing more than a hired public voice, and therefore without the integrity even of Jewett or Townsend; to this way of thinking, not only was Bennett's defense of Robinson outrageous, but his humiliations on Wall Street were well-deserved.

Bennett was of course vehement in his denial of such accusations, stating (somewhat predictably) that the editors of the *Sun, Transcript,* and various other city papers were themselves in the pay of the aristocracy, and were attempting to frame *him* along with the unlucky Robinson. Just a few days after the murder, for example, Bennett responded to a *Transcript* article accusing him of providing "easy access to petit bribery" (*Transcript* 4-14-1836) by stating that the real question was whether "the owner and editor of the *Transcript,* has been one of those regular gentlemen at Thomas Street Hotel"—and who, by implication, was involved in a payoff of Townsend and the police (*NYH* 4-15-1836). Similarly, in June Bennett suggested that the *Sun*'s Benjamin Day had been paid $450 to "prop up and sustain the character of Rosina Townsend," and that he had also received sexual favors from Townsend herself (*NYH* 6-23-1836). Again, the public disputes between the city's tabloid editors were caught up in the metaphorics of bribery and prostitution; along with issues of class, masculinity, and publicity, the debate over Jewett's murder had very much to do with issues of economic autonomy and personal integrity.

The positions being assumed by the various tabloids are also telling for the way they reflect the manner in which conflicts between men in the city often had as their site of struggle the city's brothels. As several historians of antebellum New York have shown, the first four decades of the century were marked by so-called brothel riots, most of which can be seen as struggles between contending classes of men.[18] The majority of the men involved in these riots were of the laboring classes, and most of the houses they attacked were high-priced brothels with exclusive clients. In the 1830s alone, more than forty such incidents were recorded in New York City. The year of Jewett's murder was especially violent, largely because of the activity of local gang leaders John Chichester and Thomas Hyer. Over the course of the year, Chichester organized attacks on at least three brothel houses, during which several women were beaten and threatened with murder.[19] Hyer—who would later become an influential local politician—led at least four attacks on brothels from 1836 to 1838. In one such incident, a raid on a brothel run by Ellen Holly, the physical threats were realized, as one of the women working in the house was gang-raped.

According to Timothy Gilfoyle, such attacks were often politically motivated and involved gangs hired by local ward politicians to enforce local variations on Jacksonian politics. These were probably not classical republican journeymen, but they may well have been among the group who read or were influenced by the hard money, anti-Whig narratives frequently offered in working-class organs such as *Working Man's Advocate* (which featured stock characters such as the villainous speculator "Simon Squeezem" and the carpenter "Peter Plane").[20] Frustrated by the access to high-priced prostitutes which men of the upper classes enjoyed, "gangsters" such as Chichester and Hyer were performing a sort of symbolic violence upon the women themselves. As spaces in which sex was bought and sold, such brothels acted as sites wherein privileges of class could be manifested symbolically, by virtue of an individual's buying power. Brothels such as the City Hotel were not only expensive; they were also private, frequently operating on an appointment-only basis and allowing patrons to stay the entire night with a single prostitute. Such brothels thus provided patrons with the illusion of intimacy and romance—a privilege not available to those unable to pay for it. Access to such houses therefore translated into issues of both class and masculinity, and the ability to frequent them implied a removal from often degrading concerns of bodily labor. To assault the brothels and the women who worked in them was thus a form of class struggle in which bodily violation of a brothel's inmates constituted a symbolic violation of the men wishing themselves free of such threats. As with the public confrontations between Webb and Bennett, distinctions of gender and class were being fashioned reciprocally, and considerable emphasis was being put on the symbolic power of violent action. Again, the various forms of "masculinity" available to men in the city were often contingent on registers of class in which the distinction between bodily integrity and bodily violation played a crucial role.

But the city's gangs were not the only ones resorting to such forms of violence. Several times in the months prior to Robinson's trial the city's clerks manifested their support for Robinson with violent assaults on female prostitutes and other women. In April, for example, a meeting at the New York

Moral Reform Society called to discuss the lessons of the Jewett murder was broken up by a group of young men, possibly clerks, who jeered and threw stones, causing the women in attendance to flee (*NYH* 4-19-1836). Similarly, in the days leading up to the trial, large crowds of clerks began to gather outside the courtroom, causing near-riots on several occasions. The most violent gathering occurred on May 24 following Robinson's arraignment, when a large gang of Robinson supporters confronted a group of prostitutes as they were leaving the courthouse. As described in a lengthy passage in the *Sun,*

> A number of females, some of whom attended as witnesses, on leaving the Hall, were mobbed by a collection of several hundred vagabonds of all sizes and ages—amongst whom the long lank figure of the notorious Bennett was most conspicuous—who surrounded the women and almost prevented them entirely from reaching the outside of the Park, and which was finally effected by them with great difficulty, if not danger to their persons. . . . The mob, from the Hall steps to the Park gate, kept up a deafening shout of yells and epithets of the most vulgar kind. From the former most unwise and suicidal course which some of the reckless associates of Robinson have practiced in relation to these women . . . for the purpose of frightening them from appearing to testify on the trial of their companion, there can be no doubt that the mobbing of them yesterday was got up by the same clan of reprobates for the same purpose—particularly as their purchased and super-serviceable tool, before mentioned, appeared amongst the foremost of the gang of ruffians, and encouraged them by his presence and approbatory grins. (*NYS* 5-25-1836)

Led by the seemingly ubiquitous (and "super-serviceable") Bennett, the clerks assaulting Jewett's associates were in fact waging a form of class struggle with the city's Whig-based aristocracy. For Bennett, the attack translated into a form of continued competition with the likes of the *Courier's* Webb. Already the victim of several public humiliations out on Wall Street, Bennett was able here to use Jewett's cohorts as the vehicle through which he might receive an at least imagined form of healing for his abused sense of bodily integrity and masculinity.

At the trial itself, which was presided over by Justice Ogden Edwards, a leading Whig, the clerks were especially demonstrative.[21] Attending the trial in large numbers, they overflowed the courtroom, hissing and jeering during the testimony of Rosina Townsend and other prostitutes, and cheering wildly for defense witnesses. According to former mayor and staunch Whig Philip Hone, the atmosphere was overwhelmingly—and disturbingly—pro-

Robinson: "I perceived in court a strong predilection in favor of the prisoner. He is young, good looking, and supported by influential friends. . . . There are good reasons for public sympathy, but there are others, less benevolent. There appears to be a fellow-feeling in the audience; I was surrounded by young men, about his age, apparently clerks like him, who appeared to be thoroughly initiated into the arcana of such houses as Mrs. R. Townsend's. They knew the wretched women inmates as they were brought up to testify, and joked with each other in a manner illy comporting with the solemnity of the situation" (*DPH* 210–11). Again, the clerks were engaging in a form of class warfare by appropriating public space at the expense of prostitutes such as Townsend. And in this instance the clerks found themselves on the winning side of a class struggle. Flanked by a team of expensive attorneys and by his employer, Joseph Hoxie, Robinson was able to manifest sufficient connections to property and class to distance himself from the many accusations and alleged evidence against him. Indeed, despite the imposing nature of the case compiled against Robinson, his fortunes began to change when a grocer named Robert Furlong appeared as a surprise witness for the defense. Testifying that Robinson had been in his store smoking cigars from 9:30 to approximately 10:15—exactly the time witnesses claimed he had visited the City Hotel—Furlong provided the clerk with a much-needed alibi.

Furlong's testimony was crucial. As the jury prepared to leave the courtroom for deliberation following three days of testimony, Justice Edwards instructed them to discount the evidence provided by Rosina Townsend and the other prostitutes from the City Hotel, explaining that "When persons are brought forward who lead such profligate lives their testimony is not to be credited unless corroborated by testimony drawn from more credible sources" (*CE* 6-7-1836). Without any "credible" witnesses to place Robinson at the scene of the murder, the jury thus returned a verdict of "not guilty." According to the *Herald*, the reaction was overwhelming: "The cheerings and huzzas were tremendous—in vain the court assayed to stop them" (*NYH* 6-9-1836).

Nor was Robinson the only victor in the affair: by the time of Robinson's acquittal, the *Herald*'s circulation had quadrupled from 4,000 to 16,000, a figure that did not fall off with the end of the trial.[22] By August of 1836 the *Herald* was able to double its price and join the ranks of the *Courier;* a year after the murder and two years after founding the paper, Bennett claimed his own worth at near $100,000, by which time the *Herald* was without question the leading newspaper in the city. Apparently, despite the many challenges to him on the levels of class, self-possession, and masculinity, Bennett had managed to negotiate his way through the Robinson-Jewett case with extremely advantageous results.

"A BEAUTIFUL FEMALE CORPSE":
THE AESTHETICS OF MALE ANXIETY

But if Bennett achieved through Jewett's murder a form of class triumph, the question remains as to how he negotiated his relationship with Jewett herself, especially with respect to class and gender. As the accounts above make clear, the case was caught up in a dynamic of often fierce forms of violence, both representational and actual. I thus want to understand the abuse to which Bennett was subjected as something he deployed not only upon the likes of Rosina Townsend but also upon Jewett herself—who, again, seems to have figured powerfully in Bennett's desire for economic advancement. This, it seems to me, is what lay behind Bennett's obsession with Jewett and the City Hotel in the months following the murder. Bennett was seeking a form of social affirmation and self-possession that—at least symbolically—would secure him against the sort of class and gender violence he was experiencing on the city's streets. "Access" to a high-priced prostitute such as Helen Jewett meant access to the spheres of class, reputation, and masculinity to which Bennett aspired, even as he was critiquing these spheres in his many denunciations of the Bank and its Whig supporters. The trouble, however, was that Jewett proved extremely resistant to such efforts.

In particular I want to focus on the trips to Jewett's room that Bennett describes in the *Herald* in the days following her murder. What Bennett encountered there was a scene that frustrated his efforts to classify her. As Bennett reported with seeming surprise on April 11 and April 12, Jewett's possessions included not only expensive clothing and jewelry—outer manifestations of class that could be put on and taken off—but also objects reflecting her internalization of class status. According to Bennett in an entry titled "A Visit to the Scene," Jewett's room was stocked with a range of books, periodicals, and letters, as well as several sketches and paintings—all signs that she had apparently been able to negotiate the boundaries of class and of culture, and perhaps even manipulate them. In describing the letters, Bennett seems particularly struck not only by Jewett's ability to provide "apt quotations from the Italian, French, and English poets," and to "satiriz[e] playfully the little incidents of her life," but also by the "uncommonly beautiful" nature of her handwriting (*NYH* 4-13-1836). Among the books, Bennett lists Byron's *Don Juan* ("in all the elegance of binding that London could afford" [*NYH* 4-11-1836]), Lady Blessington's *Flowers of Loveliness* (1836), and an unnamed novel by Sir Walter Scott; of the periodicals, he lists the *Knickerbocker,* the *New York Mirror,* and the *Ladies Companion.* As Bennett put it, "What an air of elegance and intellectual refinement, without the slightest approach to principles and morals, dispersed itself throughout the apartment" (*NYH* 4-11-1836). Blessington's work—which Bennett claims, perhaps dubiously, to have found beneath the sheets of Jewett's bed—may have had the greatest resonance. As Bennett explained, Blessington, "one of the most unprincipled—yet most enchanting women in the world!," had risen from poor beginnings as a promiscuous vintner's daughter serving drinks in Ireland to the status of Lady Blessington by concealing her background and eventually marrying a beguiled Lord Blessington; later, she was widely viewed as scandalous for her not-so-covert affair with her stepson, the heir to the recently (and mysteriously) deceased Lord Blessington (*NYH* 4-11-1836). Sitting on Jewett's bed, in other words, was a narrative whose contents echoed Jewett's own life of transgression at the levels of class and sex.

What all of this suggests is that Jewett, who by virtue of her cultural capital seemed far more "self-possessed" than a female prostitute ought to have been, posed a particular threat to Bennett. In an environment already heavily coded by the symbolics of class distinction, gender hierarchy, and sex, Jewett might be said here to possess the "phallus" in ways that are anxiety-producing to one such as Bennett, whose own relation to symbolic power never seems certain. As he put it two days after the murder, in a passage that performs male anxieties in particularly overt ways, "From those who have known her, we have been informed that she was a fascinating woman in conversation, full of intellect and refinement, but at the same time possessed of a very devil, and a species of mortal antipathy to the male race. Her great passion was to seduce young men, and particularly those who most resisted her charms. She seems to have declared war against the sex. 'Oh,' she would say, 'how I despise you all—you are a heartless, unprincipled set. You have ruined me—I'll ruin you—I delight in your ruin'" (*NYH* 4-12-1836). As with so many of his pieces in the *Herald,* Bennett's sensationalism is so overstated that it's difficult to know how seriously to take him. Nevertheless, the passage is telling, especially since Bennett offers such a clear link between "intellect and refinement," female seduction, and a perceived threat to "the male race." This linkage also characterizes a letter to the *Herald* signed with the alias "Julius"—which, as the above charge of forgery by the *Sun* suggests, may well have been written by Bennett himself. Titled "FIRST STEP," the letter is an account of Jewett, some four years before her murder, "playing dominoes with a pretty boy, apparently about fourteen." When Julius, who "knew Ellen well," asked what she was doing, Jewett merely "smiled," the suggestion being that she took open pleasure in seducing "pretty" young boys (*NYH* 6-17-1836). The irony here is that the boy in the scene is Richard P. Robinson; in a cruel if predictable twist, Jewett's "antipathy to the male race" turns out to be her undoing, and Robinson becomes *Jewett's* victim, rather than the other way around.[23]

But again, this is the sensational version of Helen Jewett emerging from the unstable fiscal environment of the mid-1830s—an environment in which Bennett was an important player. Seeking very aggressively to back Jackson's bullionist campaign against the U.S. Bank and the Whig party more generally, Bennett seems to have seen in Jewett the very corruption and capriciousness that he saw in the credit economy itself. Whether decked out in her green dress and expensive jewelry or luxuriating within the rarified world of the City Hotel brothel, Jewett represented a negative zone of fantasy that, supposedly backed by Whig forces, transformed the gold standard of affect (love and romance) into commodities available to anyone with the proper notes in his pocket. Hence Bennett's overt reference in 1837 to Jewett as a figure for "public credit—paper money" who has "los[t] . . . all decency, and all virtue." But Bennett's somewhat playful suggestion (offered later in the same 1837 editorial) that the paper economy be bludgeoned to death in the same way that Jewett was murdered with Robinson's hatchet suggests that Jewett was fairly anxious-making for the embattled Bennett. Indeed, Bennett's claim that Jewett's "great passion was to seduce young men" so as to "delight in [their] ruin" might be understood as a commentary on both Jewett and the paper economy more generally: in each case, the truly fearsome agent is desire itself, especially as it is being created in the unstable fiscal world of 1830s New York. Embodied here in the figure of Jewett, that desire is both titillating and anxious-making for one such as Bennett—and, it seems, for many of his readers as well.

Such anxiety is the reason I find Bennett's various depictions of Jewett's corpse so telling. The most provocative such example is the one I quote from briefly earlier, in which Bennett describes Jewett as he found her at the City Hotel. Here is an extended version of this quote:

> What a sight burst upon me! . . . On the carpet I saw a piece of linen covering something as if carelessly flung over it. "Here," said the Police Officer. "Here is the poor creature." He half uncovered the ghastly corpse. I could scarcely look at it for a second or two . . . It was the most remarkable sight I ever beheld. I never have and never expect to see such another. "My God!" I exclaimed. "How like a statue! I can scarcely conceive that form to be a corpse." Not a vein was to be seen. The body looked as white, as full, as polished as the purest Parisian marble. . . . The countenance was calm and passionless. Not the slightest appearance of emotion was there. One arm lay over her bosom—the other was inverted and hanging over her head. The

left side down to the waist, where the fire had touched, was bronzed like an antique statue. For a few moments I was lost in admiration of this extraordinary sight—a beautiful female corpse—that surpassed the finest statue in antiquity. (*NYH* 4-11-36)[24]

In addition to providing wonderful copy for his newspaper, the passage offers a telling look at the pleasure Bennett takes in viewing Jewett's dead body. "Beautiful" and "extraordinary," Jewett seems to offer Bennett an unexpectedly erotic experience—one that, as he himself says, he isn't likely to get again.

What also seems apparent is that Bennett wants his description to display a certain sense of security. This is why, as the police officer pulls the linen away, Jewett is "slowly" transformed from monstrous Other (a "ghastly corpse") into aesthetic object ("as polished as the purest Parisian marble"). Jewett not only becomes more pleasurable to view the more we see of her, she also becomes safer. For what Bennett seems to have been implying is that, as a high-priced female prostitute, Jewett's task was above all to reassure her patron of his dominance and masculinity, most particularly by being fully accessible and unthreatening. More abstractly, she was to reassure her patron that she had nothing to hide—that beneath her clothing and accessories (her green dress, for example), there was nothing that carried the potential for its own signification. Her job, in other words, was to prove that she lacked the cultural power of the phallus at the same time that she reassured men such as Robinson and Bennett that they were indeed secure in their own possession of it. Yet as the many books, periodicals, and letters Bennett encountered in her room imply, Jewett seems—surely—to be hiding *something*. Much like Poe's deathly Ligea, whose unmatched intellectual capacity is both terrifying and pleasing to Poe's narrator, Jewett seems to possess a hidden cultural capital that signifies for Bennett in terms of both class and sexuality. Another way to put this is to say that Jewett seems to be here a figure of "theft" much like that which we see in a character such as the sensational Jew. But this comparison works only in terms of the Shylock figure. For unlike the Jessica character of antebellum sensationalism, Jewett seems resistant to the compensatory strategies we so often see in this material. Hence Bennett's decision to render Jewett in terms of a safely eroticized aesthetic: threatened, apparently, by the power of a woman such as Jewett, Bennett portrays her aesthetically in order to achieve a safer, more reassuring form of erotic excitement—one that translates into not-so-subtle forms of representational violence.[25] In this sense one sees that the problem isn't *Jewett's* relation to the phallus so much as it is Bennett's panic about his own "lack" thereof.

Nor is this dynamic far removed from that of the lithographs produced by Alfred M. Hoffy, who accompanied Bennett to Jewett's room the morning of the murder. (The lithographs were offered for sale on the city's streets on April 16.) One of the images, entitled *The "Innocent Boy"* (figure 16), recreates the moments following Jewett's murder, including a capped Robinson fleeing, clutching a hatchet and his cloak about to slip from his shoulders. More clearly even than Bennett's description, *The "Innocent Boy"* manifests—if in comically exaggerated fashion—the castration anxiety associated with Jewett and her possessions. With Jewett's books and paintings spread threateningly about the room (the middle painting is a recognizable portrait of Byron) and her writing implements ready at her bedside (with pen, paper, and inkwell suggestive of cultural—and thus in this case sexual—empowerment), the hatchet poised over Robinson's crotch literalizes the castration threat Jewett poses. From this perspective, Robinson is fleeing not only the scene of his crime, but, via Hoffy and Bennett, the scene of masculine disempowerment and panic as well.

But a second lithograph, titled *Ellen Jewett* (figure 17), gives Jewett's threat its fullest articulation. In contrast to *The "Innocent Boy,"* there is in this second image only Jewett and the bed on view. All items of cultural currency have been removed, and all attention is focused on Jewett as she lies lifeless on the bed. Here we see the same scene of deathly erotics offered by Bennett in his depiction of her corpse. Indeed, with her left arm a marbleized white—Hoffy's version of the wounds inflicted by the fire—Jewett is very much the aestheticized and pleasingly erotic "antique statue" of Bennett's description. This is apparent in practically every detail of the picture: with Jewett's blankets and clothing eaten away by the now extinguished flames, her breasts are partially exposed, her hair is let down around her shoulders, and the curve of her hip is given full accent. Even more than in Bennett's written description, the viewer is invited to indulge in the pleasure not only of gazing at Jewett's body but also of gaining an imaginary access to it. For what the image seeks to prove is that—with books, pictures, and other items of cultural currency now removed—there is nothing *but* Jewett's body to be found beneath her blankets. There is only the nude and accessible body of a high-priced female prostitute, one that men such as Bennett might represent as a way of vying for self-possession and advantage in the competitive world of New York's sensational public sphere.

Bennett's misogyny is thus complex indeed. For what it reflects is the difficulty men such as Bennett were having negotiating their own social positions during this period. Struggling for economic advancement, Bennett seemed to experience a form of gender "panic" inextricable from insecurities of class and culture as they were evolving in the climate of 1830s fiscal

Figure 16 *The "Innocent Boy".* 1836 by Alfred M. Hoffy. Printed and published by H. R. Robinson. Reproduced with permission of the New York Historical Society.

Figure 17 *Ellen Jewett.* 1836 by Alfred M. Hoffy. Printed and published by H. R. Robinson. Lithograph, hand-colored; image and text 27 x 35 cm. Reproduced with permission of the American Antiquarian Society.

anxiety. Thus while reflecting powerfully the desire to categorize Jewett and provide readers (and perhaps himself) with a compensatory narrative of male dominance, the various depictions Bennett provides of her murdered corpse—from the imagined removal of her from her grave to the murder scene narratives and their accompanying lithograph images—reflect also the considerable anxiety motivating that desire. What had to be proved by representing Jewett as disinterred or murdered was that the ghostly Jewett was actually "there," so that the category of the female prostitute might offer a reliable referent in the vexed effort to experience oneself publicly as "self-possessed." Already the victim of a particularly gendered and public form of class violence and humiliation, Bennett was seeking to ensure he did not continue to suffer that fate. Jewett, however, offered him little assurance on this score. Instead, what Bennett saw in the City Hotel was a figure marked in unsettling ways by a culture in which economic competition between men, often violent, could not be evaded—even in the realm of a high-priced prostitute such as Helen Jewett.

CODA:
CAPITALISM AND THE FEMALE CORPSE IN
THE BLITHEDALE ROMANCE

The form of sensational masculinity staged by Bennett in the pages of the *Herald* receives a powerful echo in Hawthorne's *The Blithedale Romance*. Indeed, while the novel narrates an attempted return to a life of labor and use value—it is of course famously based on George Ripley's Brook Farm effort to construct a utopian socialism, an effort in which Hawthorne participated for a short time—the story might in fact be read as an extended allegory of the speculative, paper money masculinity spawned by the 1837 Panic. Various critics have cited *Blithedale* as a text that operates according to a consumerist logic, but we might also consider it in relation to the period's debates over political economy and the U.S. Bank.[26] Indeed, Hawthorne's 1852 narrative actually recounts events that are twelve years in the past, which places the novel's events at about 1840, a postpanic moment of intense economic depression and uncertainty, and the period just following the Helen Jewett case. And as with Bennett's tabloid sensationalism, *Blithedale* stages a market-based masculinity in terms of an obsession with very public women (Zenobia and Priscilla) who act as sites of possible "investment" (both financial and psychic) for the various men of the novel.[27] "It was purely speculative," Coverdale says of his attraction to Zenobia, "for I should not, under any circumstances, have fallen in love with Zenobia" (48).

The distinction Coverdale makes here is crucial for the economies of both money and gender circulating within this narrative. Though offering "love" as a kind of hard currency—which suggests, somewhat deceptively, that it is the novel's gold standard of emotional value—Coverdale nevertheless makes it clear that he is antibullionist in orientation, preferring instead the anxious pleasures of playing the market.

Nor is this surprising, for Zenobia is to some extent the very figure of market desire. The eldest daughter of Fauntleroy—once "a man of wealth" and "prodigal expenditure" who ends up losing his fortune so that he can only stand by and watch as "the wreck of his estate was divided among his creditors" (182–83)—Zenobia acts as a figure through whom various dreams of economic prosperity can be played out. As her father, now named Moodie, puts it, "Let the world admire her, and be dazzled by her, the brilliant child of my prosperity! It is Fauntleroy that still shines through her!" (192). Zenobia, that is to say, does an important sort of fantasy work for the various men who take an interest in her. Numerous critics have investigated Coverdale's penchant for voyeurism (what Zenobia refers to as "eye-shot" [47]), a neurosis that allows him to control his anxieties—especially those related to castration—by means of an object-controlling gaze.[28] Put simply, Coverdale objectifies the people he views and places them within a field of fantasy that allows him the pleasures of visual access without having to make physical contact with them. But the voyeurism Coverdale engages in is also analogous to economic speculation precisely in that, while providing him with a detached (and largely dematerialized) relationship to the present world of real bodily encounter, it also allows him a fantasy about future rewards.[29]

And to be sure, Coverdale is not the only male in the novel who operates according to a logic that conflates speculation and femininity. Indeed, this link is expressed even more clearly in Coverdale's accusation to Hollingsworth that his romance with Zenobia is driven solely by his interest in her inheritance. According to Coverdale, Hollingsworth's plan is to use this money to buy up the Blithedale land as the site for his proposed prison. "But whence can you, having no means of your own, derive the enormous capital which is essential to this experiment?" Coverdale asks pointedly. "State-street, I imagine, would not draw its purse-strings very liberally, in aid of such a speculation" (132). Like Coverdale, Hollingsworth is banking on Zenobia in ways that suggest he is uninterested in the gold standard of love; instead, Zenobia is quite literally a source of investment for him.

And certainly this logic pertains to Westervelt, who extends these relations even further. For Westervelt is in many ways the embodiment of the false nature of the credit economy, something Coverdale discovers after encountering Westervelt lurking in the woods near Blithedale one day. As Coverdale explains with clear distaste, "In the excess of his delight, he opened his mouth wide, and disclosed a gold band around the upper part of his teeth; thereby making it apparent that every one of his brilliant grinders and incisors was a sham. This discovery affected me very oddly. I felt as if the whole man were a moral and physical humbug; his wonderful beauty of face, for aught I knew, might be removable like a mask" (95). Like the depiction of so many paper money men in antebellum sensationalism (Colonel Fitz-Cowles in *The Quaker City*, for example), Westervelt is all exterior and no substance. Or—to pick up on Coverdale's reference to Westervelt as a "humbug"—the professor is like the spurious "shinplaster" banknotes circulating in the wake of the 1837 suspension of specie by New York banks. The general cynicism about these notes is captured in an 1837 lithograph satire of the shinplaster notes titled *Fifty Cents. Shin Plaster* (figure 18), in which we see a desperate Andrew Jackson riding a pig over a cliff as he chases after a "gold humbug." As Mihm points out in a short reading of this lithograph, the banknote itself is dated the day the banks suspended specie payments, and, rather than a pledge to redeem the note in gold or silver, it offers a promise to pay "in counterfeit caricatures" (*Counterfeiters* 152). The implied insubstantiality of the lithography note extends to Westervelt, who is a "sham" echo of the often untrustworthy paper economy.

Even the products that Westervelt peddles—the Veiled Lady and mesmerism—resonate with the language of the paper economy. This is especially evident in the scene late in the novel in which Westervelt introduces the Veiled Lady at a "village-hall" performance that Coverdale attends. As Westervelt explains, "That silvery veil is, in one sense, an enchantment, having been dipt, as it were, and essentially imbued, through the potency of my art, with the fluid medium of spirits. Slight and ethereal as it seems, the limitations of time and space have no existence within its folds. . . . She beholds the Absolute!" (*Blithedale* 201). The veil provides the very properties of capital itself: though seemingly ethereal and without real substance, it is able, like the new economy, to perform the seemingly magical feat of accessing what are apparently incredibly distant sites and populations in ways previously unimaginable. In *Worlds Apart* (1986), Jean-Christophe Agnew writes that by the mid-eighteenth century, "The attributes of materiality, reality, and agency ordinarily assigned to the sphere of social relations (or to God) were implicitly reassigned to the sphere of commodity relations, as supply and demand took on a life of their own"; in this sense, he argues, markets became "placeless" in that they were transformed from temporally and spatially specific sites to abstract processes no longer available or accessible to lived experience (56; 202). Understood in this way, the

Figure 18 *Fifty Cents. Shin Plaster.* 1837 printed and published by H. R. Robinson. Lithograph on wove paper; 26.1 x 44.6 cm. Reproduced with permission of the American Antiquarian Society.

act of "behold[ing] the Absolute" implies an almost unthinkable access to the "placeless" space of the free market itself, as it circulates unbounded in mid-century America and beyond. The fact that the veil requires the aid of Westervelt's "art" to achieve such an astonishing transcendence merely highlights Westervelt's role as a figure for speculation and paper money men in antebellum America.

But the figure of the Veiled Lady also reminds us that it is the female body that stands in for the abstract and mysterious nature of the credit economy. Much like Helen Jewett, the Veiled Lady (Priscilla) is a figure of public access, one through whom various fantasies and desires can be played out. This is something we see played out most fully in Zenobia's "Legend" about the Veiled Lady, a story-within-a-story that acts as the novel's central exploration of the links between gender and the period's political economy. Told by Zenobia to a group of listeners at Blithedale, the story revolves around a young man named Theodore. After hearing the "wild stories that were in vogue" (108) among young men about the Veiled Lady (stories we might even read as metaphors for rumors about valuable speculative schemes), Theodore makes what is apparently the crucial mistake of refusing to act on "trust." Sounding very much like a wary bullionist, he claims boldly that "Nobody, unless his brain be as full of bubbles as this wine, can seriously thinking of crediting that ridiculous rumor" (109). In order to debunk the rumor as a humbug, Theodore proceeds to sneak into the Veiled Lady's dressing room. As with so much else in the novel, the encounter resonates with the period's intersecting languages of political economy and gender. Certainly the Veiled Lady's activity echoes the weightless nature of the paper economy: "so impalpable, so ethereal, so without substance," we are told, she "floated, and flitted, and hovered about the room;—no sound of a footstep, no perceptible motion of a limb;—it was as if a wandering breeze wafted her before it, at its own wild and gentle pleasure" (111–12). But as a variety of critics have pointed out, the Veiled Lady also acts here as an ideal of Victorian womanhood, in particular as this womanhood conjoins an incorporeal and nonthreatening version of femininity that promises nevertheless (or as a result) a certain amount of erotic appeal.[30] Even off-stage Priscilla is a "ghost-child" with "a lack of human substance in her" (87; 185), but onstage as the Veiled Lady, floating about in a strange sort of bondage to Westervelt, she provides for the (male) viewer a safely eroticized performance of disembodiment. Brown puts it thus: "Both an anonymous apparition and a public performer, she elicits and eludes sexual and epistemological discovery" (*Domestic* 122). Thus in each case—fiscal and feminine—Priscilla offers an idealized form of insubstantiality, one that promises transcendence over the material constraints of the body, whether laboring or sexual.

But again, Theodore's skepticism about such magical properties—and about the Veiled Lady's promise that in "pledging himself" to her he will ensure that they experience "all the felicity of earth and of the future world" (113)—leads him to insist on peeking beneath the veil before committing to her. Brown argues that Theodore's insistence on peeking before committing aligns him with a consumerist desire: "Taking her on faith . . . would mean aligning desire to a purpose, curiosity to investment" (119). I would argue something similar: that Theodore's skepticism is actually more analogous to that of an investor wishing to read up on the financial reports of a company before purchasing its stock—something a character such as Charles Dickens's Martin Chuzzlewit would have been wise to do, for example, before buying into a phony land scheme in America and becoming what Dickens refers to sarcastically as "a landed proprietor in the thriving city of Eden" (*Chuzzlewit* 423). Yet this skepticism is also tinged with a certain amount of anxiety, something reflected in Theodore's concerns about kissing the Veiled Lady through her veil. "A delightful idea, truly, that he should salute the lips of a dead girl, or the jaws of a skeleton, or the grinning cavity of a monster's mouth!" (113) we are told in words that capture Theodore's unspoken thoughts. Picking up on the various rumors circulating that the veil conceals "the face of a corpse," "the head of a skeleton," or "a monstrous visage, with snaky locks, like Medusa's" (110), Theodore's fears suggest a very real terror of both women *and* the paper economy—one felt not only by him but also by the class of "young gentlemen" of whom he is a representative (108). And as the reference to Medusa and her "snaky locks" makes clear, his fears are coded by castration anxiety. As Freud puts it in a well-known passage, "To decapitate = to castrate. The terror of Medusa is thus a terror of castration that is linked to the sight of something. . . . The hair upon the Medusa's head is frequently represented in works of art in the form of snakes, and these once again are derived from the castration complex" ("Medusa" 273–74). The "sight" that causes Theodore such anxiety (and which he conceals by means of the veil-as-fetish) is thus the sight of his own possible "lack." And this lack is made doubly terrifying in that it seems to carry with it a particularly ferocious form of female potency—one that, as with Helen Jewett in her brothel room at the City Hotel, threatens to disrupt the fantasy of male viewers such as Theodore and James Gordon Bennett. Here, in fact, it may be that this castration anxiety is what works to absorb or displace a broader complex of concerns about the period's political economy—which, again, is the very force that has sent the novel's various characters to Blithedale in the first place.

Theodore is both right and wrong about what lurks beneath the veil. For what he sees is not "the face of a corpse," nor of Medusa; rather, he glimpses what we might think of as the face of desire itself. "[J]ust one momentary glimpse," we are told, "and then the apparition vanished, and the silvery veil fluttered slowly down, and lay upon the floor. . . . His retribution was, to pine, forever and ever, for another sight of that dim, mournful face . . . to desire, and waste life in a feverish quest, and never meet it more!" (114). On one level, then, Zenobia's story—and, by extension, Hawthorne's novel—offers here a sentimentalized morality play about romantic trust: the Veiled Lady (Priscilla) demands a pledge of true love in order to receive what Lori Merish describes as an "antidote to [her] bondage" to Westervelt (*Sentimental* 185). From this perspective, Theodore must suffer the pangs of unrequited love as the penalty for his lack of trust in her unknown identity. But we might also understand Theodore as having entered into the very logic of capital, the result being that, following his glimpse beneath the veil, he is himself thrust into a form of market bondage very similar to that worried over by reformers such as Timothy Shay Arthur and Henry Ward Beecher, whom I discuss in chapter 3. "The gratification of one desire only makes way for another still more exacting," Arthur warns (*Advice* 31), words that do much to capture the hapless state into which Theodore has fallen. For what he finds is that he cannot stop his intense desire for the fleeting and quite ghostly residue of fulfillment that he has glimpsed in the image left behind by the Veiled Lady. We might thus say that, while Theodore does not find the terrible figure of a corpse beneath the veil, he does locate something equally horrifying: he finds that *there is no hidden hand beneath the veil of the paper economy;* rather, it is truly without substance. But, of course, fulfillment and substance are precisely what the speculative, credit economy cannot allow, any more than it can condone the kinds of restraints that a Jackson-style specie policy would impose. In this sense the absence that Theodore views beneath the veil is actually quite similar to the castrating image of Medusa: in each case Theodore faces an image of "lack" and longing that signals his own impotence as a young man in antebellum America.

Nor, perhaps, is this surprising, for the legend of Theodore is after all Zenobia's story. Coverdale spends a considerable amount of time in this novel critiquing Zenobia's skill as a writer, but even he concedes that she has real talent as a public speaker (120). The legend she tells at Blithedale reflects this talent, for what she manages is a critique of the speculative masculinity by which she is surrounded, both in town and at Blithedale. But what she also reveals is that the pleasures of speculation embraced by men such as Coverdale, Hollingsworth, and Westervelt are indeed anxious: as Coverdale puts it in reference to that crucial index of Zenobia's market value, her virginity, "The riddle made me so nervous, however, in my sensitive condition of mind and body, that I most ungratefully began to wish that she would let me alone" (48). The "nervous" condition Coverdale describes is related to that which we have seen in characters such as Ichabod Crane, the Gentile men of the Shylock and Jessica narratives, and so on: it is the nervousness of paper money manhood. And here, as with these other texts, the stakes are apparently high, something reflected in the novel's climactic scene when Coverdale encounters the horrific sight of Zenobia's corpse after she is dredged up from the river near Eliot's Pulpit. "She was the marble image of a death-agony," Coverdale says. "Ah, that rigidity! It is impossible to bear the terror of it!" (235). Deploying language strikingly similar to Bennett's description of Jewett's corpse ("as polished as the purest Parisian marble," Jewett's dead body is alternately "ghastly" and "beautiful"), Coverdale's description suggests that his speculative efforts have failed, giving way to a form of "terror" that seems to conflate gender panic and financial panic.

What is it that Coverdale encounters in the horrific sight of Zenobia's corpse? Russ Castronovo argues compellingly that Zenobia "practices radical democracy," by which he means that she, much like the farmer-laborer Silas Foster, insists on a labor-based materiality that runs counter to the market-driven and largely speculative desires of men such as Coverdale and Hollingsworth (*Necro-Citizenship* 144). We need to add that Zenobia's corpse also undermines the speculative logic of the paper economy itself, precisely in the sense that it insists on its very solidity and materiality. Thus, in death, Zenobia and Helen Jewett do a similar form of work for men such as Coverdale and James Gordon Bennett. For in each case what we see is a thwarted form of male desire, and thus an anxious form of professional manhood. And, at least in Coverdale's case, it is a haunted form of manhood. "Tell him he has murdered me!" Zenobia says to Coverdale in bitter reference to Hollingsworth. "Tell him that I'll haunt him!" (226). Zenobia's words might also apply to Coverdale, who informs us that the image of Zenobia's corpse has remained with him "for more than twelve long years," so forcefully in fact that he is able even in the narrative present to "reproduce it as freshly as if it were still before my eyes" (235). Like Bennett, Coverdale thus represents the difficulties and anxieties faced by the paper money man who, seeking compensation via the figure of the female body, finds himself faced with the very terrors of capital he has sought to repress and deny.

"Success" and Race in
The House of the Seven Gables

> "What's that you mutter to yourself, Matthew Maule? . . . And what for do you look so black at me?"
>
> "No matter, darkey! . . . Do you think nobody is to look black but yourself?"
>
> —Exchange between Young Matthew Maule and Scipio, slave of Gervayse Pyncheon, in Hawthorne's *The House of the Seven Gables*

Failure, Race, Manhood

What role does race play in the compensatory fictions of the sensational public sphere? As my discussion of the capitalist Jew in chapter 2 suggests, the sensationalism produced in the wake of the 1837 Panic frequently seeks to redress masculine crises of self-possession by recourse to figures of racial alterity. By way of continuing this analysis, I want to turn in this final chapter to narratives in which masculine anxieties about the paper economy were managed by enlisting parallel anxieties about the distinction between the racial categories of whiteness and blackness. Michael O'Malley refers to the relationship between political economy and racial economy as that existing in nineteenth-century America between "specie and species." As he explains, "[I]f many seemingly solid things melted into air, other more nebulous ideas grew more certain as capitalism advanced. . . . The shared language of race and money suggests that the freer market society became, the farther its promises extended, the more it demanded racial categories that resisted exchange or negotiation" ("Specie" 373). For O'Malley, in other words, the putative racial purity of whiteness was offered as a kind of compensatory "gold standard" in antebellum America, such that narratives about race and racial purity act as a kind of fantasy bribe, whereby anxieties about the period's radically unstable economy can be displaced onto similar concerns about racial instability—the latter of which are often represented as far more manageable than those associated with the period's panic-prone economy.

Here in this chapter I want to build on and complicate O'Malley's important discussion, in particular by exploring more fully the way in which the sensational public sphere puts race into service as a means of negotiating fiscal insecurity and masculine dispossession. For, much as with the capitalist Jew, the category of blackness—especially as embodied in the sensational black male—acts as a crucial and quite fungible fantasy space for the paper money male, one that is accessed again and again as a means of negotiating both white identity and, more specifically, white manhood during this period. But in ways that O'Malley doesn't quite account for, the relationship between whiteness and blackness is during this period extremely volatile and fluid, a fact that makes whiteness far less able to "resist[] exchange or negotiation" than he suggests. Indeed, the sensational black body of this period proves even more labile than the fiscal Jew, especially in the material produced in and around 1850—the period in which the Fugitive Slave Law was enacted, and the period in which legal definitions of selfhood and self-sovereignty were increasingly affected by legal definitions of both race *and* money. With respect to the former, the Fugitive Slave Law transformed the entire country into a territory hostile to black people, as both escaped slaves and those suspected or accused of being runaways could be sold into the Southern slave system. As Frederick Douglass famously put it, "Under this law the oaths of any two villains (the capturer and the claimant) are sufficient to confine a free man to slavery for life" (*Life and Times* 200). With respect to the latter, bankruptcy and debt were coming more and more to feel like a form of servitude, so much so that those seeking legislation for debt relief and a change in bankruptcy laws invoked the language of race to make their case. Sandage puts it thus: "White slaves, wage slaves, debt slaves: specters of dependent manhood proliferated after 1820. Trade unionists co-opted the slavery metaphor from their employers, the debtor classes of manufacturers and merchants" (*Losers* 194). And as David Roediger makes clear, this was not an effort to establish a shared bond between white men and black slaves. "[A] term like white slavery," he explains, "was not an act of solidarity with the slave but rather a call to arms to end the inappropriate oppression of whites" (*Wages* 73). The cover of an 1840 pamphlet titled *White Slavery!! Or Selling White Men for Debt!* provides powerful visual confirmation of the heightened racial rhetoric that accompanied the plight of the debtor male (figure 19).[1] Depicting a small group of ragged and nervous-looking debtors standing huddled together while an auctioneer takes bids for their purchase, the image makes aggressively clear the linkage between the black slave and

From the Globe.

WHITE SLAVERY!!

OR SELLING

WHITE MEN FOR DEBT!

June 27, 1840.

We have received from Indianapolis a certified copy, under the 'broad seal' of the State of Indiana, of the 11th, 30th, and 31st sections of the act of 1807, approved by General Harrison, providing for the sale of white men and women in certain cases ; and also the third section of an act regulating elections, approved in like manner, requiring a property qualification in voters for Representatives, &c. The copy is in the following words, viz :

AN ACT RESPECTING CRIMES AND PUNISHMENTS.

SEC. 11. If any person shall unlawfully assault or threaten another in any menacing manner, or shall strike or wound another, he shall, upon conviction thereof, be fined in a sum not exceeding one hundred dollars ; and the court before whom such conviction shall be had, may, in their discretion, cause the offender to enter into recognizance with surety for the peace and good behaviour, for a term not exceeding one year.

Sec. 30. When any person or persons shall, on conviction of any crime or breach of any penal law, be sentenced to pay a fine or fines, with or without the costs of prosecution, it shall and may be lawful for the court, before whom such conviction shall be had, to order the sheriff to sell or hire the person or

Figure 19 Cover of *White Slavery!! Or Selling White Men for Debt!* 1840. Reproduced from The Library of Congress, Rare Book and Special Collections Division.

the white debtor. For each group—black slaves and white debtors—self-possession had become alienable, a fact that suggested an implicit shift in identity itself. The white men depicted in *White Slavery!!* had, it seemed, slipped into an economic zone in which their very sense of whiteness had begun to fade into the alternative racial category of blackness. And to be sure, this was a concern that directly addressed the professional male, something we see in an 1864 quote such as the following from the antislavery *Independent*: "one hundred thousand good business men—mostly white men—are now in bondage, praying, at the doors of Congress, that their chains may be broken. They love freedom [as much as] black men" ("Bankrupt," *Independent* 4-7-1864; quoted in Sandage, *Losers* 199).

The twin concerns about race and money in the negotiation of professional manhood find especially resonant expression in a variety of sensational urban novels from the early 1850s. My main text here will be Nathaniel Hawthorne's *The House of the Seven Gables* (1851), which I will argue provides one of the period's most complex—and most uneasy—examinations of the fraught boundary between masculine whiteness and masculine blackness. Indeed, I want to suggest that *The House of the Seven Gables* is valuable as an object of study precisely because it stages this racial boundary directly in the context of the period's emergent market economy. Before turning to Hawthorne's novel, however, I want to look at a text that is in many ways less complicated, if more aggressively ideological. This is J. B Jones's *The City Merchant; or, the Mysterious Failure* (1851). As I mention in chapter 3, Jones's text is one of many sensational "Wall Street" novels from mid-century that revolve around the lives of professional men, and that thematize crises of debt and fiscal panic. Here, though, what we see is a fascinating display of the linked thematics of financial and racial panic—concerns that pass, seemingly inevitably, through the endlessly nervous category of professional manhood.

The novel opens in the months preceding the 1837 Panic, and focuses on the cautious fiscal practices of a merchant named Edgar Saxon. Specifically, we learn that on the eve of the 1837 Panic, Saxon makes the unexpected and quite unorthodox announcement that his wholesale supply house will conduct business on a specie-only basis. This decision, we learn, is sparked by the advice left by his father in a series of journal entries about his catastrophic financial failure in the 1819 Panic, a calamity that eventually took his life. In times of fiscal uncertainty, the journal says, "*lose no time [in the] conversion of your means into gold and silver, or other equally secure and imperishable substance*" (30; emphasis in original). Saxon follows this advice to the letter: refusing to either receive or extend credit of any kind, he demands instead that his agents convert all outstanding accounts into actual gold or silver specie, regardless of any short-term loss that might be incurred. So insistent is Saxon on this hard money or "bullionist" approach to his finances that he even refuses the entreaties of U.S. Bank president Nicholas Biddle to buy back the large number of shares in the Bank that he has sold—even at a large discount (Biddle is concerned that word of Saxon's lack of confidence in the U.S. Bank will spread, thus creating a panicky run on the nation's central specie supply). As Saxon puts it in a private conversation with Biddle, "Van Buren will be elected, and Jackson's policy will be adhered to. . . . They can and will break you down; and in doing so they will destroy the credit of the country, and a loss of confidence will involve the destruction of fortunes depending always so much upon its maintenance" (76). Soon Saxon is proved correct: while his overextended competitors fail in the Panic, he acquires "immense amounts of gold and silver" and is eventually referred to as a "one of the FIRST MERCHANTS in the country" (214). In this sense Saxon is the exception that proves the rule: his ability to retain a rational, bullionist posture as a merchant in 1830s America is almost radically unusual, to the point where the broader message seems to be that a more normative selfhood is one that falls prey to the temptations and passions of the marketplace.

But Saxon's fiscal and affective restraint is in fact maintained and bolstered in large part by virtue of the psychic work performed by the novel's various figures of racial alterity. On the one hand this is staged in the figure of a "cunning Jew" named Abraham Ulmar (66). Circulating in a section of Philadelphia "where the Jews were as thick as blackberries, and almost as dark," Ulmar is one of "four or five of the most opulent Jews of the city" (91), a status he has achieved by placing himself at the center of the local paper economy. Buying up and selling notes held against merchants such as Saxon at discounted rates, Ulmar is a sort of commodities trader, seeking to make a profit by speculating on the rise and fall of the reputations of the city's businessmen. But though Ulmar has been able to profit off of most of the city's merchants, he finds that the merchant Saxon is seemingly impervious to the excessive desires of the paper economy. Working in league with a broker named Grittz (who is "really a Jew," but who "affect[s] to be a Christian, and attended the Christian churches" [235]), Ulmar attempts to capitalize on Saxon's rumored vulnerability by selling a note he holds against Saxon at a thirty-three percent discount. But when "the discomfited Jew" (97) finds out that Saxon has in fact received a letter of praise from Bank president Biddle—a strong indication of Saxon's financial strength—Ulmar realizes he has been had. Worse, he finds that, because Saxon has paid off all of his debts and refused to circulate any new notes of credit, there is no leverage to be had against the savvy merchant. "Curse tem all!" Ulmar says, a comment echoed by the other Jewish traders, who "join[] him in bitter denunciation[] . . . of Mr. Saxon, and all Christians in general" (97–98). Further efforts by Ulmar to undermine Saxon's fiscal security—and thus his manhood—are similarly unavailing.[2]

Here then we see a narrative in which fiscal desire as embodied in the Jew, though able to permeate Saxon's world, is ultimately held in check; Saxon's internal registers of integrity make the Shylock figure less threatening than he often is in the period's sensational fiction. But we might understand Saxon's position as fairly anxious nevertheless. For while Saxon stays one step ahead of both Ulmar and Andrew Jackson in their respective efforts to undermine his financial status, he is also plagued by a different and more urgent threat. This is the specter of racial amalgamation, a threat that eventually leads to a city-wide race riot at novel's end. And what we see is that, for Saxon, the two concerns are intimately related, so much so that we are being asked to understand that financial panic is being negotiated by—and displaced onto—various forms of racial difference.

Anxieties about amalgamation begin about halfway through the novel, when Saxon's two young nieces, Alice and Edna Sandys, are approached by a pair of men whom Jones describes as "fashionable . . . mulatto exquisites, [who] had the effrontery to step forward and offer their arms" to the women. Saxon's nieces indignantly refuse the offer—when the men persist Alice tells them, "you'll be horsewhipped for this!" (131). But it is only when the men are brutally beaten by a working-class (and stereotypically Irish) family friend named Paddy Cork that the two sisters are able to make their way home unimpeded. According to Jones's narrator, the incident is one of many taking place on the streets of Philadelphia in 1836 and 1837. "For several days the abolitionists had been engaged in an unwonted jubilation in the city," we are told. "They had been addressed by Mr. Thompson, the British emissary—not the emissary of the government, but of a class of English and Scottish fanatico-philanthropists" (128). The result of this abolitionist rhetoric, the narrator continues, has been to promulgate notions of racial equality among the city's black population—notions that extend to sexual interaction between whites and blacks. Voicing concern about the provocative sight of "Lucretia Mott walking by the side of Frederick Douglas [*sic*]" (131), the narrator explains as follows: "The negroes themselves, both the free and the fugitive, credulous by nature, and utterly incapable of restraint when their passions are roused, believed a day was coming, nay, that it was at hand, when they would be on an equality in every respect with the white people of the north. And for several days great strapping negro fellows were seen promenading the streets in social attitudes and familiar converse with white women, while white men walked the pavements with sooty-faced

African women hanging on their arms!" (130). The description echoes and reinforces anxieties over racial mixing displayed with increasingly regularity in Philadelphia and other northeastern cities during the late 1830s. For example, in one of a series of seven lithographs produced by Edward Clay in 1839 titled *Practical Amalgamation,* we see two mixed-race couples in various stages of amorous relations (figure 20). As with each of the lithographs in this series, the image depicts precisely the concerns over miscegenation Jones taps into in his retrospective narrative (indeed, one suspects that the white and black dogs to the left of the image are intended as a comic mirror of the couples, and thus act as a reminder that interracial sex is understood as base and animalistic).[3]

In *The City Merchant,* the middle-class parlor trappings offered in "Practical Amalgamation" are abandoned, as Jones's narrative eventually realizes the fears that black men are incapable of restraining their sexual passions. Late in the text, Alice and Edna are kidnapped by the same two "mulatto exquisites" who accosted them in the street, and whisked off to a predominantly black section of the city, where, presumably, they will be raped. "That part of the city at that time was inhabited chiefly by the colored people," we are told ominously, "who, in moments of excitement and passion, could be roused with great unanimity to the commission of terrible deeds" (188). Fortunately for the girls, however, they are soon rescued by a young (and white) medical student named Edmund Scarboro, who then locks himself and the girls into the top floor of an abandoned building. In an image provided within the text, we see Scarboro literally holding the door shut as the black would-be rapists seek to break into the room, and the two girls huddle together in the room's far corner—the symbolics of heroic and manly white resistance to racial assault are quite clear. Perhaps not surprisingly, Scarboro buys just enough time to save them all; in a violent confrontation that eventually turns into a race riot, Scarboro and the girls are rescued by the police and various groups of white vigilantes who have tracked them to the black portion of the city. As Jones's narrator puts it, "it was literally carrying the war into Africa, but not exactly as Scipio did. There was no Hannibal to contend against" (192). Accordingly, after a lengthy battle that lasts long into the night, the "sooty rabble" (189) is eventually routed, and a large portion of the city's black population flees to nearby New Jersey.

What we therefore see is the intersection of the narratives of race and money. For just as Saxon's fiscal integrity is threatened by the irrational passions of the paper economy, so too is his family's sexual and racial integrity threatened by the similarly irrational passions of the rapacious black male. We might say that financial panic and racial panic are virtually synonymous in this novel. And here, we see that the language of racial purity (something

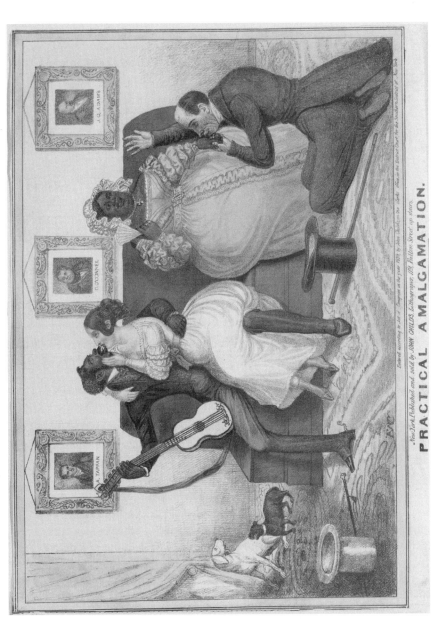

Figure 20 *Practical Amalgamation.* 1839 by Edward Clay. Lithograph, hand-colored; 24 x 32 cm. Reproduced with permission of the Library Company of Philadelphia.

referred to, of course, by Edgar Saxon's very name) works to stave off anxieties about the perceived movement away from a specie-based gold standard, as well as the various forms of masculine failure and emasculation attendant upon the new economy. Indeed, the novel, which goes on to narrate the marriage of Saxon's niece Alice to the young, white Edmund Scarboro, offers a sensational literary form we might think of as a "bank romance." Here in this conservative subgenre, the hard facts of political economy are transferred to the removed realm of white upper-class domestic enclosure; simultaneously, the disquieting threat of racial amalgamation drops away once it has done the hard work of absorbing the looming threat of fiscal panic.

In this compensatory fiction, then, it is the racial category of whiteness that is the fantasy trade-off for fiscal anxiety. But it's worth wondering whether the very project of displacing the fiscal onto the racial doesn't bespeak the very anxiety by which such a move is motivated. For if racial affect is asked to absorb fiscal affect in order to instantiate a stable form of white professional manhood, we might therefore understand the passionate, rapacious bodies of the "mulatto exquisites" who abduct Saxon's nieces as serving a function quite similar to that performed by Abraham Ulmar and the other capitalist Jews circulating "as thick as blackberries" on the edges of Philadelphia. In each case, racial difference might well act as a displaced figure of Saxon's *own* market-driven passions and desires, themselves repressed in answer to the stern dictates of the journal entries written by his financially failed father. Certainly these passions are received here in this very racist text as monstrous. Indeed, the "mulatto exquisites" are very much related to figures of "theft" we have seen throughout this study. Living on the outskirts of Philadelphia—imagined so sensationally as a kind of "Africa"—these men are the projected figures of stolen white enjoyment. Accordingly, in rescuing the two girls from this space of Otherness, Saxon and his white allies stage a kind of retrieval. This may not be the fantasy of recuperation we see in the Gentile theft of Jessica from her Shylock daughter, but it performs a kind of compensatory satisfaction nevertheless. It is as though some precious part of a paper money manhood has been retrieved, an act that is directly paralleled by Saxon's ability to beat the market panic and accumulate vast stores of gold bullion. But the continued efforts of the abolitionist project—bringing with them troubling assumptions about equality and, by extension, racial mixing—suggests *inter alia* that these passions might return. And this, in turn, is another way of saying that fiscal panic and masculine failure are ever-present threats. Saxon, that is to say, must be ever-wary and ever-anxious: in paper money America, apparently, success has its price.

"GO-AHEAD" MANHOOD AND RACE IN
THE HOUSE OF THE SEVEN GABLES

Another text from 1851 that negotiates the twin masculine concerns of fiscal and racial decline is Hawthorne's *The House of the Seven Gables*. Indeed, Hawthorne's novel is in many ways a roadmap for the various trajectories of manhood available during this period. From the working-class Maules, to the upwardly mobile Holgrave, to the declining Pyncheon aristocracy, we see a fraught drama that revolves in many ways around the following question: what do masculine "success" and "failure" look like in mid-century America? We might begin to answer this question by positing that, at least for Hawthorne, each of these categories is linked to the dream of locating treasure. For, much as with the search for gold in texts such as Irving's "The Golden Dreams of Wolfert Webber" and Poe's "The Gold-Bug" (both of which I discuss in the introduction), Hawthorne's narrative revolves in large part around the search for the missing deed to the territory of Waldo County in Maine. As Hawthorne's narrator explains, the deed was signed over to the Pyncheons by the "several Indian sagamores, and convey[ed] the Colonel Pyncheon and his heirs, forever, a vast extent of territory at the eastward" (316). The document, we are told, will return the Pyncheon family to aristocratic status; Holgrave's magazine story claims that the land "would be worth an earldom" (199). Thus, much like Captain Kidd's missing treasure, the deed also promises to provide the Pyncheons the more abstract benefit of allowing them to return, if in imagined or symbolic form, to the earlier "stage of commerce" described by Jameson. And, as I also suggest in the introduction, what such a return provides is the fantasy ability to transcend the modern world of capital, in which success and failure are internalized states that produce the kind of anxious male subjectivity we see (however differently) in characters such as Jaffery Pyncheon, Clifford Pyncheon, and Holgrave, the last surviving descendant of the Maule family.

In his preface to the novel, Hawthorne famously writes that he would "feel it a singular gratification, if this Romance might effectually convince mankind (or, indeed, any one man) of the folly of tumbling down an avalanche of gold, or real estate, on the heads of an unfortunate posterity" (2). This might seem like a posture that renounces the notion of treasure. But—and as I will demonstrate—Hawthorne's warning refers to money as it might exist once in circulation. At novel's end, of course, the deed is actually located, but it has no value for the Pyncheons. "It is what the Pyncheons sought in vain, while it was valuable," Holgrave says, *"and now that they find the treasure, it has long been worthless"* (316; emphasis mine). The message here seems clear: in the absence of found treasure (or gold bullion of the sort stored away by Edgar Saxton in *The City Merchant*), both the Pyncheons and the Maules must continue to negotiate the modern "stage of capital."

Another way to put this is to say that the various characters in this novel—the male characters in particular—must come to terms with the psychologies of "success" and "failure" as meted out by the unstable paper money world of antebellum America. And, much as in *The City Merchant,* one of the more subtle ways in which this is negotiated is via the related category of whiteness. But as I will suggest, even this is elusive; in the sensational urban world that Hawthorne depicts in his quirky gothic novel, all that is solid has indeed melted into air, even the putative securities of race and racial difference. Indeed, specifically because of its engagement with various racial (and racist) tropes available within mass culture—from the wide-eyed black servant and the dancing figure of Jim Crow, to the enfeebled "Anglo-Saxon" aristocrat and the white virgin heroine whose "unsullied purity" is violated (203)—the novel offers a telling example of how the period's sensationalism (of which Hawthorne's is an important if more "highbrow" version) was tapping into the malleable and frequently unsettling energies and fantasies of race, both "black" and "white," developing during this period as a means of managing anxieties over manhood and fiscal insecurity.

The result is that we need to complicate our understanding of the way in which race operates within the sensational public sphere. Recent scholarship on the politics of whiteness has done much to help us recognize the ways in which, as Toni Morrison so eloquently argues, "Americans choose to talk about themselves through and within a sometimes allegorical, sometimes metaphorical, but always choked representation of an Africanist presence" (*Playing* 17). And certainly this is what we see in a novel such as *The City Merchant,* in which figures of blackness provide the fantasy pathway to bolstered white manhood. In *The House of the Seven Gables,* however, the "Africanist presence" Morrison describes is unstable. Indeed, rather than act in the enabling way Morrison suggests—"thoroughly serviceable" and "companionably ego-reinforcing" to white self-presence (8)—the Africanist presence imagined by Hawthorne in *The House of the* Seven Gables, lifted as it is from the protean world of white racial fantasy, repeatedly ends up destabilizing the very distinctions of sensibility and culture it seems to have been deployed to bolster. Hawthorne's gothic romance thus represents a "racial gothic," in which the ghosts inhabiting the House of the Seven Gables are the uncanny figures of race and racial passion, returning to capitalist America to disrupt the very categories of gender and whiteness from which they were cast off and repressed.

Perhaps not surprisingly, the ambivalent racial negotiations I am describing take place in *The House of the Seven Gables* at moments when categories of class seem most unstable. The first such example comes in the pivotal scene in which Hepzibah Pyncheon makes her initial sale from the cent shop she has established on the side of the House of the Seven Gables. As Gillian Brown argues, the scene enforces Hepzibah's corporeal "enslavement" to the forces of the financial market with which she is finally forced to make actual physical contact (*Domestic* 81–86). But it's important to note that the vicissitudes of market embodiment reflected here are both facilitated by and routed through the figure of Jim Crow, who enters the narrative in the form of the Jim Crow gingerbread cookies Hepzibah offers for sale in her newly opened shop. Described as "Impish figure[s]" who can be seen "executing [their] world-renowned dance" in the cent shop window, the cookies advertise Hepzibah's entrance into the world of retail exchange, but they also act as the first goods exchanged between the Pyncheons and the working classes (51; 36).

Tellingly, the first customer they entice into the shop is Ned Higgins, a working-class boy whose repeated requests for the cookies eventually force Hepzibah to charge him money for the goods. Here is how Hawthorne depicts Hepzibah's first sale: "The new shopkeeper dropped the first solid result of her commercial enterprise into the till. It was done! The sordid stain of that copper coin could never be washed away from her palm. The little school-boy, aided by the impish figure of the Negro dancer, had wrought an irreparable ruin. The structure of ancient aristocracy had been demolished by him" (51). Described in specifically working-class terms as "dressed rather shabbily . . . in a blue apron, very wide and short trousers, shoes somewhat out at the toes, and a chip-hat" (*Gables* 49–50), Ned Higgins is a caricature of the working-class corporeality Hepzibah finds so threatening. Indeed, when, a short time after the young boy leaves the shop, Hepzibah waits on a "man in a blue cotton frock" who is "much soiled" and smells of alcohol, it seems clear that we are seeing a grown-up version of the boy as Hawthorne envisions him in future years. Imagined by Hepzibah to be the husband of a "care-wrinkled woman" she has seen earlier, one whom "you at once recognize as worn to death by a brute," the man terrifies Hepzibah both because of his "brutal" nature, and because she imagines he is the overly fertile father of "at least nine children"—all of whom will no doubt turn out like himself (and thus like Ned Higgins), and all of whom will threaten to overrun the degenerated and barren Pyncheon family line (53).

But Hawthorne's description of Hepzibah's first sale is also telling because "the impish figure of the Negro dancer" mediates her contact with the working-class embodiment represented by customers such as Ned Higgins. This is true on a literal level, in that Jim Crow is the commodity that passes between the classes and who thus "aid[s]" in forcing the Pyncheon family into the material world of retail exchange. But this is also true in the more figural sense that Jim Crow introduces race as a factor in the relations between the two classes. Here, this is especially evident in that Hepzibah is actually marked by her commodity exchange with "the lower classes," the surest sign of which is of course the "sordid stain" she receives from Ned Higgins's coin—a mark which those lucky enough to remain free of such contact are able to avoid (55). For example, a few moments after Hepzibah experiences her Eden-like "fall" into commerce, she sees a female member of "the idle aristocracy" walking with "ethereal lightness" down the street, and poses the following question to herself: "Must the whole world toil, that the palms of *her* hands may be kept white and delicate?" (55). The answer of course is "Yes," but what is especially telling here is how issues of class and labor are figured in terms very much like racial markings, and how the unwashable "stain" of Ned Higgins's working-class money separates Hepzibah from the "white and delicate" sphere of aristocratic racial purity. Class, in other words, is being made by Hawthorne into a racial issue, a fact that makes blackness a crucial third term in the effort to imagine a distinct difference between working-class whiteness, and whiteness of the kind inhabited by the "idle aristocracy."[4] But, and just as interestingly, money is itself being made here into a racialized topic. Indeed, it seems that contact with actual money leaves one with markings very much like a racial taint. Here, then, we see a modification of the scenario depicted in *The City Merchant*. Whereas in that text (and in visual images such as the cover of *White Slavery!!*) it is the absence of money that threatens one's relationship to whiteness, here it is contact with what Hepzibah might term "filthy lucre" that has racial implications. This, perhaps, is why Hawthorne can in his preface speak with confidence about the problems associated with "an avalanche of ill-gotten gold"—from the rarified perspective of this novel, anything that circulates, even gold bullion, is tainted. This is also the reason that, in a text such as *Uncle Tom's Cabin*, we are told that the slave trader Haley carries the papers for his slave transactions in a "greasy pocket-book" (236): this is literally money tainted by contact with the marketplace, and money that, by extension, taints those who make contact with it.

But whether it is the absence of money or actual contact with it, what we see is that economic decline figures the threat of racial decline. Indeed, from the perspective of the Pyncheons—and especially, perhaps, of Hepzibah—only the discovery of treasure (such as the missing map of Waldo County) will now retrieve the family's lost whiteness. Hence, of course, the irony inherent in the fact that she continues even in her now impoverished state to maintain a "hereditary reverence" (59) for the portrait of Colonel Pyncheon that hangs on the wall of the House of the Seven Gables. For what we find at novel's end is that the portrait is quite literally backed by the now-worthless deed of Waldo County. Again, the logic of this novel suggests that whiteness not backed by treasure (which is to say the fantasy of money—of fiscal security—that is located outside actual circulation) is vulnerable to market intrusion and, *inter alia,* to racial tainting.

The unsettling conflation of race and money for the Pyncheons is furthered later in the novel. This comes as Clifford Pyncheon (recently released from prison after serving thirty years for the alleged murder of old Jaffrey Pyncheon) watches from a balcony window of the House of the Seven Gables as a young Italian organ grinder performs on the street in front of the Pyncheon home. Clifford, who is variously described in terms of his "pale" and "yellowing" skin, "lack of vigor," "filmy eyes," and his tendency to "burst into a woman's passion of tears" (112; 113), is in many ways a hyperbolic extension of the enfeebled, degenerated male imagined by reformers such as Catherine Beecher and Horace Greeley.[5] Indeed, the descriptions Hawthorne provides of Clifford's fragile physical and mental condition also echo warnings by antebellum reformers such as John Todd against the evils of masturbation, the ultimate effect of which was thought to be impotence. Advising against the "habit of reverie" as the pathway to "evils which want a name, to convey any conception of their enormity," Todd describes states ranging from nervousness to melancholia and poor memory, all of which speak to Clifford's enfeebled status after his release from jail (*Student's Manual* 88, 146–47).[6]

But Clifford is also, and perhaps more obviously, a figure for the male who has proved incapable of achieving the much-discussed "go-ahead" attitude of the early 1850s. A term used to connote the energy and drive of the successful businessman, "go-aheadism" captured the capitalist ethos of the paper money man. As Sandage explains, "Supposedly open to any white man who did not 'lack energy,' this fraternity hooted and hollered about 'our go-ahead spirit' and 'American *go-aheadism.*' Even the staid *Scientific American,* founded in 1846, warned of 'the fearful blot of a wasted life' and beat the drum for 'Yankee go-ahead-ativeness.' . . . In competitive markets, to lack the 'go ahead spirit' (in reality or allegedly) counted as a fatal flaw. In 1851, a credit-rating agency blacklisted a New Yorker, noting 'R. is not a 1st rate business man, has not enough energy to be a business man'" (*Losers* 84). The language used to depict the go-ahead male is clearly antithetical to that we see in descriptions of Clifford as "lacking in vigor," or when, terrified at the notion of a confrontation with his aggressively masculine cousin Jaffrey Pyncheon, he cries out to Hepzibah, "[G]o down on your knees to him! Kiss his feet! Entreat him not to come in! Oh, let him have mercy on me! Mercy!—mercy!" (129). At one point in the novel Clifford is "startled into manhood and intellectual vigor" when he and Hepzibah leave the House of the Seven Gables and, taking a trip on a railroad car, discover an exciting world of technological advance (258). But this new and invigorated manhood quickly fades, and we see that, "with a torpid and reluctant utterance" (266), Clifford asks Hepzibah to lead him home. Again, Clifford is profoundly unsuited for the modern world of capitalist competition, and the forms of manhood that seem necessarily to accompany it. Instead, he is a figure of the aesthete, whose removal from actual market production Hawthorne seems to find absurdly impractical. Indeed, characterized by qualities of aesthetic appreciation "so refined" they seem to provide him a form of "spiritual" disembodiment (108), Clifford represents an old-world aesthetic sensibility Hawthorne clearly seeks to mark as incompatible with the modern world of industrialization and mass culture looming close by outside the House of the Seven Gables.

This contrast is perhaps best exemplified by Clifford's practice of blowing soap bubbles from the second-story window, miniature creations Hawthorne describes in terms that highlight the fleeting nature of the aesthetic Clifford represents. "Little impalpable worlds were those soap-bubbles," Hawthorne explains, "with the big world depicted, in hues as bright as imagination, on the nothing of their surface" (171). Composed of an interior logic that the outer world is unable to penetrate without ruining it altogether (in such instances Hawthorne describes the bubble as having "vanished as if it had never been" [171]), the soap bubbles suggest an antimarket aesthetic resistant to reproduction and circulation of the kind taking place in Hepzibah's cent shop. And it is precisely this fragile aestheticism that is at issue when Clifford views the Italian organ-grinder who circulates in the neighborhoods surrounding the House of the Seven Gables. At first it appears that the boy will provide Clifford a picturesque image of life on the streets, in particular because the boy's barrel organ contains a number of miniature mechanical figures that perform the very kind of utopia Clifford longs for, a kind of mercantilist *Gemeinschaft* in which community and labor-value coincide. "In all their variety of occupation—the cobbler, the blacksmith, the soldier, the lady with her fan, the toper with his bottle, the milk-maid sitting by her cow—this fortunate little society might truly be said to enjoy a harmonious existence, and to make life literally a dance" (163). But while the boy's barrel organ appeals to Clifford's sensibilities, the other attraction he offers does not. This is the monkey that accompanies him, a creature Hawthorne marks by tellingly anthropomorphic signs of race, gender, and even sexuality. Described as having a "strangely man-like expression" on his face, "perform[ing] a bow and scrape" for passing pedestrians, and "holding out his small black palm" for money (164), the monkey is an only thinly veiled caricature of a performative but also fairly aggressive black masculinity, one Hawthorne seems to have expected his readers to recognize. While he does not explicitly "jump Jim Crow," his theatrical "bow and scrape," coupled with his "man-like expression" and his overtly "black" skin, make it clear that Hawthorne is again tapping into the charged images of the performing black male body so ubiquitous throughout antebellum mass culture, in particular within minstrel shows. The connections between the monkey and the bawdy tropes of minstrelsy are even stronger when one realizes that the monkey is marked by an overdetermined sexuality that his Highland pant suit is literally unable to conceal. Characterized three times in two paragraphs for the "enormous tail" protruding beneath his suit pants (Hawthorne describes it as a "preposterous prolixity . . . too enormous to be decently concealed under his gabardine" [164]), the monkey offers the sort of excessive caricature of black male sexuality that, as Eric Lott and others have shown, was so common within the period's minstrel performances. The effect of all of this on Clifford is dramatic: having taken a "childish delight" in the Italian boy, he becomes "so shocked" by the "horrible ugliness" of the monkey that he "actually beg[ins] to shed tears" (164).

What is it that Clifford weeps over, exactly? Hawthorne's narrator tells us that his tears represent "a weakness which men of merely delicate endowments—and destitute of the fiercer, deeper, and more tragic power of laughter—can hardly avoid, when the worst and meanest aspect of life happens to be presented to them" (164–65). My sense is that this "weakness" (and the tears it produces) is being contrasted with the forms of aggressivity associated with the figure of black manhood we see in the Italian boy's monkey—an aggressivity that is here understood as "the worst and meanest aspect of life." On the one hand, of course, this has to do with the seeming sexual potency the monkey represents. But Clifford's unease is also related to the image of the monkey's "small black palm" held outward in expectation of monetary reward: this is the figure of insistent monetary desire, one made all the more troubling because of its very link to blackness and to black sexuality.[7] Late in the novel, the Italian boy and his monkey return to the House of the Seven Gables, only to find that Clifford and Hepzibah have departed (though as it turns out, this is only temporary). But again we see the monkey "bow[] and scrape[] to the bystanders, most obsequiously, with ever an observant eye to pick up a stray cent" (293). Much as with Hepzibah in her cent shop exchange with Ned Higgins, Clifford is confronted in his interaction with the Italian boy's monkey the hard facts of economic exchange. And—again as with the cent shop scene—this exchange is routed through the stereotyped figure of the performing black male. Apparently, market relations are for Hawthorne negatively associated with race.

Here then we are in the confusing terrain inhabited by the infamous Black Guinea in Melville's *The Confidence-Man* (1857). A "grotesque negro cripple" aboard the riverboat Fidèle, Black Guinea appeals to potential donors by performing the shocking trick of catching pennies in his mouth (15). "Hailing each expertly-caught copper with a cracked bravura from his tambourine," we are told, "he grinned, and only once or twice did he wince, which was when certain coins, tossed by more playful almoners, came inconveniently nigh to his teeth" (17). Like the Italian boy's monkey, Black Guinea is a "grotesque" figure of economic appetency, one who negatively reflects the market world of desire back to his white observers. And indeed, the fact that Black Guinea, like the Italian boy's monkey, seems to emerge out of the performative aesthetics of blackface minstrelsy only underscores his role in this regard (as one cynical observer comments, "He's some white operator, betwisted and painted up for a decoy" [20]). For the link to minstrelsy reminds us that the form of blackness we see in such characters is simply a nervous fantasy, one that assigns and deploys racial stereotypes specifically as a means of assuaging white anxieties. And in this case, these anxieties revolve around the uneasy status of manhood in the go-ahead period of economic development. Sandage suggests that a minstrel songster image such as the 1834 *Zip Coon on the Go-Ahead Principle* (figure 21) reflects the felt "absurdity" (and hence the putative humor) of a professionally ambitious black male (*Losers* 85). But, and especially for one such as Clifford, a black dandy character such as Zip Coon also bespeaks a certain *anxiety* about the attenuated nature of white manhood, especially in the face of the go-ahead demands of the emerging market economy. Perhaps, the songster seems to be saying, one must lose one's whiteness in order to succeed in the economic marketplace (hence, perhaps, Zip's anti-Biddle lyrics).[8]

And in this we might understand such images as doing psychic work quite similar to that performed by the "mulatto exquisites" in *The City Merchant*. For surely such figures of sensational blackness, linked as they are to both sexuality and money, represent the perceived theft of enjoyment that is, we might say, at the root of the psychological and emotional crisis facing the Pyncheon family (and with it, of course, white America itself). Again, then, we see the sensational public sphere staging figures of sensational Otherness—here the black male—as a means of negotiating anxieties over an imperiled form of manhood. Here, though, unlike a narrative such as *The City Merchant*, retrieving stolen enjoyment is far less straightforward than staging a race riot. Indeed, we might ask, is there a compensatory fantasy available to readers of *The House of the Seven Gables*? Clearly, and as I have been suggesting, the novel understands race in relation to money. But in the absence of both secure racial boundaries and reliable sources of economic security, the answer to this question is both uncertain and anxious.[9]

ZIP COON

ON THE GO-AHEAD PRINCIPLE.

I went down to Sandy hollar t'other arternoon,
I went down to Sandy hollar t'other arternoon,
I went down to Sandy hollar t'other arternoon,
An de first man I chanc'd to meet war ole Zip Coon,
  Ole Zip Coon he is a larn'd scholar,
  Ole Zip Coon he is a larn'd scholar,
  Ole Zip Coon he is a larn'd scholar,
For he plays upon de banjo, "Cooney in de hollar."
    Tudle tadle, tudle, tadle, tuadellel dump,
    O tuadellel, tuadellel, tuadellel dump,
    Ri tum tuadellel, tuadelleldee.

Cooney in de hollar an racoon up a stump,
  Cooney in de hollar, &c.
And all dose 'tickler tunes Zip use to jump.
  Oh de Buffo Dixon he beat Tom Rice,—(repeat.)
And he walk into Jim Crow a little too nice.

Ole Sukey Blueskin she is in love with me,
  Ole Sukey Blueskin, &c.
An I went to Suke's house all for to drink tea,
  An what do you think Sue and I had for supper,
  An what do you think, &c.
Why possum fat an hominy, without any butter.

My old missus she's mad wid me,
  My ole missus, &c.
Kase I wouldn't go wid her into Tennessee.
  Massa build him a barn to put in fodder,
  Massa build him, &c.
'Twas dis ting an dat ting, one thing or odder.

Did you eber see he wild goose sailing on a ocean,
  Did you eber, &c.
De wild goose motion is a mighty pretty notion,
  De wild goose wink and he beacon to de swallow,
  De wild goose wink, &c.
An de wild goose hollar google, google goliar.

I spose you heard ob de battle New Orleans,
  I spose you heard, &c.
Whar ole gineral Jackson gib de British beans;
  Dare the Yankee boys de de job so slick,
  Dare de Yankee, &c.
For dey cotch Pakenham, an row'd him up de creek.

Away down south dare close to the moon,
  Away down, &c.
Dare lives a nullifier what they call Calhoun,
  When gineral Jackson kills Calhoun,
  When gineral, &c.
Why de berry next President be ole Zip Coon.

He try to run ole Hickory down,
  He try to run, &c.
But he strike a snag an run aground,
  Dis snag by gum war a wapper,
  Dis snag by, &c.
And sent him into dock to get a new copper.

In Phil a del fie is old Biddle's Bank,
  In Phil a del fie, &c.
Ole Hickory zamin'd him an found him rather crank
  He tell Nick to go and not make a muss,
  He tell Nick to go, &c.
So hurrah for Jackson he's de boy for us.

Possum on a log play wid im toes,
  Possum on a log, &c.
Up comes a guinea hog and off he goes,
  Buffalo in cane break, ole owl in a bush,
  Buffalo in a canebreak, &c.
Laffin at de blacksnake trying to eat mush.

Nice corn's a growing, Sukey loves gin,
  Nice corn's a growing, &c.
Rooster's done crowing at ole niggars shin,
  Oh Coone's in de hollar and a Possum in de stubble,
  Oh Coone's in the hollar, &c.
And its walk chalk ginger blue, jump double trouble.

Oh a bullfrog sot an watch an alligator,
  Oh a bullfrog sot, &c.
An jump upon a stump an offer him a tater;
  De alligator grinned an tried for to blush,
  De alligator grinned, &c.
An de bullfrog laughed an cried oh hush.

Oh if I was president ob dese Nited States,
  Oh if I was, &c.
I'd lick lasses candy and swing upon de gates,
  An does I dina like why I strike em off de docket,
  An does I dina like, &c.
De way I ns'd em up was a sin to Davy Crocket.

Sold wholesale and retail, by L. DEMING, at the sign of the Barber's Pole, No. 62, Hanover Street, Boston, and at MIDDLEBURY, Vt.

[1832 - 1837]

Figure 21 *Zip Coon on the Go-Ahead Principle.* 1834, sold by Leonard Deming. Sheet music; 1 page; 22.9 x 15.6 cm. Reproduced with permission of the American Antiquarian Society.

RACIAL VAMPIRISM?

I would suggest that the fate of both whiteness and professional manhood in this novel hinges on the actions of the character Holgrave. For despite his working-class roots (as a Maule), Holgrave is perhaps better understood as a version of the upwardly mobile male of the professional classes. Indeed, Holgrave is in many ways a version of the go-ahead male of the early 1850s. Daguerreotypist, short-story writer, mesmerist, and sometime political activist (Hepzibah has "read a paragraph in a penny paper . . . accusing him of making a speech full of wild, disorganizing matter, at a meeting of his banditti-like associates" [84]), he is both entrepreneurial and, it seems, intensely canny about his role as a male subject under advancing forms of capitalism. We might even think of him as an updated version of the New York *Herald's* James Gordon Bennett Jr., who as I discuss in chapter 4 was instrumental in carving out the very form of sensationalism that Holgrave manipulates in his role as writer of pulpy gothic fiction. Holgrave, that is to say, occupies the far end of the sensational fraternity of professional men I have been outlining over the course of this study. As such, I want to understand him as a key point of reference in detailing how masculinity was being organized under the paper economy. For again, Hawthorne's novel suggests that the masculine sensibility of the emergent professional classes was intertwined in complicated and often vexed ways with the sensational sensibilities and passions of blackness. And with Holgrave what we see is a character who seems to understand this relationship, and who is, I will argue, willing to manipulate it.

Holgrave thus represents an important addition to the outline of paper money manhood I have been describing. For he seems to understand that, in the confusing and uncertain world of antebellum America, successful manhood requires an incredible amount of dexterity at the levels of both class and race. Indeed, the tropes of racial appropriation that accompany the references to Jim Crow and blackface minstrelsy in the above-described scenes might also help us understand the way in which Holgrave negotiates the various registers of class, race, and manhood that are at stake in this novel. In the world according to Holgrave, that is to say, the smug fiscal and racial certainties of characters such as Edgar Saxon and (as we will see) Jaffrey Pyncheon are simply not realistic. Holgrave wants to "go ahead," but—like a kind of confidence man—he will do what is necessary in order to get there.

Much of what we learn about Holgrave comes from the sensational-gothic short story that he writes, and which Hawthorne inserts into the pages of his novel in the form of a reading Holgrave gives to Phoebe. As

Holgrave explains upon learning that Phoebe has not read any of the fiction he has published, "Well, such is literary fame! Yes, Miss Phoebe Pyncheon, among the multitude of my marvellous gifts I have that of writing stories; and my name has figured, I can assure you, on the covers of Graham and Godey, making as respectable an appearance, for aught I could see, as any of the canonized bead-roll with which it is associated. In the humorous line, I am thought to have a very pretty way with me; and as for pathos, I am as provocative of tears as an onion" (186). Very much in the manner of a tabloid such as the *Herald* or a novel such as *The Quaker City,* Holgrave seeks to use the pulpy discourse of gothic sensationalism in order to stage masculine class conflict within antebellum culture. He is, that is to say, a contributor to the very sensational public sphere that, via Hawthorne, he inhabits as a character. Here, his goal is to provide background to the feud between the Maules, who have been dispossessed of their land, and the Pyncheons, who engineered this displacement by accusing Matthew Maule of witchcraft. We might say that the story provides a rationale for the continued sense of failure that his family—and especially its men—have suffered for some two hundred years. "They were generally poverty-stricken," we are told early on of the Maules, "always plebian and obscure . . . living here and there about the town, in hired tenements, and coming finally to the alms house, as the natural home of their old age" (25). This is the burden that Holgrave carries with him, and one thus suspects that Holgrave's fiction acts as a kind of projected space in which to work out the very notions of success and failure that are so central to his culture—but also to his very sense of selfhood—at mid-century.

The story is set some forty years after the execution of the founding Maule, and dramatizes the meeting between Young Matthew Maule, Holgrave's grandfather many times removed, and Gervayse Pyncheon, Phoebe's equally distant uncle. Tellingly, however, the story also provides significant commentary about the role of race in sensational constructions of antebellum manhood. In particular I am interested in the encounter Holgrave narrates between Maule and "black Scipio," whom Holgrave describes as one of the black slaves whose "shining, sable face[s]" can be seen "bustling across" the "cheery" windows of the Pyncheon home (191).[10] The brief exchange between the two men is significant: "What's that you mutter to yourself, Matthew Maule?" Scipio asks after delivering a message to Maule to come see Gervayse Pyncheon, the owner of the House of the Seven Gables. "And what for do you look so black at me?" But Maule's response—"No matter, darkey! . . . Do you think nobody is to look black but yourself?"—has a meaning beyond the straightforward notion of looking angrily at someone (188). For Maule is also implying that to "look black" is to bear the burden of class inferiority and of service in a way that is racially marked, something about which he is reminded by the basic—and to Maule highly insulting—fact that Scipio is even willing to address him in such a manner. Maule, in other words, is claiming a position analogical to racial victimage, one intended to highlight his felt sense of class oppression as he receives a summons to the House of the Seven Gables.

The ensuing visit that Maule makes to the front door of the Pyncheon home might thus be read as a precursor episode to the pivotal crisis scene that William Faulkner stages in *Absalom, Absalom!* (1936)—the childhood moment when Thomas Sutpen is "barred" from the front door of the plantation Big House by the "monkey dressed nigger butler" who tells him "never to come to that front door again but to go around to the back" (187; 188). As Hortense Spillers suggests in her reading of this scene, Sutpen's rejection by the Big House slave forces upon him not only the shocking recognition that he "has" "race" but, more disturbingly, that class and race are inextricably linked to his sense of masculinity ("Who Cuts the Border?" 10–14). In Sutpen's case, this results in a variety of violences, just as it does in the case of Maule, who, after gaining entrance to the Pyncheon home, mesmerizes Alice Pyncheon in an action that looks very much like a rape motivated by his emasculated class status. Pressing a "slow, ponderous, and invisible weight upon the young maiden," Maule penetrates the spheres of her "unsullied purity," and places her "in a bondage more humiliating, a thousandfold, than that which binds its chains around the body" (204; 203; 208). In what follows, Alice is forced by Maule to perform a variety of demeaning acts for him, including waiting on Maule's bride the night of his wedding. But the most horrific of these acts is perhaps a stereotypically working-class ethnic dance Maule repeatedly commands her to perform. Described as a "high-paced jig, or hop-skip rigadoon, befitting the brisk lasses at a rustic merry-making" (209), the dance links Alice directly to the sullied nineteenth-century bodies of the Irish Ned Higgins and the vagrant Italian boy (the latter of whom is described by Hawthorne's narrator in terms of his "dark, alien countenance" [294]). Accordingly, the dance suggests powerfully that the highly charged mesmerization by Maule has left her tainted by the racialized markings of class difference. This point is driven home most dramatically in Alice's untimely and highly sentimental death by consumption. A fate brought on when, en route to Maule's wedding, her "gossamer white dress" becomes wet as she "trod[s] the muddy sidewalks" of Maule's working-class neighborhood (209), Alice's death seems to be the direct result of the racial tainting she has received from the lower classes. Unlike Alice and Edna Saxon in *The City Merchant,* who are saved from their "mulatto exquisite[]" kidnappers at the last moment, Alice is left alone to suffer her fateful violation and death.

And what this suggests is that, at least in the sensationalism produced by Holgrave, whiteness is not available as compensation for readers seeking fantasy redress from the more general climate of economic anxiety and failure. Instead, projecting his antebellum present backward onto his ancestor's colonial past, Holgrave seems here to be embracing and manipulating the racial anxieties experienced by citizen-subjects such as the Pyncheons. Indeed, what we see in Maule is in many ways a version of Jacksonian-era masculine class politics projected backward into the colonial American past—politics that involve once again the tropes of minstrelsy and racial performance. Specifically, in referring to himself as "black," Maule is in effect blacking himself up in ways not unlike the white performers blacking themselves up to appear as stock urban black dandy characters such as Zip Coon or Jim Brown.[11] An 1842 minstrel songster titled *Jim Brown* is instructive in this regard (figure 22). "I play upon de fife,—I play upon de fiddle / I'm opposed to de Bank and don't like Biddle," Jim Brown says, an anti-Whig, anti-Bank posture that, offered as it is in a blackface guise, might be understood as very much related to the political sensibilities that Holgrave, via Maule, seeks to express. But as the violence of his story indicates, Holgrave is also interested in suggesting that he poses a very real threat to the Pyncheons. It is as though he is implying that, by putting on (and thus appropriating) blackness, he is accessing the very forms of passion and desire that are so troubling to characters such as Clifford and Hepzibah Pyncheon (to say nothing of Gervayse Pyncheon and his daughter Alice).[12]

Certainly this is what black dandy minstrel characters such as Jim Brown implied. As we have seen with the Italian boy's monkey and Melville's Black Guinea, they embodied a relation to pleasure and enjoyment unavailable to the white audience (and perhaps the performer himself), except in the imaged fantasy space of blackface. "De wenches in de city, dey all run arter me / I lite on dar affections like a possum on a flea," Jim Brown says in the above-cited songster. "Dey can't suck in dis child, I don't know how it be / For nothing less dan white gals will eber come to tea." Here, the excesses of pleasure are sexual rather than fiscal, but the repeated emphasis in such songsters on political economy ("I'm opposed to de Bank and don't like Biddle") suggests again that the two spheres of desire—sexual and economic—intersect. Putting on blackface or watching its performance, that is to say, gives the anti-Bank (or at least anti-aristocratic) white male imagined access to the very spheres of pleasure and enjoyment that men such as Edgar Saxon and Clifford Pyncheon have either renounced or repressed. This

[1832 – 1837]

Figure 22 *Jim Brown*. 1842, sold by Leonard Deming. Sheet music; 1 page; 26 x 22 cm. Reproduced with permission of the American Antiquarian Society.

contradiction is something Lott discusses in his analysis of the ambivalent fascination displayed by working-class audiences of blackface performances. "[T]he repellent elements repressed from white consciousness and projected onto black people were far from securely alienated," he says. "[T]hey are always 'inside,' part of 'us.' Hence the threat of this projected material, and the occasional pleasure of its threat" (*Love* 149). Lott's formulation helps us understand the complicated dynamic we encounter with Holgrave. For here we see a character who understands that he has been racially marked by his history—primarily his family's history—of economic failure. But he seems nevertheless to represent a version of the go-ahead male of the mid-century period. Indeed, he may even be the new and quite aggressive face of professional manhood.

But what we see, of course, is that Holgrave ends up renouncing the sort of aggression that he stages in his depiction of his ancestor Maule. Seeing that Phoebe has been partially mesmerized by listening to his story, Holgrave resists the urge, so "seductive to a young man," to take advantage of Phoebe's vulnerability and "twine that one link more, which might have rendered his spell over Phoebe indissoluble" (212). Instead, he suggests that he will burn his short story: "the manuscript must serve to light lamps with," he says (212). More dramatically still, Holgrave and Phoebe become romantically involved, a plot shift that hastens the "developement [*sic*] of emotions" (305) necessary to secure middle-class distance from the outside world of commerce and racial difference. By novel's end Holgrave has renounced his previous opposition to permanent homes built for posterity (184), and moves with Phoebe to live in the country home of the deceased Judge Pyncheon. The exchange between Phoebe and Holgrave over this contradiction sums up the dramatic shifts that take place in the wake of Holgrave's reading of his magazine story to Phoebe: "[H]ow wonderfully your ideas are changed!" she says, to which Holgrave ("with a half-melancholy laugh") replies as follows: "You find me a conservative already! Little did I ever think to become one" (315). Holgrave, it would appear, has settled on a form of manhood not at all unlike the conservative posture we see modeled by Edgar Saxon in *The City Merchant*. Here too, it would seem, we encounter a "bank romance," a form wherein Holgrave's "success" revolves around the repression of his racially tainted working-class blood and its attendant passions, and the "developement [*sic*] of emotions" that are romantic and middle-class in nature.[13]

But isn't it possible to understand Holgrave as conducting yet another form of racial performance, one in which he has smuggled himself into the Pyncheon house wearing a kind of *whiteface* mask? As various critics have pointed out, the novel is obsessed with false countenances: Uncle Venner advises Hepzibah to put on a "bright face" for her cent shop customers (66);

the portrait of Colonel Pyncheon is said to reveal the "indirect character of the man" (58); and Jaffrey is several times described as wearing a false face for the local community, one that hides a darker self below the surface (57; 116–19).[14] Indeed, with regard to Jaffrey, Gilmore suggests that *he* assumes a kind of whiteface: "[T]he Judge essentially reverses the masking of white performers as minstrels and harlequins," he says. "By polishing his face into a benign smile, the Judge can pass as 'white,' . . . hiding his 'black and damnable' interior under a layer of white respectability" (*Genuine* 134). I would argue that a similar dynamic of racial deception is at work with Holgrave. For again, and especially within the logic of this novel, Holgrave's link to the working classes suggests that he is *himself* somewhat less than fully or purely white. Perhaps, indeed, Holgrave actually *has* mesmerized Phoebe, this as a means of accessing the spheres of middle-class enclosure offered by the Pyncheons. Certainly this would help explain Phoebe's somewhat dazed admission of love to the inquiring Holgrave. "You look into my heart," she says. "You know I love you!" (307). If nothing else, Holgrave's entrance into the Pyncheon family has the odd feel of a performance, of something not quite right. Critics have long pointed out that the marriage effectively ends the feud between the two families, and thus represents a disavowal of the political and imaginative possibilities Hawthorne opened up so suggestively with Holgrave's character. But, and as Cathy Davidson points out, Hawthorne arrived at this resolution only after considerable difficulty finishing the novel, a problem that seems to have begun after writing the famous scene in which Holgrave takes his postmortem daguerreotype image of the dead judge. Davidson suggests that during this period Hawthorne was facing "his own, direst apprehension about representation," concerns that extend to the ethical politics not only of artistic reproduction but also of subjectivity itself in the mid-nineteenth century ("Photographs" 691).

I find this reading compelling, but I want to extend this idea, and suggest what this particular scene might also imply about the connections between class and race in the age of commerce and paper money masculinity I have been describing here. For Holgrave's photographing of the judge's corpse represents an exchange not at all unlike what occurs when he incapacitates Phoebe by reading his magazine story to her. Here, however, the transaction is much more violent, as, vampirelike, Holgrave utilizes another form of mass culture—the daguerreotype—in order to steal the judge's image as "a pictorial record" for his own keeping (302). "This is death!" exclaims Phoebe when she sees the image produced by Holgrave's creepy handiwork. "Judge Pyncheon dead!" (302). But Holgrave's response makes it clear that Phoebe has experienced a momentary confusion over the represented and the actual. "Such as there represented," he says to her, referring to the daguerreotype. "[H]e sits in the next room" (302). Holgrave is being ironic, but his emphasis on the need to distinguish between the reproduced image of Judge Pyncheon and his actual corpse is telling, for it is a reminder that for many the daguerreotype raised just such questions. Indeed, as Davidson points out, early commentators on the new technology of photography often suggested that the photographer was sometimes suspected of having stolen the actual soul of the subject whose image had been taken.[15] I would suggest that Hawthorne participates in this line of thinking, but in ways that involve the fraught status of race and manhood in this novel.

What does Holgrave want with an image of the dead Judge Pyncheon? My suggestion is that at least a portion of his motivation can be detected in the narrator's description near novel's end of the dead judge, in which he turns to an unexpected discussion of the actual pigmentation of the judge's skin as he sits still upright in his chair in the parlor. As he explains, "The gloom has not entered from without. . . . The judge's face, indeed, rigid, and *singularly white,* refuses to melt into this universal solvent. . . . Has it yet vanished? No!—yes!—not quite! And there is still the *swarthy whiteness*— we shall venture to marry these *ill-agreeing words*—the *swarthy whiteness* of Judge Pyncheon's face. The features are all gone. There is only *the pale- ness* of them left. And how looks it now? There is no window! There is no face! An infinite, inscrutable *blackness* has annihilated sight! Where is our universe? All crumbled away from us" (276; emphasis added). At once play- fully overstated and remarkably serious, the passage is perhaps Hawthorne's most profound effort to address the issue of race in the novel. For what he provides here is a last, lingering moment in the history of the "Anglo-Saxon" aristocracy the Pyncheons represent. Moving from "singularly white" to an "ill-agreeing" state of "swarthy whiteness" to a featureless "paleness" and then (finally) to "blackness," Judge Pyncheon's face seems here to be the face of elite white American culture "itself." Increasingly diluted by differences of class and race, that face appears here to reflect a failed last moment in the maintenance of upper-class whiteness.

Holgrave's photographic "vamping" of the judge might thus be read as a rather radical act of appropriation, one that involves both class and race. For, while seizing the judge's "soul," Holgrave should also be thought of as appro- priating that which is most dear to those of the judge's class—the conception of white racial purity. It might be said, in other words, that captured on the magically depthless surface of Holgrave's daguerreotype plate is the image of the Pyncheons' lost whiteness "itself," merged rather dramatically now with yet another document of the sensational public sphere. And I would suggest by extension that Holgrave (who is, after all, replacing the deceased judge as the head male of the Pyncheon family) is himself now wearing this whiteness—a racial determinate that is, again, a kind of mask. Working in tandem with the "conservative" posture he assumes before Phoebe, this mask allows Holgrave access to the more rarified world of whiteness occupied by the likes of *The City Merchant*'s Edgar Saxon, even as he seems to have retained contact with the sullied world of capitalist desire and racial difference. Holgrave, it seems, is able to have his enjoyment, and disavow it at the same time.

Hawthorne's imagined resolution thus has its nightmarish underbelly. For like a true vampire, Holgrave, once invited across the threshold of his victim's habitation, will never leave. Instead, the House of the Seven Gables (as well as, perhaps, the novel of the same name) will continue to be haunted by the differences of race and class that it has sought, generation after generation, to repress and displace—Hawthorne's imagined version of an Africanist presence notwithstanding. "Pretty good business!" observes the local laborer, Dixie, as Holgrave and company ride off to their new home. "Pretty good business!" (319). Dixie is correct. For Holgrave—who seems to have known all along that there was no "treasure" of any value to be found within the Pyncheon home—understands that success for the paper money man at mid-century necessitates the following combination: a "conservative" posture of middle-class affect (the "development of emotions" Hawthorne describes), as well as continued access to the passions and appetencies of capitalism itself. Here these passions are displaced onto figures of blackness, but they remain central to the organization of middle-class desire and selfhood nevertheless. No wonder there is such tension between Holgrave's story and Hawthorne's novel. Like a repressed form of cultural knowledge forcing its way to conscious enunciation, Holgrave's story makes its uncanny appearance within *The House of the Seven Gables* in order to tell Hawthorne what he seems not to want to know: that compensatory fictions are tenuous creations requiring consistent forms of ideological maintenance, lest they give way to the scandalous reality of paper money manhood in antebellum America.

EPILOGUE

BARTLEBY'S BANK

I mean no mischief, seek the gratification of no heartless curiosity, thought I; besides, the desk is mine, and its contents, too, so I will make bold to look within. . . . The pigeon holes were deep, and removing the files of documents, I groped into their recesses. Presently I felt something there, and dragged it out. It was an old bandanna handkerchief, heavy and knotted. I opened it, and saw it was a savings' bank.

—Herman Melville, "Bartleby the Scrivener: A Story of Wall-Street"

One of the most fascinating representations of money in the antebellum sensational public sphere comes in Herman Melville's "Bartleby the Scrivener: A Story of Wall-Street" (1853). This is the moment when the story's attorney-narrator discovers in the "recesses" of Bartleby's desk a small "savings' bank" that has been hidden way inside of "an old bandanna handkerchief, heavy and knotted" (110). This is not a cache of treasure. Rather, it is money stored and maintained as a hedge against the vicissitudes of the Wall Street world of speculative economic activity that is the story's setting. And, judging at least from the weight of the bundle, it seems as though the contents of this "bank" is primarily hard currency. It is, that is to say, a form of money quite different from the thirty-two dollars in paper "bills" that the exasperated attorney attempts to give to Bartleby as a kind of severance pay, but which Bartleby refuses (116). "Why," the attorney exclaims upon returning to his office and discovering that Bartleby has not left the premises, "you have not even touched the money yet" (119). Understood in the context of the period's discourse of political economy, Bartleby's refusal to "touch[] the money" suggests a crisis for the narrator: unwilling to accept or even make contact with the attorney's proffered bills, Bartleby displays an unwillingness to partake of the paper system itself. His is, it would seem, a mercantilist mind-set, one that reflects a desire to resist the ceaseless circulation and exchange of modern capitalism. The attorney, meanwhile, who as a conveyancer does a "snug business among rich men's bonds and mortgages and title-deeds" (93), is the very embodiment of this new capitalism. Indeed, while the attorney makes the provocative comment that he likes the name John Jacob Astor because it "rings like unto bullion" (93), he is himself no bullionist when it comes to political economy. The attorney's unexpected discovery thus stages a question that we have seen in various other texts throughout this study, both "Wall Street" narratives such as *The City Merchant,* and more general forms of sensationalism such as "The Legend of Sleepy Hollow" and *The Quaker City:* how do the tensions between an older form of mercantilism and a modern form of capitalism influence and shape professional manhood in antebellum America?

In a brilliant reading of this story, Gillian Brown suggests that Bartleby—who of course perishes at story's end when he refuses to eat—is analogous to the very disturbing figure of the anorectic; seeking to control desire and thus maintain some sort of insulation and self-possession against the intrusions of the marketplace, Bartleby, like the anorectic, refuses to consume (*Domestic* 189–95). But while Bartleby might, as Brown argues, provide a disturbing mockery of sentimental self-possession (192), we need to understand as well the way in which Bartleby's resistant stance poses a more general threat to the very form of white-collar professional selfhood the attorney represents. For although Bartleby might be thought of as a fairly powerful figure of renunciation, we might also understand him as a figure of "theft" similar to those we have seen throughout this study. Indeed, much as with the other sensational versions of Otherness I have examined here—the Headless Horseman, the capitalist Jew, and the appetitive black male, and so on—Bartleby seems to have access to modes of enjoyment that the attorney believes he has either lost, or has had stolen from him. Saving rather than spending, renunciatory rather than greedy, Bartleby is a figure of alterity both to the attorney, and to the paper money man of antebellum America.

Hence, it seems to me, the feelings of anxiety and even terror that Bartleby evokes in the attorney. For the attorney is haunted by Bartleby, much in the way that Ichabod Crane, Irving's representative paper money man of the 1819 era, is haunted by the horrific and castrating figure of the Headless Horseman. Described variously as "the apparition in my room" (122) and "this man, or rather ghost" (123) who "persists in haunting the building" (125), Bartleby makes gothic the scene of Wall Street precisely because he represents a return of the repressed for the attorney narrator: "[H]e *was always there,*" the attorney says (107; emphasis in original). And, as Naomi Reed rightly suggests, Bartleby is apparitional precisely in that he is a figure for the specterlike nature of the commodity in its alienated form ("Specter" 247–63).

But Bartleby is also ghostly in that he is a figure of the uncanny nature of the attorney's own desires, which is to say that the attorney is haunted by his clerk precisely because Bartleby is a figure for his lost enjoyment, returned to him now in familiar but unrecognized form. And again, much of this seems to revolve around the attorney's discovery of Bartleby's "savings' bank." "My first emotions had been those of pure melancholy and sincerest pity," he tells us shortly after his search of Bartleby's desk. "[B]ut just in proportion as the forlornness of Bartleby grew and grew to my imagination, did that same melancholy merge into fear, that pity into repulsion. So true it is, and so terrible too, that up to a certain point the thought or sight of misery enlists our best affections; but, in certain special cases, beyond that it does not" (111).

Here, the "certain special case[]" is Bartleby, but Bartleby as linked to the period's political economy. For what he calls attention to are the attorney's own excessive capitalist desires. Žižek describes a similar form of inversion in accounting for American anxieties about the Japanese in the late 1980s and early 1990s. Citing the general sense in the United States that "the Japanese don't consume enough," he argues that the real psychological problem stems from the perception that "their very relationship between work and enjoyment is strangely distorted. *It is as if they find an enjoyment in their very renunciation of pleasure*" (*Tarrying* 205–6; emphasis in original). Bartleby too seems, at least from the attorney's perspective, to take a perverse pleasure in the very renunciation of pleasure. And he is thus a figure of intense fascination for the attorney, precisely because it is in the scrivener that he encounters in inverted form his own relationship to the desires, passions, and appetencies of the paper economy itself. *This* is what the attorney finds fearful and repulsive.

Thus, while the main question that seems to pervade this story is "what does Bartleby want?," the real topic here is the attorney and his modes of desire. But this, of course, is what the attorney can't admit to himself, lest he give conscious articulation to the fact that what he finds repulsive in Bartleby is in fact the projected image of his own excesses under the sign of the period's speculative paper economy. What we see instead is a kind of affective overload—a form of panic that is in many ways coincident with the Wall Street atmospherics of market panic. Indeed, while the attorney critiques the affective excesses of the murderous debtor John Colt, who as I mention in chapter 3 became a penny paper sensation in the mid-1840s ("imprudently permitting himself to get wildly excited," the attorney tells us, "[Colt] was at unawares hurried into his final act" [120]), he himself gives over to extremes of emotionality when dealing with Bartleby. "I could not, for the very soul of me, avoid falling into sudden spasmodic passions with him," he says at one point (107). Describing himself by turns as "fearful" (127), "fairly flying into a passion" (126), and suffering "a state of nervous resentment" (119), the attorney models what we might think of as a kind of Wall Street hysteria—a condition highlighted late in the story when, after Bartleby has refused the attorney's offer to lodge at his own house, the attorney flees his Wall Street office altogether. "[E]ffectually dodging everyone by the suddenness and rapidity of my flight, [I] rushed from the building, ran up Wall-street towards Broadway, and, jumping into the first omnibus was soon removed from pursuit" (127). Sounding more like gothic maiden than self-possessed professional, the attorney here reminds us not only that he is haunted by Bartleby but also, as he twice puts it in an earlier scene, that he has been "unmanned" by his clerk's uncanny presence in his Wall Street office (109). For again, like so many texts within the sensational public sphere, this is a story about professional manhood and its vexed status in antebellum America.

And, at least in the Wall Street world that Melville creates in this story, manhood remains unstable. For though the dream of recovering lost enjoyment drives a great deal of the sensational material I have described over the course of this study, "Bartleby" suggests that the self-and-Other divide that informs paper money manhood cannot be overcome. Toward story's end the attorney seeks to deploy the sentimentalizing balm of domesticity, one that echoes the sought-after closure of a text such as *The House of the Seven Gables*. "Will you go home with me now—not to my office, but my dwelling?" he asks (127). But Bartleby refuses to be incorporated into the attorney's private sphere. Instead, intensely located in the world of mid-century professional life, Bartleby gives the lie to the ideology of compensatory fictions. "I know you," he says to the attorney once he has been removed to the Tombs, "and I want nothing to say to you" (128). The comment seems to include both the baffled attorney, and the equally confused reader of the original version of the story as it appeared in *Putnam's Monthly* in 1853. "Reader," Bartleby seems to be saying, "[T]his is not a story in which you'll find fantasy compensation for your concerns about life under modern capitalism. Whatever precious part of yourself that you're trying to find or replace can't be found here." Hence the power of the attorney's well-known final lines: "Ah Bartleby! Ah, humanity!" (131). Though easily read as indicating a lack of sincerity, they might also reflect a final moment of pained realization. Perhaps, that is to say, he understands that Bartleby and his "savings' bank" in fact offered a brief glimpse of a now vanished form of completed, premarket selfhood. No wonder compensatory fictions were so pervasive: they helped manage the realization that figures such as Bartleby and the Headless Horseman would continue to haunt Wall Street, and the paper money manhood it produced, far into the future.

NOTES

INTRODUCTION

1. Sellers, *The Market Revolution;* Sandage, *Born Losers;* Mihm, *Nation of Counterfeiters.*

2. See, for example, Rotundo, *American Manhood;* Smith-Rosenberg, "Beauty, the Beast, and the Militant Woman" and "Sex as Symbol in Victorian Purity"; Nelson, *National Manhood;* Cohen, "Unregulated Youth"; Ditz, "Shipwrecked; or, Masculinity Imperiled"; Gilfoyle, *City of Eros;* Newfield, *The Emerson Effect;* Thomas Augst, *The Clerk's Tale;* Carnes, *Secret Ritual and Manhood;* Kimmel, *Manhood in America;* Stansell, *City of Women;* and Horlick, *Country Boys and Merchant Princes.* For a related and quite useful examination of later-nineteenth- and early-twentieth-century manhood, see Bederman, *Manliness and Civilization.* For valuable overviews of the rise of the professional middle classes during this period, all of which have been useful to me here, see Blumin, *The Emergence of the Middle Classes;* Ryan, *Cradle of the Middle Class;* and Halttunen, *Confidence Men and Painted Women.*

3. Nelson's work is, it seems to me, in closest conversation with Christopher Newfield's *The Emerson Effect,* a study that reads the emergent form of liberal masculinity in the antebellum period through the lens of corporate relations, or what he terms "submissive individualism."

4. For extended analysis of the panics of 1819, 1837, and 1857, see especially Sellers, *The Market Revolution.* On the relations between Jacksonian economic and social policy more generally, see Remini, *Andrew Jackson and the Bank War;* Watson, *Liberty and Power;* Rousseau, "Jacksonian Monetary Policy"; Fabian, "Speculation on Distress"; and Wilentz, *Chants Democratic,* 299–325. For insightful readings of nineteenth-century American and British literature in relation to the climate of economic panic, see David Zimmerman, *Panic!;* and Gail Turley Houston, *From Dickens to Dracula.*

5. For a related though quite different reading of the "Money Diggers" sequence, see Jennifer Baker, *Securing the Commonwealth,* 157–67.

6. My thanks to Christopher Looby for suggesting Bird's text to me.

7. In a related discussion, Franco Moretti suggests that the hoard of treasure that Jonathan Harker discovers in Dracula's Transylvanian castle should be understood as old money that the Count has brought back to life in the form of capital. "This and none other is the story of Dracula the vampire," he says. "The money of Dracula's enemies is money that *refuses to become capital*" . . . . "It must have . . . a moral, anti-economic end. . . . This idea of money is, for the capitalist, something inadmissible" (emphasis in original). Moretti, *Signs Taken for Wonders*, 93–94.

8. James Thompson also examines this passage in *Models of Value*, 8–9, and I owe my awareness of it to him.

9. There were occasional counters to this longing for gold. Thus Benjamin Franklin, writing in 1729 as the Busy-Body, critiques the "peculiar Charm in the conceit of *finding* Money" by quoting his friend Agricola, who leaves his son a plot of land with the following caveat: "I have found a considerable Quantity of Gold by Digging there; thee mayest do the same. But Thee must carefully observe this, *Never to dig more than Plow-deep!*" (*Writings of BF* 130; 132). For the Franklin of this narrative, in other words, labor is more important to success than even found gold.

10. For detailed histories of the fiscal crises and "bank wars" surrounding the panics of 1819 and 1837, see Sellers, *Market*, 103–201; 301–63; Mihm, *Counterfeiters*, 103–56; and Schlesinger, *Age of Jackson*.

11. *Jack and the Beanstalk* was first sold in America in 1809 as the title *The History of Mother Twaddle, and the marvellous atchievments* [sic] *of her son Jack*. For early American versions of the story aside from the ones I list in the text, see the collection at the American Antiquarian Society. Note that there are various spellings for "Beanstalk" (open, hyphenated, and closed) in the titles of different versions of the text and that I use these specific styles when discussing individual texts. But note as well that I use the closed style here and elsewhere when making generic reference to the story.

12. Anonymous, *The Surprising History of Jack and the Bean Stalk*. Listed in Works Cited by title.

13. For a compelling Freudian reading of *Jack and the Beanstalk*, one that has been useful to me here, see Bettelheim, *The Uses of Enchantment*, 183–93. Bettelheim also discusses the related *Jack and His Bargains*, but I have been unable to determine whether this narrative was commonly read in antebellum America.

14. Listed in Works Cited under H.A.C.

15. Anonymous, *Jack and the Bean Stalk*. Listed in Works Cited by title.

16. Anonymous, *Jack and the Bean-Stalk*. Listed in Works Cited by title.

17. Published by William Raine, and listed in the Works Cited under his name.

18. Here I am building on the capacious archival work conducted by David Reynolds in *Beneath the American Renaissance*. Reynolds argues that the pulpy sensationalism of the antebellum period was located "beneath" the more refined aesthetic work of writers such as Hawthorne, Poe, and Melville, who were able to draw on this raw material and provide more complicated and ultimately more compelling narratives out of it. I disagree with the general nature of this claim, and I will be seeking instead to show how high-culture works such as "Bartleby" are inextricable from the thick context of urban novels, short stories, plays, penny newspapers, and other materials that imagine the lives of professional men. But the value of Reynolds's work is incontestable, and it has been of considerable use to me here.

19. Fraser, "Rethinking the Public Sphere"; Schudson, "Was There Ever a Public Sphere?"; Ryan, *Women in Public;* Berlant, *The Queen of America Goes to Washington City.*

20. Other titles include the *Sunday Flash, The Whip, and Satirist,* the *Libertine,* and the New York *Sporting Whip.* The complete history of these interesting papers has yet to be written, but for excellent analyses of their cultural impact, see Horowitz, *Rereading Sex,* 159–93; Cockrell, *Demons of Disorder,* 92–139; and Gilfoyle, *City of Eros,* 92–116.

21. Hendler offers a related analysis in *Public Sentiments* of antebellum temperance narratives, suggesting that "Habermas virtually precludes consideration of the performative, theatrical, and spectacular forms that political discourse took in the Jacksonian era, and similarly militates against consideration of women's participation in the public sphere" (47). I am suggesting that we understand the period's sensationalism—and in particular the sensational public sphere—in the sort of "performative" and "spectacular" context that Hendler describes.

22. Roediger, *The Wages of Whiteness;* Saxton, *The Rise and Fall of the White Republic.*

23. Reynolds argues that the penny news industry is crucial to the rise of a sensationalist aesthetic in nineteenth-century America, and I have benefited from this background in formulating my understanding of the penny presses and the sensational public sphere. See in particular chapter 6 of *Beneath the American Renaissance,* "The Sensational Press and the Rise of Subversive Literature," 169–210. There is a wealth of historiography on the Jewett case, most of which I cite in chapter 4.

24. Various critics have argued that U.S. sensationalism often offers a counter to the aesthetics of sentimentality, in particular as the former is usually masculine in orientation, while the latter is usually geared toward a feminine audience. See, for example, Streeby, *American Sensations;* Reynolds, *Beneath the American Renaissance;* and Elmer, *Reading at the Social Limit.* But one of the things I hope to do here is show how the sensational public sphere designates a representational space in which these two discourses—the sensational and the sentimental—overlap, and perform a fairly specific kind of cultural work. Indeed, rather than trying to isolate the sensational, the urban gothic, or the gothic from the sentimental or the melodramatic, I will be tracing a range of texts that seek to produce a form of reading that responds affectively—"sensationally"—to the many crises of capitalist selfhood faced by the modern male of the mid-nineteenth century. For in fact, as Ann Cvetkovich puts it in her study of the British sensation novel of the 1860s, sensationalism is "not really a distinct genre" at all (*Mixed Feelings* 14). Rather, it is a discursive formation that informs a range of subgenres, most of them mass-produced, but some part of the now-canonical literature that bears an elitist or highbrow stamp. See also in this regard Christopher Looby, who suggests that the sentimental and the (urban) gothic are in fact thoroughly intertwined in antebellum sensationalism. As he puts it in a compelling discussion of George Thompson's sensational fiction, "[Thompson] wants both to mount a powerful critique of the status quo and to endorse some of its fundamental values; he wants to affirm sentimental domestic norms even as he violates them, expose moral hypocrisy even as his fiction succumbs to it" ("Romance" 653).

25. Eric Lott has shown that the staged excesses of the minstrel show represent a similar instance of ambivalence for white male audiences. As he puts it in an analysis

that is also informed by Žižek's notion of "theft," white subjectivity "was and is . . . absolutely dependent on the Otherness it seeks to exclude and constantly open to transgression, although, in wonderfully adaptive fashion, even the transgression may be pleasurable" (*Love* 150).

CHAPTER ONE

1. In a related discussion, Plummer and Nelson suggest that Crane is "an intrusive male . . . representative of a bustling, practical New England who threatens imaginatively fertile rural America with his prosaic acquisitiveness" ("Girls" 175). I will be seeking here to extend this analysis, and I understand this story more accurately as an attempt by Irving to narrate the debt-based and frequently humiliated forms of masculinity emerging out of the new economy.

2. In *An Enquiry into the Causes of the Present Commercial Embarrassments in the United States* (1819), the aptly self-titled "Anti-Bullionist" argues that a currency supported by specie was dangerously unstable because cheaper labor elsewhere in the world would inevitably result in domestic supplies of specie being "drawn off" to those markets where labor, and hence commodities, were cheapest. Arguing instead that a national paper currency not backed by specie reserves would free the country from the fluctuating value of precious metals and hence from anxieties that specie would disappear from the country's bank vaults, the writer insists that "[W]e must from necessity abandon the agency of the precious metals, as a check to our circulating medium; and . . . a well-regulated paper-money must be established in its stead" (*Enquiry* 2; 7). A creative variation of this argument was offered by James Swan, who argued in 1819 for a new form of "national paper" issued by a national loan office at three percent interest, one that would replace both specie and the current paper money in circulation. "Who can doubt the solidity of the bills proposed?" he asks. "The Banks which are now in a suspension of payment, have not the power to imprint on their bills the value of specie; but the United States by lending their bills will give to them the action of circulation, and spread at once over our county, a money really superior in value to the precious metals" (*Address* 13).

3. For a useful history of the split between more traditionally Jeffersonian Republicans and the emergent National Republicans, see Sellers, *Market,* 97–102.

4. For a useful history of the ensuing Depression of 1819–22, see Rezneck, "The Depression of 1819–1822."

5. In this sense *The Sketch Book* echoes Burke's lament in *Reflections on the Revolution in France* (1790) over the fate of Marie Antoinette and, as Claudia Johnson puts it, "the fall of sentimentalized manhood, the kind of [chivalric] manhood inclined to venerate her" (*Equivocal* 4).

6. This vulgarity is even more evident in the depiction we receive of the citizen's two sons, who seem to represent a posterity that is if anything further removed from Federalist masculinity. "They were arrayed in the extremity of the mode," Crayon tells us of the man's offspring, "with all that pedantry of dress, which marks the man of questionable pretensions to style. . . . Art had done everything to accomplish them as

men of fashion, but nature had denied the nameless grace [of the] true gentlemen" (*SB* 82).

7. In a compelling study of Irving's use of the bachelor type in his negotiation of masculinity and an emergent form of American authorship, Bryce Traister contends conversely that Ichabod's appetite is here "a metaphor for sublimated sexual desire," wherein "the bachelor's motivating sensuality is represented as appetitive and consuming, rather than sexual and procreative" ("Wandering" 118). For another discussion of Irving in relation to masculinity and bachelorhood (one that does not include "Sleepy Hollow"), see Banks, "Washington Irving," 253–65.

8. For a reading of *Arthur Mervyn* as an allegory of anxieties over speculation (especially as related to the overseas slave trade), see Goddu, 31–51. For a more general analysis of early republican fiction in relation to concerns over speculation during the 1790s, one that includes an analysis of *Dorval*, see Weyler, "A Speculating Spirit," 207–42.

9. For a useful outline of the history of libertine discourse in early America, see Tennenhouse, "Libertine America," 1–28.

10. Similar links between fiscal humiliation and male castration mark the early republican period. See for example Sara Wood's 1801 *Dorval*. Here a gold advocate named Colonel Morely—whose virtue is reflected in his earlier decision to buy up the worthless paper scrip of revolutionary war soldiers for "gold and silver"—loses his entire estate when he is seduced by Dorval into speculating on the infamous Yazoo land scheme in Georgia (13). Unable to pay his creditors, Morely is arrested and sent to debtors' prison, where, "unmanned" and humiliated, he soon dies (140). Morely's real humiliation, however, comes when the widowed Mrs. Morely actually marries the speculator Dorval. After attempting repeatedly to seduce and then rape Morely's daughter, Dorval eventually murders his new wife, stabbing her in Colonel Morely's bed with his sword. With Dorval's "naked sword" (244) standing in for the rapacious phallus of the speculator and the blood-soaked bedding violently mocking Mrs. Morely's lack of virtue on her wedding night, the republican family romance is transformed rather decisively into something more closely resembling gothic horror—a sensational format overtly linking the evils of speculation with the humiliation and symbolic castration of men such as Colonel Morely.

CHAPTER TWO

1. This image is not pictured here. Noah was frequently derided for his pro-Bank sympathies and close ties to Bank president Nicholas Biddle, but he was also the target of various anti-Semitic slurs. See, for example, the 1828 lithograph "City of New-York. Mordecai M. Noah." Arranged as a parody of a public notice, the image depicts Noah as being beaten ("cow-skinned") by a rival news editor, Elijah Roberts. A playbill on the wall behind them advertises "The Jew," "I Act of the Hypocrite," and "End with the face of The Liar."

2. Levine, *Highbrow/Lowbrow;* see in particular chapter 1, "William Shakespeare in America," 11–82. Harap's *The Image of the Jew in American Literature* provides an

especially capacious body of research on representations of the Jew in early American culture, and has been invaluable to me in laying the groundwork for this chapter.

3. The closest we get is the Wandering Jew of Hawthorne's *The Marble Faun* (1860). For an extended discussion of *The Marble Faun* in this context, see Harap, 107–18.

4. See also Jones's *The City Merchant; Life and Adventures of a Country Merchant;* and *The Western Merchant.*

5. Consider the concerns voiced by popular political economist Edward Kellog in his 1841 *Remarks upon usury and Its Effects.* Beginning ominously with an epigraph quoting Shylock's famous lines about his hatred for Antonio—"I hate him for he is a Christian / But more, for that in low simplicity / He lends out money gratis, and brings down / The rate of usance here with us in Venice" (1.3.42–45)—Kellog complains as follows:

> [T]he money-lenders predict approaching scarcity of money, and begin to draw their deposits from [the] bank; perhaps even draw a few hundred thousand dollars in specie, which creates some little alarm; the banks begin to call in their loans on stocks, and stocks fall in the market. They curtail their discounts, and an unusual demand for money, and a depreciation in the means of procuring it, ensure, and again the usurer begins to exact his own treble compensation for the temporary loss of interest he chose to submit to; and now, again, he becomes a competitor at bank for discounts, and, by the same means as before, a usurious system of plunder worse than robbery is begun and maintained, to the utter destruction of hundreds otherwise prosperous men. The predictions of the usurers have been verified. Money is, indeed, exceedingly scarce, and is worth (upon the usurer's rule of value "what it will bring") what it will destroy any class of business men to pay. (32)

For Kellog, the usurer is a danger not simply because he might ruin America's many unwise debtors. More importantly, he is a danger at the level of the general economy; this because he is able, by withholding specie during periods of fiscal "scarcity" and then raising rates on it, to control the actual supply of money in circulation, and thus provoke economic crisis—"the utter destruction of hundreds otherwise prosperous men."

Edward Palmer offers a similar view in a sermon pamphlet entitled *Usury, the Giant Sin of the Age* (1865). As he puts it in words that echo Kellog's, "[Usury] is a system which is subversive of all true and equitable commerce, and wholly incompatible with permanent commercial prosperity.... [U]nder its operation there comes a time every few years when the interest due to capitalists upon obligations then maturing, amounts to more than all the money in circulation. Then, of course, there is a great revulsion in commercial affairs. The crisis is sometimes temporarily postponed by financial maneuvering, but only to be the more disastrous when it comes, as come it must. Then the 'money market is tight,' and rates of interest are enormously increased. *The Shylocks must have the amount of their bonds*" (16; emphasis added).

Like Kellog, Palmer views usury as exerting a choke hold on the nation's money supply, and thus precipitating economic panics. For both authors, in other words, it is usury that is at the heart of the nation's economic woes. And what this suggests is that the image of the Jewish usurer so common to the period's sensationalism is in fact the virtual embodiment of the much more prevalent and insidious form of high-interest lending practiced by the nation's banks and other "capitalists," and thus the screen against which to project both anxiety and anger about the scarcity of money circulating within the unsteady economy. This is why both Kellog and Palmer are able, almost in passing, to offer the figure of the capitalist Jew ("the Shylocks") as a stock stand-in for high interest rates, and for usury more generally. For again, what this figure represents is a negative form of political economy, one that acts as a direct threat to the nation's economic health.

6. *The Emerald, or, Miscellany of Literature*, 389.

7. Jonathan Freedman provides a similar argument in his discussion of later-nineteenth-century authors such as Anthony Trollope, George du Maurier, and Henry James. As he explains in outlining what he terms "literary versions of economic anti-Semitism," "The passions ascribed to the Jew in the culture of capitalism . . . may serve as a powerful way of distancing the affects unleashed by this system from the normative life of Christian culture and gentile commerce. Indeed, the affect-drenched, passionate, lascivious Jew becomes a literal embodiment of all the irrationalities, the perversities, the greeds and lusts, that are arguably the motor, and undoubtedly the consequences, of an economic system that presents itself as a self-correcting and rational mechanism for the maximally efficient delivery of goods and services" (*Temple* 73; 69). Freedman's work—easily the most nuanced of the many valuable studies of Jews in America and the American imagination—has been especially influential to me here as I have sought to understand the antebellum period's obsession with a population of Jews that historians suggest was no more than fifty thousand. The return form of Gentile "theft" that I describe below is thus an attempt to build on Freedman's study.

8. The form of projection Žižek describes might also help explain the contradiction one encounters in realizing that the penchant for hoarding gold ascribed to the sensational Jew mirrors the faith in gold so often voiced by Jacksonian Democrats, and just as frequently mocked by anti-Jackson detractors. From this perspective the sensational Jew is in many ways a dramatic extension of these hard-money Jacksonians: like the Jew hoarding his cache of gold bullion, Jackson and his followers adhered to a strict mercantilist gold policy that bordered on the obsessional. But the mirrored reflection of Jacksonian fiscal policy provided by the sensational Jew clearly went unrecognized. Instead, the Jew remained an uncanny figure that haunted antebellum culture with the very image of its own quite repressed relationship to gold bullion, even as—or precisely because—he acted as the figure who had stolen that money in the first place.

9. For a similar but more extended discussion of Marx's essay, see Freedman, *The Temple of Culture*, 65–67.

10. See for one of many examples John Todd's "The Jew" in *Simple Sketches*. Here a sick Jewish daughter beseeches her father to convert to Christianity as she lies on her deathbed, the implication being that she herself has converted. One might note, however, the various tales in which the Jewess refuses, even in the face of death, to convert. See for example "Myrrah of Tangiers" by "Caroline C—." In this story, Myrrah, "the daughter and sole heiress of the wealthy and excellent Raguel" (125), is accused by a jealous Muslim man of religious infidelity, and is burned at the stake.

11. On castration in *The Merchant of Venice*, see in particular Penuel, "Castrating the Creditor."

12. A similarly overt moment appears in Ned Buntline's *Morgan; or The knight of the black flag. A strange story of by-gone times.* (1861). Here a group of "brawny ruffians" (20) storm the home of Solomon the moneylender after he has refused to loan their leader a large sum of money ("he called me a cursed Jew," Solomon explains, "and swore he would raise a mob to pull the roof down about mine ears!" [19]). The goal of the raid is to seize Solomon's gold, but in the ensuing scenes we see that the men are just as intent on raping Solomon's daughter, Miriam. As the libertine leader of the crew puts it in explaining why he doesn't wish to burn down the Jew's home, "I do not wish to melt his gold, and there is a fairy within whose ebon tresses I would not scorch for a thousand sovereigns" (21). The "ruffians" are driven off by the "black knight" Morgan, but the mob's desire for both the Jew's gold and his daughter underscores the collective belief in the Jew's hoarded riches as well as the link between the nation's missing gold bullion and the alluring figure of the Jewess.

13. Tellingly, Miriam's father goes on to inform her that her love for a Gentile repeats the sin of her own mother, who, he explains, had an affair with a Christian years before ("a Gentile, unclean dog as he was" [*Agnes* 44–45]).

14. This anxiety is also evident in Buntline's "Miriam" narratives. For example, in *Agnes; or, the beautiful milliner*, Miriam is locked into a sealed-off attic room where, in what is perhaps Buntline's sensational zenith, she finds her mother's skeleton. Miriam thus realizes that she has entered her mother's death chamber, as well as her own. At first she believes that she will be left to starve, but soon a perfumed gas begins to fill the room, and she understands that her father intends to poison her. Paired with her mother in this makeshift tomb, the horrified Miriam highlights the Jew's perverse (and perhaps, given the link with her mother, incestuous) desire. But she also underscores the more general form of cultural work performed by the Jewess in antebellum culture. And that is to act as an image of excess, one that, at least in the sensational world constructed by Buntline, is simply too volatile for entrance into Gentile culture. Thus, rather than imagining Jessica's conversion, Buntline, like various other antebellum authors, depicts her as stolen from Gentile culture, but apparently irretrievable from the clutches of the Shylock figure. Simultaneously fascinating, desirable, and fearful, she embodies the very qualities that antebellum culture—and antebellum manhood in particular—has disavowed in itself. In yet another narrative, *Rose Seymour; or, the Ballet Girl's Revenge* (1865), the Miriam character is violently whipped for attempting to escape from her father's home. "Naked to her waist, the lovely young Jewess was fastened up against the wall," we are told. "A hideous old hag was flogging her with savage ferocity" (46). See also *Miriam; or, the Jew's daughter* (1860s–70s[?]).

15. This narrative was substantially expanded from the 1828 version of the text, entitled "Judith Bensaddi, a Tale Founded in Fact," and appearing in *The Souvenir* in 1828.

16. James Shapiro, "The Jew's Daughter." Unpublished Paper. My thanks to Professor Shapiro for sharing his work with me.

17. Beginning with an epigraph from *The Merchant of Venice*—"Antonio and Shy-

lock, stand forth!"—*Abednego* tells the story of a young man named Basil Annesley who owes money to Abednego Osalez, a Jewish moneylender who seems to have in his debt nearly every wealthy person in the city of London. Basil's goal in borrowing this money is to lend financial support to a poor young Jewish woman named Esther, with whom he has fallen in love. Unbeknownst to Basil, however, Esther is the niece of the childless Abednego—she is, that is to say, a kind of daughter substitute in the Jessica genre.

18. As with the death of the Shylock figure, the looting of the Jew's home is fairly common to this material, so much so that we might read the depiction of mob violence as reflecting a latent—and here displaced—desire within Jacksonian America for collective Gentile action against the nation's mercantile Jews.

19. This passage is also cited in Harap, and it is to his scholarship that I am indebted for this passage.

20. A similar anxiety over the linked categories of Jewishness and blackness is displayed in Edgar Allan Poe's famous short story "Ligeia" (1838). As Joan Dayan has discussed, Ligeia is marked throughout the text by signs of "black" blood. But, and importantly, Ligeia is also described in terms of Jewish characteristics. As Poe's narrator puts it, "I looked at the delicate outlines of the nose—and nowhere but in the graceful medallions of the Hebrews had I beheld a similar perfection. There were the same luxurious smoothness of surface, the same harmoniously curved nostrils speaking the free spirit" ("Ligeia" 63–64). As with Hawthorne's description of the Jewess he sees in London, or Robert Byng's racist description of the villain Densdeth, blackness and Jewishness seem to serve as referents for one another, and blackness lurks menacingly behind Jewishness as a kind of fearful and only indirectly named presence, one that, especially in "Ligeia," threatens to emerge and overwhelm the unsuspecting Gentile male (Dayan, "Amorous Bondage" 239–73).

21. Garame's anxieties about Judith's racial makeup are further suggested on the day he and Judith depart for what is supposed to be a short separation before their planned marriage. At this point Garame has already begun to experience misgivings about the engagement, all of which revolve around his understanding of Judith as racially distinct. Such feelings emerge as he climbs into his coach, and looks up to see Judith watching him from her bedroom window. As he explains, "On taking my seat I looked up at Judith's window—it was lighted—her sadly declining form was distinctly *shadowed* forth upon it. . . . '*Shade* of my beloved,' said I in my full heart, '*shade* of my beloved, fare thee well, fare thee well.' The whip cracked, the wheels rattled over the pavement, and I no more saw even the *shade* of my beloved" (*Benasaddi* 119; emphasis added). Marking Judith with racially suggestive terms such as "shadow" and "shade," Garame—much like Hawthorne in his journal entry—negotiates the vexed terrain of race and desire into which he has entered by transforming Judith into a sort of two-dimensional figure of blackness, one that stands in for the racial miscegenation with a Jew that he both longs for and abhors. Indeed, this is the last time Garame sees Judith in the novel, leading one to suspect that the subsequent revulsion he experiences at the thought of marrying her is at least partially informed by this haunting image of her racially distinct shadow-presence.

CHAPTER THREE

1. There is a wealth of information available on the Webster-Parkman case. The most comprehensive text is Bemis, *Report of the Case of John White Webster* (1850). For an extremely compelling analysis of the case, one that links it to changes in conceptions of liberal selfhood in the nineteenth century, see Karen Halttunen, *Murder Most Foul*, 126–32.

2. It's worth noting that although American newspapers were almost uniformly moved by Webster's confession, the *London Times* was much more cynical. Referring to Webster's "insincerity," the paper described the text as "written with a vast deal of unction and sentiment," and went on to state that "it is difficult to see how the writer could have regretted its [the *Confession's*] publicity, before his fate was finally sealed" (7-8-1850).

3. See also Colt, *Life, Letters, and Last Conversation* (1842).

4. Joseph Fichtelberg provides a similar perspective in his discussion of Emerson's response to the debt he incurred following the 1837 Panic. "For many conservatives, the lesson of the panic was quite clear: retrench, repent, reform," he explains. "But other writers, both men and women, sense a more powerful change in these circumstances that no mere assertion of reason could forestall. With insolvency, these writers saw, an older vision of the autonomous self was also waning, and newer conceptions of a more plastic, deft, market-molded individual were demanded" (*Critical* 117–18).

5. See also Jackson's *A Week in Wall Street* (1841).

6. The main pamphlet for Robinson's trial is *Trial, Confession, and Execution of Peter Robinson* (1842). I would like to thank Peter Molin for calling my attention to this text, and for sharing with me his unpublished paper on the Robinson murder and Sedgwick's novel, "'Genteel Crime Fiction': The Case of Catherine Sedgwick's 'Wilton Harvey.'"

7. For similar advice to young men from moral reformers, see William A. Alcott, *A Young Man's Guide* (1833), and Catherine Sedgwick, *The Poor Rich Man and the Rich Poor Man* (1836).

8. The well-known phrase "structure of feeling" comes from Raymond Williams, *Marxism and Literature* (1977). I am also drawing on Hendler's use of this notion in *Public Sentiments*. See especially his introduction, 1–26.

9. On the rhetoric and ideology of male submission in antebellum culture, see Christopher Newfield, "The Politics of Male Suffering," and *The Emerson Effect*.

10. For a more detailed history of events surrounding the issuance of the Specie Circular, see Sellers, *Market*, 332–63.

11. *The Quaker City* sold 60,000 copies its first year of publication, and 10,000 per year for the next decade. The novel went through twenty-seven American printings, and was pirated in Germany and England, under slightly altered titles. For more on Lippard and the publication of *The Quaker City*, see Reynolds, introduction to *The Quaker City*, i–xvi.

12. See Denning, *Mechanic Accents*, 85–117; and Streeby, "Haunted Houses."

13. Nelson argues that this novel reflects the "gynecological projection onto women's bodies" of male anxieties about class and gender (*National* 137). For her full discussion of this dynamic, see 143–60.

14. See in particular Shelley Streeby, "Haunted Houses"; Walter Benn Michaels, *The Gold Standard and the Logic of Naturalism*, 87–112; and Paul Gilmore, *The Genuine Article*, 125–50.

15. Lori Merish provides a similar point in suggesting the influence of Scottish enlightenment philosophers such as Adam Smith on narratives of female submission within the period's domestic sentimentalism. As she explains, "[T]he objectification of women as male property is internalized as a psychic mechanism through which men managed their feelings of powerlessness and their developmental dependence on women" (*Sentimental* 39–40).

16. My information on these early American counterfeiters comes from Mihm, *Counterfeiters*.

17. See Mihm, *Counterfeiters*, 113–25.

CHAPTER FOUR

1. The Helen Jewett case is often mentioned in histories both of prostitution and of journalism, but the only sustained analysis is Cohen's *The Murder of Helen Jewett*. See also by Cohen the following: "The Helen Jewett Murder," and "Unregulated Youth." For a briefer analysis that places the murder more specifically in the context of antebellum prostitution, see Gilfoyle, *City of Eros*, 92–102. For a discussion of the case in relation to the history of journalism, see Stevens, *Sensationalism in the New York Press*.

2. To the best of my knowledge, virtually all editorial material in the *Herald* is, unless otherwise indicated, authored by Bennett. I have therefore consolidated all *Herald* references under Bennett's name in the Works Cited. Each of these references is cited parenthetically within the text.

3. For readings of the various female reform movements and auxiliary publications proliferating in reaction to the perceived problems posed by the newly mobile "Jacksonian male" and the prostitution industry in general, see Christine Stansell, *City of Women;* and Smith-Rosenberg, "Beauty, the Beast, and the Militant Woman," and "Sex as Symbol in Victorian Purity."

4. For a useful and provocative reading of the cult of the female corpse in America and Europe in the nineteenth century, one that revolves largely around the work of Poe, see Elisabeth Bronfen, *Over Her Dead Body*.

5. In addition to the *Herald*, full proceedings were published in the New York *Sun*, the New York *Courier and Enquirer*, and the New York *Tribune*. The transcripts were also published in *The Trial of Richard P. Robinson*, 1836.

6. The pamphlets are as follows: *The Thomas Street Tragedy* (1836); *An Authentic Biography of the Late Helen Jewett* (1836); *The Life of Ellen Jewett* (1836); *A Sketch of the Life of Richard P. Robinson* (1836); *Sketch of the Life of Miss Ellen Jewett* (1836); *Trial of Richard P. Robinson* (1836). For a detailed reading of these pamphlets, which I do not go into here, see Cohen, "The Helen Jewett Murder."

7. See, for example, *NYH* 5-14-1836; and the New York *Sun* 5-6-1836.

8. George Wilkes, publisher of the crime periodical *The Police Gazette*, mentions the Robinson caps in his 1849 pamphlet *The Lives of Richard P. Robinson and Helen Jewett;* quoted in Alexander Saxton, *Rise and Fall of the White Republic*, 207–8. Saxton

also provides a description by David O'Meara of David Broderick, a local Irish political leader, wearing a "Helen Jewett mourner" hat as a symbol of anti-Whig political sympathies when he led a delegation of New York Democrats to meet President Polk during a visit to Perth Amboy (*Rise* 208).

9. My information on Bennett and his career as a journalist comes from three main sources: Crouthamel, *Bennett's New York Herald*; Carson, *The Man Who Made News*; and Stevens, *Sensationalism*. The information below on the early history of the penny presses comes from the above titles, as well as from Schiller, *Objectivity and the News* (1981); and Saxton, *Rise and Fall of the White Republic*, 95–108.

10. Owned and edited by Benjamin Day, the New York *Sun* began publication September 3, 1833, with the aim of providing a form of news from which mercantile and trade information, as well as partisan politics, would be absent. By all accounts the *Sun* enjoyed immediate success: within four months it equaled the most popular mercantile papers in circulation, and by 1834, with the aid of increased print technology, its circulation was up to ten thousand. Created in imitation of the *Sun* in 1834, the *Transcript* was the most successful of the penny copycats until the *Herald* was started. For more on the early history of the *Sun* see Crouthamel, *James Watson Webb*, 69–81. Note that I have listed the *Sun* under Day's name in the Works Cited section.

11. The cash-and-carry policy was crucial to the success of the newly emergent penny papers such as the *Herald* and the New York *Sun*. Instead of having to subscribe to a newspaper, customers were able for the first time to buy editions by the copy. The young boys selling the papers so aggressively on the street would purchase a bundle of one hundred papers for sixty-two and one-half cents, which left them a fairly decent profit margin, provided they sold all of their copies (Crouthamel, *James Watson Webb* 67–81).

12. As with Bennett and the editorials in the *Herald*, Webb seems to have been the author of most if not all of the editorials in the *Courier and Enquirer* during this period. I have therefore listed the *Courier and Enquirer* under Webb's name in the Works Cited section. For a fuller account of the "Moral War" waged against Bennett, see Crouthamel, *Bennett's New York Herald*, 34–38; and Crouthamel, *James Watson Webb*, 84–86.

13. The most famous such encounter occurred in 1842, when Webb fought in a duel with Congressman Thomas F. Marshall of Kentucky. Following a series of barbed exchanges over the national bankruptcy act (which Webb himself had made use of and defended vehemently), the two met in the woods outside of Washington to settle their differences. Both men missed their first shot, Webb firing intentionally into the air; but on the second shot, though Webb again fired into the air, Marshall hit Webb in the hip. Webb was not seriously injured, but he was indicted by the New York District Attorney for violating an ordinance against leaving New York State to fight in a duel. Webb was sentenced to two years in prison for his crime but pardoned not long afterward by New York governor William Henry Seward. For more on this duel and various other confrontations between the city's newsmen, see Crouthamel, *James Watson Webb*, 67–94.

14. For Bennett's description of his encounter with Townsend, see *NYH*, October 8, 9, 17, 1836; for an account of his beating by Leggett, see *NYH* 1-5-1836. For a very general contextualization of these fights, see Crouthamel, *Bennett's New York* Herald, 26.

15. For a useful biographical account of Poe's many rivalries in the publishing world, see Silverman, *Edgar A. Poe.*

16. As Bennett put it in one of many such entries on Townsend, "Mrs. T., I understand, had borrowed money of Ellen—and yet it is said she intends to administer on her property. Ellen had many valuables about her—she had a large amount of jewelry—her wearing apparel was splendid, and worth probably $1,500. What has become of all this property?" (*NYH* 4-14-1836).

17. This claim was never pursued or proved; the following day Bennett reported that Chancellor, though in fact an ex-lover of Robinson's who had been enticed by him to run away from her parents, was sent by her parents to South Carolina when the affair was discovered. Bennett further reported that Chancellor had later returned to the city, even visited Robinson while he was in prison, and perhaps left the city with him after his acquittal in June.

18. Most of the information below on brothel "riots" comes from Gilfoyle, *City of Eros,* 76–91; 321–29.

19. Chichester's reputation as a ruffian involved in the politics of the city's brothels is something Bennett takes advantage of in his early coverage of the murder, when he provides an ironic depiction of a conversation between Robinson and Chichester while the two were supposedly housed next to one another the first few days of Robinson's incarceration (*NYH* 4-18-1836).

20. Cited in Wilentz, *Chants Democratic,* 240.

21. In one of the most significant moments for labor politics in the antebellum period, Judge Edwards, immediately following the Robinson trial, ruled against twenty-five journeyman tailors for conspiring to strike, a decision that resulted in days of mass demonstration and violence throughout the city. For a history of the strike and Edwards's verdict, one that provides interesting commentary on Bennett's role in the events, see Wilentz, *Chants Democratic,* 255–96.

22. The circulation and financial figures below come from Stevens, *Sensationalism,* 29–53.

23. In an 1843 fictionalization of the Jewett story, Joseph Holt Ingraham echoes Bennett's narrative, explaining that "*She* was the seducer, *not* he. . . . Her beauty was her power, and she triumphed in it. She felt a sort of revenge against the other sex, and used every art to tempt and seduce and ruin young men." *Frank Rivers;* cited in Gilfoyle, *City of Eros,* 151. For more on the sensational story of the revengeful prostitute as it evolved in the years following the Jewett case, see especially Gilfoyle, *City of Eros,* 150–57; and Keetley, "Victim and Victimizer."

24. This quote, as well as most of Bennett's coverage of the murder from April 11 and 12, is reprinted in *The Thomas Street Tragedy.*

25. Bennett's strategy here was not an isolated one during the period. As critics such as Nancy Cott have discussed, the ideologies of female "passionlessness" and purity were frequently invoked within middle-class Victorian culture, specifically as a means of maintaining a masculine sense of security against the contaminating influences of the "public" spheres of economic competition (Cott, "Passionlessness"). Perhaps the most famous example of such a representation is Hiram Powers's *The Greek Slave,* a statue that toured the United States in the late 1840s to the fascination and possibly the sexual titillation of an estimated one hundred thousand paying patrons. Depicting

a young Greek woman standing naked as she is about to be sold into slavery to the Turks, the statue was hailed by critics as a model image of sexual purity and chastity, in particular because of the way the figure's expression suggested an otherworldly detachment that lifted her beyond the sordid realities of her present situation. For a particularly insightful reading of the cultural politics surrounding the reception of this statue, see Kasson, "Narratives of the Female Body."

26. Brown, *Domestic Individualism,* 96–132; Goddu, *Gothic,* 105–16; and Merish, *Sentimental,* 172–90. Further citations to Brown are parenthetical within the text. Goddu's market reading is closest to my own here, and I have benefited greatly from her insightful analysis.

27. For a compelling reading of *Blithedale* that places the novel in the context of female celebrity and antebellum mass culture more generally, see Brodhead, *Cultures of Letters,* 62–82.

28. See especially Brown, *Domestic,* 96–132; and Bronfen, *Dead Body,* 241–49.

29. Brown refers to Coverdale's anxiety about bodily contact as "self-protective consumerism" (*Domestic* 113–14).

30. Russ Castronovo, for example, argues that like the consumptive and increasingly spiritual body of Little Eva in Stowe's *Uncle Tom's Cabin,* Priscilla offers "the airy insubstantiality of an adolescent girl" (*Necro-Citizenship* 118).

CHAPTER FIVE

1. For a related and compelling discussion of this image, see Sandage, *Losers,* 198.

2. *The City Merchant* is yet another text that follows the romantic career of the Jew's daughter. Here, though, we see a fascinating variation of the Jessica narrative that I outline in chapter 3. In this version of the story, we see that Rachel, the daughter of the Jew Ulmar, is married to Billy Grittz, the son of the broker Grittz. The union links the families of the two Jewish brokers, but it has the effect of thinning, or dissipating, Jewishness nevertheless. This is most overt with Rachel, who "being born and bred in the city, had none of the Jew-German thickness of speech, nor any of their avaricious cunning" (*City* 94); the implication here is that her children will assimilate fairly easily into the world of sensibility ruled over by the racially "pure" Edgar Saxon. This is also true of Billy, who is described as "a descendant of Japhet, as well as of Canaan," in whom "the blood of both races mingled harmoniously" (235). Billy's Jewish ancestry helps explain the almost reverential attitude he displays toward hard money when working at Saxon's counting house. "The boy could not help feeling exceedingly proud when accompanying a dray load of gold and silver," we are told. "[A]s if by instinct, which seemed to be innate, his eyes and ears were open to observe and hear everything which passed among the revenue officers" (214). At the same time, however, the "Japhet" portion of his blood promises that the avariciousness of his father will also fade out in future generations. Thus, even this substory of Jones's racial romance demonstrates how the crises both of the Jew and the unstable economy of the Jacksonian moment are defused, the result being that Saxon's own masculine selfhood and integrity are retained intact.

3. For an excellent discussion of the rhetoric and politics of miscegenation during this period, one that includes examination of Clay's "Racial Amalgamation" series, see Lemire, *"Miscegenation."*

4. Hawthorne's reliance on a metaphoric slippage between blackness and whiteness in relation to issues of class and labor also informs several of his comments about manual labor in his letters and journal entries from the 1840s and 1850s. This is particularly true of his descriptions of his work as a surveyor in the Salem Custom House, a position that often placed him aboard cargo ships bearing loads of coal. Complaining that his "coal-begrimed visage" or the "sable stains" of his profession give him qualities in common with "chimney sweepers," or with "the black-faced demons in the vessel's hold" (he also describes the longshoremen as looking "like the forgemen in Retsch's Fridolin" [*American* 296]), Hawthorne seems drawn to the ways in which the coal dust he encounters provides metaphoric connections between manual labor and the racial markings of blackness—markings that he seems quite willing to ascribe to the white working-class men along Salem's waterfront. This is also evident in letters Hawthorne writes from the Custom House to his wife, in which he expresses how unsuited she is to visit the working-class world of the waterfront. As he puts it in one such letter when informing her that the day's shipment will be salt rather than coal, "Sweetest Dove, fly hither sometime, and alight in my bosom. I would not ask my white dove to visit me on board a coal vessel; but salt is white and pure—there is something holy in salt" (*American* 345). Though certainly playful, Hawthorne's comment also reflects his desire—similar to that in his description of the "sordid stain" left by Ned Higgins's money—to keep the "pure" categories of upper-class "whiteness" clear of the debasing marks of labor, marks that Hawthorne seems willing to discuss in ways that suggest a relation to racial difference.

5. For contemporary commentary on the perceived threat of upper-class degeneracy at mid-century, see Beecher, *Letters to the People on Health and Happiness;* and Greeley, *An Address Before the Literary Societies of Hamilton College.*

6. As Todd and other reformers made clear, the only cure for this disease was heterosexual intercourse within the bounds of marriage. But as Hawthorne explains, Clifford, "who had never quaffed the cup of passionate love[,] . . . knew now that it was too late" (*Gables* 141)—a fact that highlights the reproductive crisis facing not only the Pyncheon family but, at least symbolically, upper-class white men in general. For readings of antebellum culture in relation to male moral reformers addressing masturbation, see Bertolini, "Fireside Chastity"; and Smith-Rosenberg, "Sex as Symbol." My thanks to Professor Rosenberg for pointing out to me the connections between Clifford's enfeeblement and the rhetoric of male sexual purity advocated by moral reformers.

7. Brown makes a related point in discussing Hepzibah's cent shop, observing that "Miserliness, the preoccupation with hoarding and holding money, highlights the role of the hands in trade, the fact of burst physicality in the touch and love of money, and this is also emphasized in Hawthorne's depiction of the grasping hand of the organ-grinder's monkey, noted as well for its 'too enormous tail' and 'excessive desire'" (*Domestic* 83).

8. Lott argues something similar about Zip Coon and the period's other black dandy characters. "The black dandy literally embodied the amalgamationist threat of

abolitionism," he says, "and allegorically represented the class threat of those who were advocating it; amalgamation itself, we might even say, was a partial figuration of class aspiration" (*Love* 134). Here, in an analysis that certainly reflects usefully on a novel such as *The City Merchant*, the locus of anxiety is the upwardly mobile white man, whose aspirations are projected onto the dandy character. But again, the Pyncheon family experiences these concerns from the top, down; they are the ones who are threatened with a form of racial tainting that is itself understood in relation to actual contact with class struggle and, *inter alia*, contact with actual money.

9. One version of a less troubling form of racial difference is offered by Hawthorne in a journal entry from 1838, one suggestively similar to his depictions of Hepzibah's Jim Crow cookies and the Italian boy's monkey. Describing a variety of working-class members of a crowd outside of a commencement ceremony at Williams College, he turns to a description of a group of black men who are also part of the crowd. Here is his description of one of the men: "I saw one old negro, a genuine specimen of the slave-negro, without any of the foppery of the race in our parts; an old fellow with a bag, I suppose of broken victuals, on his shoulders; and his pockets stuffed out at his hips with the like provender—full of grimaces, and ridiculous antics, laughing laughably, yet without affectation—then talking with a strange kind of pathos, about the whippings he used to get, while he was a slave—a queer thing of mere feeling, with some glimmering of sense" (*American* 112). More direct than his representation of the Italian boy's monkey, Hawthorne's depiction of the "genuine specimen of a slave negro" reflects a cartoon version of black male subjectivity. Here, this image seems intended to counter concerns of the sort raised by the figure of the black dandy (whose type is referred to in Hawthorne's mention of black "foppery"). "Laughing laughably," with pockets clownishly overstuffed, and engaged in a stock routine of "ridiculous antics," the man is depicted in terms of a two-dimensional aesthetic that seems designed to provide Hawthorne with a kind of security about his own, more interior form of white self-possession—one perhaps challenged by the sometimes raucous festivities of the working-class members of the crowd at the Williams commencement. Perversely, this form of assurance comes most powerfully in the "strange kind of pathos" the man is said to display over "the whippings he used to get." For though on the one hand the description seems to suggest a sympathy extended across lines of race to one whose feelings might signal an internal—and perhaps shared—form of suffering and pain, it should more accurately be read as a sentimentalized and nostalgic return to the plantation South, perhaps of the sort imagined in "Plantation Melodies" by Stephen Foster such as "My Old Kentucky Home, Good-Night!" (1853), or "Massa's in de Cold Ground" (1852)—products of mass culture in which the body of the black male acts as a reliable space of difference in the efforts of men such as Hawthorne to make their own relation to class and whiteness cohere.

10. As Gilmore points out, the slaves remind us that the Pyncheon fortune seems to have been derived at least in part from slave labor (*Genuine* 133; 225n19).

11. For more on the relation between Jacksonian politics and blackface minstrelsy, see Lott, *Love and Theft*; and Saxton, *The Rise and Fall of the White Republic*, 165–82.

12. Of course, this exchange between Maule and Scipio also suggests once again that white America's racial imagination is circumscribed by basic tropes of minstrelsy and racial performance. It may be true that Maule's comment to Scipio about a shared

"blackness" is motivated by the theft of his family's property by the Pyncheons. But his comment also signals a rather profound act of racial *appropriation*. Claiming blackness, Maule appropriates the absolute victimage of this category for its affective resonance; there is simply no more powerful metaphor for pain, abjection, and dispossession in antebellum culture. Indeed, Scipio's very name, which is repeated throughout Holgrave's magazine story, is rarely offered without the race-fixing prefix "black" (as in "black Scipio"), a fact that has the double function of taking away what it enforces: Scipio is Other because he is "black," but his "blackness" is appropriable in ways he is unable to control. Scipio, meanwhile, does not have the option of choosing whether to wear the sign of his abjection. And as suggested by the description of Scipio showing the "whites of his eyes" (*Gables* 192) when Maule arrives at the Pyncheon front door, Scipio too is rendered in terms of a performed, minstrelized blackness: for Holgrave (and probably for Hawthorne), there is no real difference between the real and the represented of race.

13. Gilmore argues similarly: "Race, rather than class, or, perhaps more properly, race understood in terms of middle-class morality, now defines respectability, so that the historical class differences separating Phoebe and Holgrave no longer matter" (*Genuine* 146–47).

14. For excellent analysis of the multiple tensions in this novel between surface and depth models of selfhood, see Davidson, "Photographs of the Dead." Focusing on the new technologies of photography Hawthorne foregrounds, Davidson suggests that the novel represents Hawthorne's meditation on the status of representational art at mid-century, one that led him to pose often anxious-making questions not only about the distinctions between "high" and "low" art but also about subjectivity in the age of mechanical reproduction.

15. As Oliver Wendell Holmes put it in the *Atlantic Monthly* in 1859, the photographer was a "great white hunter" who gathered the images of his quarry like the head and skins of his prey ("The Stereoscope and the Stereograph").

Adams, John Quincy. *Memoirs of John Quincy Adams. Comprising Portions of His Diary from 1795 to 1848.* Volumes 4 and 5. Edited by Charles Francis Adams. Philadelphia: J. B. Lippincott & Co., 1875.

Agnew, Jean-Christophe. *Worlds Apart: The Market and the Theater in Anglo-American Thought, 1550–1750.* New York: Cambridge University Press, 1986.

Alcott, William A. *A Young Man's Guide.* Boston: Lily, Wait, Colman and Holden, 1833.

The American. June 9, 1819.

Anti-Bullionist. *An Enquiry into the Causes of the Present Commercial Embarrassments in the United States. With a Plan of Reform of the Circulating Medium. In Two Letters, Addressed to the Secretary of the Treasury.* United States: n.p., 1819.

Arthur, Timothy Shay. *Advice to young men on their duties and conduct in life.* Boston: E. Howe, 1848.

———. *Debtor and Creditor; a Tale of the Times* [1847]. New York: C. Scribner, 1852.

Augst, Thomas. *The Clerk's Tale: Young Men and Moral Life in Nineteenth-Century America.* Chicago: University of Chicago Press, 2003.

An Authentic Biography of the Late Helen Jewett, A Girl of the Town who was murdered on the 10th of April, 1836: Together with a full and accurate statement of the circumstances connected with that event by a Gentleman Fully Acquainted with her History. New York: n.p., 1836.

Baker, Jennifer. *Securing the Commonwealth: Debt, Speculation, and Writing in the Making of Early America.* Baltimore: Johns Hopkins University Press, 2005.

"A Bankrupt Law." *Independent American,* April 1, 1818.

Banks, Jenifer S. "Washington Irving, the Nineteenth-Century American Bachelor." In *Critical Essays on Washington Irving,* edited by Ralph M. Alderman. Boston: G. K. Hall, 1990: 253–65.

Beckett, S. B. "The Jewess of Cairo." *Ladies Home Companion,* 15–16 (1840–41): 270–81.

Bederman, Gail. *Manliness and Civilization. A Cultural History of Gender and Race in the United States, 1880–1917.* Chicago: University of Chicago Press, 1995.

Beecher, Catherine. *Letters to the People on Health and Happiness.* New York: Harper, 1855.

Beecher, Henry Ward. *Lectures to Young Men, on Various Important Subjects.* Boston: J. P Jewett, 1846.

Bemis, George. *Report of the Case of John White Webster.* Boston: Little and Brown, 1850.

Benjamin, Walter. *Illuminations.* New York: Schoken Books, 1969.

Bennett, James Gordon. The New York *Herald.* Multiple Dates.

Berlant, Lauren. *The Queen of America Goes to Washington City: Essays on Sex and Citizenship.* Durham, NC: Duke University Press, 1997.

Bertolini, Vincent J. "Fireside Chastity: The Erotics of Sentimental Bachelorhood in the 1850s." *American Literature,* 66 (December 1996): 707–37.

Bettelheim, Bruno. *The Uses of Enchantment: The Meaning and Importance of Fairy Tales.* New York: Alfred A. Knopf, 1976.

Bird, Robert Montgomery. *Sheppard Lee: Written by Himself* [1836]. Edited by Christopher Looby. New York: New York Review of Books, 2008.

Bloch, Ernst. *The Principle of Hope.* Volume 1. Translated by Neville and Stephen Plaice, P. Knight. Oxford: Blackwell Press, 1986.

Blumin, Stuart. *The Emergence of the Middle Classes: Social Experience in the American City 1760–1900.* New York: Cambridge University Press, 1989.

The Boston Evening Transcript. July 1, 1850.

Boucicault, Dion. *The Poor of New York.* In *American Melodrama* [1857], edited by Daniel C. Gerould. New York: Performing Arts Journal Publications, 1983. 31–74.

Brantlinger, Patrick. *Fictions of State: Culture and Credit in Britain, 1694–1994.* Ithaca, NY: Cornell University Press, 1996.

Brodhead, Richard H. *Cultures of Letters: Scenes of Reading and Writing in Nineteenth-Century America.* Chicago: University of Chicago Press, 1993.

Bronfen, Elisabeth. *Over Her Dead Body: Death, Femininity and the Aesthetic.* New York: Routledge, 1992.

Brougham, John. *Much ado about a merchant of Venice. From the original text—a long way.* New York: Samuel French [French's Minor Drama, no. 308], 1858.

Brown, Charles Brockden. *Arthur Mervyn; or, Memoirs of the Year 1793: first and second parts* [1799–1800]. Kent, OH: Kent State University Press, 2002.

Brown, Gillian. *Domestic Individualism: Imagining Self in Nineteenth-Century America.* Berkeley: University of California Press, 1990.

"Brutus." "Hints from the Observer." Philadelphia *Aurora.* January 24, 1818.

Buntline, Ned. *Agnes; or, the beautiful milliner.* New York, Hilton and Co., n.d. [1860s–70s?].

———. *Miriam, or, the Jew's daughter. A tale of city life.* New York: Dick and Fitzgerald, n.d. [1860s–70s?].

———. *Morgan; or, the knight of the black flag. A strange story of by-gone times.* New York: Robert M. De Witt, n.d. [1871–76?].

———. *Rose Seymour; or, the Ballet Girl's Revenge: A Tale of the New York Drama.* New York: Hilton and Company, 1865.

Burke, Edmund. *Reflections on the Revolution in France* [1790]. Edited by L. G. Mitchell. New York: Oxford University Press, 1999.

C[—], Caroline. "Myrrah of Tangiers." *Graham's American Monthly Magazine* 32, no. 2 (February 1850): 125–32.

Carnes, Mark. *Secret Ritual and Manhood in Victorian America.* New Haven, CT: Yale University Press, 1989.

Carson, Oliver. *The Man Who Made News: James Gordon Bennett.* New York: Duell, Sloan, and Pearce, 1942.

Castronovo, Russ. *Necro-Citizenship: Death, Eroticism, and the Public Sphere in the Nineteenth-Century United States.* Durham, NC: Duke University Press, 2001.

Chapman, Mary, and Hendler, Glenn, eds. *Sentimental Men: Masculinity and the Politics of Affect in American Culture.* Berkeley: University of California Press, 1999.

Citizen of Pennsylvania. *An Examination of the Causes and Effects, of the Present State of the Circulating Medium, and of the Remedy for its Depreciation.* Doylestown, PA: Asher Miner, 1816.

Cockrell, Dale. *Demons of Disorder: Early Blackface Minstrels and Their World.* Cambridge: Cambridge University Press, 1997.

Cohen, Patricia Cline. "The Helen Jewett Murder: Violence, Gender, and Sexual Licentiousness in Antebellum America." *NWSA Journal,* 2 (Summer 1990): 374–89.

——. *The Murder of Helen Jewett: The Life and Death of a Prostitute in Nineteenth-Century New York.* New York: Vintage Books, 1998.

——. "Unregulated Youth: Masculinity and Murder in the 1830s City." *Radical History Review,* 52 (Winter 1992): 33–52.

"Colloquy between a Bank Note and a Gold Coin." *New England Magazine,* 8 (January 1835): 45–49.

Colt, John Caldwell. *Life, Letters, and Last Conversation of John Caldwell Colt, who Committed Suicide at the New York City Prison, Nov. 18, 1842, Just Before the Time Appointed for his Execution for the Murder of Samuel Adams, Printer, in the 18th Sept., 1841.* New York: n.p., 1842.

——. *Trial of John C. Colt for the murder of Samuel Adams.* New York: n.p., 1842.

Cott, Nancy. "Passionlessness: An Interpretation of Victorian Sexual Ideology, 1790–1850." In *A Heritage of Her Own,* edited by Nancy Cott and Elizabeth Pleck. New York: Simon and Schuster, 1979. 168–92.

Crouthamel, James L. *Bennett's* New York Herald *and the Rise of the Popular Press.* Syracuse, NY: Syracuse University Press, 1989.

Crouthamel, James. *James Watson Webb: A Biography.* Middletown, CT: Wesleyan University Press, 1969.

Cumberland, Richard. *The Jew: or, Benevolent Hebrew: A Comedy. As performed with universal applause, at the New Theatre, in Philadelphia* [1794]. Philadelphia: Henry and Patrick Rice, and James Rice and Co., 1795.

Cvetkovich, Ann. *Mixed Feelings: Feminism, Mass Culture, and Victorian Sensationalism.* New Brunswick, NJ: Rutgers University Press, 1992.

"The Dandy and the Soap-Fat Man." *The Weekly Rake,* October 1, 1842.

"The Daughter of Israel." *Ladies National Magazine* 8, no. 5 (November 1845): 174–77.

Davidson, Cathy N. "Photographs of the Dead: Sherman, Daguerre, Hawthorne." *South Atlantic Quarterly* 89, no. 4 (Fall 1990): 667–701.

Davies, Benjamin. *The Bank Torpedo, or Bank Notes Proved to be a Robbery on the*

Public, and the Real Cause of Distresses Among the Poor . . . . New York: M'Carty and White, 1810.

Day, Benjamin. New York *Sun.* Multiple dates.

Dayan, Joan. "Amorous Bondage: Poe, Ladies and Slaves." *American Literature* 66, no. 2 (June 1994): 239–73.

Defoe, Daniel. *Review* [6-14-1709]. In *The Best of Defoe's Review,* edited by William L. Payne. New York: Columbia University Press, 1951. 117–19.

Denning, Michael. *Mechanic Accents: Dime Novels and Working-Class Culture in America.* London: Verso Press, 1987.

Dickens, Charles. *The Life and Adventures of Martin Chuzzlewit* [1843–44]. Edited by Patricia Ingham. New York: Penguin Classics, 1995.

Ditz, Toby. "Shipwrecked; or, Masculinity Imperiled: Mercantile Representations of Failure and the Gendered Self in Eighteenth-Century Philadelphia." *Journal of American History* (June 1994): 51–80.

Douglass, Frederick. *The Life and Times of Frederick Douglass, His Early Life as a Slave, His Escape from Bondage, and His Complete History to Present Time* [1892]. New York: Dover Books, 2003.

Duganne, A. J. H. (Augustine Joseph Hickey). *The Tenant House, or, Embers from Poverty's Hearthstone.* New York: R. M DeWitt, 1857.

The Dying Jewess. New York: Mahlon Day and Co., n.d. [1839–1845?].

Edward Scissorhands, dir. Tim Burton (1990; 20th Century Fox).

Ellison, James. *The American Captive; or, the Siege of Tripoli. A Drama in Five Acts.* Boston: Joshua Belcher, 1812.

Ellison, Julie. *Cato's Tears: The Making of Anglo-American Emotion.* Chicago: University of Chicago Press, 1999.

Elmer, Jonathan. *Reading at the Social Limit: Affect, Mass Culture, and Edgar Allan Poe.* Stanford: Stanford University Press, 1995.

The Emerald, or, Miscellany of Literature 1, no. 3 (December 13, 1806): 388–90.

Fabian, Ann. "Speculation on Distress: The Popular Discourse of the Panics of 1837 and 1857." *Yale Journal of Criticism,* 3 (Fall 1989): 127–42.

Faulkner, William. *Absalom, Absalom!* [1936]. Edited by Noel Polk. New York: Vintage International, 1986.

Fay, Theodore Sedgwick. *Sidney Clifton; or, Vicissitudes in both Hemispheres. A Tale of the Nineteenth Century.* New York: Harper, 1839.

Fichtelberg, Joseph. *Critical Fictions: Sentiment and the American Market, 1780–1870.* Athens and London: University of Georgia Press, 2003.

Fisk, Theophilus. *The Banking Bubble Burst, or the Mammoth Corruptions of the Paper Money System Relieved by Bleeding* . . . . Charleston, SC: n.p., 1837.

———. *Labor, the Only True Source of Wealth; or the Rottenness of the Paper Money Banking System Exposed, Its Sandy Foundations Shaken, Its Crumbling Pillars Overthrown.* Charleston, SC: Office of the Examiner, 1837.

Foster, Hannah Webster. *The Coquette* [1797]. New York: Oxford University Press, 1986.

Franklin, Benjamin. *The Writings of Benjamin Franklin,* edited by Albert Henry Smyth. New York: Haskell House, 1970.

Fraser, Nancy. "Rethinking the Public Sphere: A Contribution to the Critique of Actually Existing Democracy." In *The Phantom Public Sphere,* edited by Bruce Robbins. Minneapolis: University of Minnesota Press, 1993. 1–32.

Freedman, Jonathan. *The Temple of Culture: Assimilation and Anti-Semitism in Literary Anglo-America.* New York: Oxford University Press, 2000.

Freud, Sigmund. "Character and Anal Eroticism." In volume 9 of *The Standard Edition of the Complete Psychological Works of Sigmund Freud,* translated by James Strachey, Anna Freud, Alix Strachey, and Alan Tyson. London: Hogarth Press, 1959. 168–175.

———. "Dreams in Folklore." In volume 12 of *The Standard Edition of the Complete Psychological Works of Sigmund Freud,* translated by James Strachey, Anna Freud, Alix Strachey, and Alan Tyson. London: Hogarth Press, 1958. 175–203.

———. "Medusa's Head." In volume 18 of *The Standard Edition of the Complete Psychological Works of Sigmund Freud,* translated by James Strachey, Anna Freud, Alix Strachey, and Alan Tyson. London: Hogarth Press, 1940. 273–274.

Gaspey, Thomas. *Calthorpe; or, Fallen Fortunes. A Novel.* Philadelphia: n.p., 1821.

Gilfoyle, Timothy. *City of Eros: New York City, Prostitution, and the Commercialization of Sex, 1790–1920.* New York and London: Norton, 1992.

Gilmore, Paul. *The Genuine Article: Race, Mass Culture, and American Literary Manhood.* Durham, NC: Duke University Press, 2001.

Goddu, Teresa. *Gothic America: Narrative, History, and the Nation.* New York: Columbia University Press, 1997.

Gore, Catherine. *Abednego, the Money-Lender. A Romance.* New York: Wilson and Company, 1843.

Gouge, William. *A Short History of Paper Money and Banking in the United States* [1833]. New York: Augustus Kelly, 1968.

Greeley, Horace. *An Address Before the Literary Societies of Hamilton College on "The Discipline and Duties of the Scholar."* Clinton, NY: n.p., 1844.

———. New York *Tribune.* Multiple dates.

Habermas, Jürgen. *The Structural Transformation of the Public Sphere: An Inquiry into Bourgeois Society.* Translated by Thomas Burger and Frederick Lawrence. Cambridge, MA: MIT Press, 1989.

H.A.C. *The history of Mother Twaddle, and the marvellous atchievments* [sic] *of her son Jack.* Philadelphia: Wm. Charles, 1809.

Halttunen, Karen. *Confidence Men and Painted Women. A Study of Middle-Class Culture in America, 1830–1870.* New Haven, CT: Yale University Press, 1982.

———. *Murder Most Foul: The Killer and the American Gothic Imagination.* Cambridge, MA: Harvard University Press, 1998.

Harap, Louis. *The Image of the Jew in American Literature: From Early Republic to Mass Immigration.* Philadelphia: The Jewish Publication Society of America, 1974.

Hawthorne, Nathaniel. *The American Notebooks.* Edited by Claude Simpson. Volume 8 of *The Centenary Edition of the Works of Nathaniel Hawthorne.* Columbus: The Ohio State University Press, 1972.

———. *The English Notebooks.* Edited by Randall Stewart. New York: Russell and Russell, 1941.

———. *The Blithedale Romance* [1852]. Edited by Annette Kolodny. New York: Penguin Classics, 1983.

———. *The House of the Seven Gables* [1851]. Edited by Milton Stern. New York: Penguin Classics, 1986.

———. *The Marble Faun: or, the Romance of Monte Beni* [1861]. Edited by Richard Brodhead. New York: Penguin Classics, 1990.

Henderson, Andrea K. *Romantic Identities: Varieties of Subjectivity, 1774–1830*. Cambridge: Cambridge University Press, 1996.

Hendler, Glenn. *Public Sentiments: Structures of Feeling in Nineteenth-Century American Literature*. Chapel Hill: University of North Carolina Press, 2001.

Herbert, Christopher. "Filthy Lucre: Victorian Ideas of Money." *Victorian Studies* 44, no. 2 (Winter 2002): 185–213.

Holcroft, Thomas. *The Road to Ruin*. New York: David Longworth, 1819.

Holmes, Oliver Wendell. "The Stereoscope and the Stereograph." *Atlantic Monthly* (June 1859): 738–49.

Hone, Philip. *The Diary of Philip Hone, 1828–1851*. Edited by Allan Nevins. New York: Dodd, Mead and Company, 1936.

Horlick, Allan Stanley. *Country Boys and Merchant Princes: The Social Control of Young Men in New York*. Lewisburg, PA: Bucknell University Press, 1975.

Horowitz, Helen Lefkowitz. *Rereading Sex: Battles over Sexual Knowledge and Suppression in Nineteenth-Century America*. New York: Alfred A. Knopf, 2002.

Houston, Gail Turley. *From Dickens to Dracula: Gothic, Economics, and Victorian Fiction*. New York and Cambridge: Cambridge University Press, 2005.

Independent American. April 1, 1818.

Ingraham, J. H. (Joseph Holt). *The Clipper Yacht; or, Moloch the Money Lender! A Tale of London and the Thames*. Boston: H. L. Williams, 1845.

———. *Frank Rivers; or, The Dangers of the Town*. Boston: E. P. Williams, 1843.

Irving, Washington. *Letters, Volume I: 1802–1823*. Edited by Ralph M. Aderman. Volume 23 of *The Complete Works of Washington Irving*. Boston: Twayne Publishers, 1978.

———. *The Sketch Book of Geoffrey Crayon, Gent*. Edited by Haskell Springer. Volume 8 of *The Complete Works of Washington Irving*. Boston: Twayne Publishers, 1978.

———. *Tales of a Traveller*. Edited by Judith Giblin Haig. Volume 10 of *The Complete Works of Washington Irving*. Boston: Twayne Publishers, 1987.

Jack and the Bean Stalk. New York: John McLoughlin, 1857.

Jack and the Bean-Stalk: Illuminated with ten pictures. Volume 5 of *Hewet's illuminated household stories for little folks*. New York: H. W. Hewet, 1856–57[?].

Jack the Giant Killer, n.d.

Jackson, Andrew. "Farewell Address" [1897]. In Volume 3 of *A Compilation of Messages and Papers of the Presidents, 1789–1897*, edited by James Richardson. New York: Johnson Reprint Corporation, 1968. 292–308.

Jackson, Frederick. *The Victim of Chancery: or a Debtor's Experience*. New York: University Press, 1841.

———. *A Week in Wall Street. By One Who Knows*. New York: Booksellers, 1841.

Jameson, Fredric. *Ideologies of Theory: Essays 1971–1986*. Minneapolis: University of Minnesota Press, 1988.

———. "Reification and Utopia in Mass Culture." *Social Text* 1, no. 1 (Winter 1979): 130–48.

Jefferson, Thomas. *The Writings of Thomas Jefferson.* Edited by Paul Leicester Ford. Volume 10. New York: G. P. Putnam's Sons, 1892–99.

"The Jewess of Constantina." *The Union Magazine of Literature and Art* 2, no. 1 (January 1848): 35–39.

Johnson, Claudia. *Equivocal Beings: Politics, Gender, and Sentimentality in the 1790s.* Chicago: University of Chicago Press, 1995.

Jones, J. B. (John Beauchamp). *Border War. A Tale of Disunion.* New York: Rudd and Carleton, 1859.

———. *The City Merchant; or, the Mysterious Failure.* Philadelphia: Lippincott and Grambo, 1851.

———. *Life and Adventures of a Country Merchant.* Philadelphia: Lippincott and Grambo, 1854.

———. *The Western Merchant.* Philadelphia: Lippincott and Grambo, 1849.

Journal of Commerce. Multiple dates.

Kasson, Joy. "Narratives of the Female Body: *The Greek Slave.*" In *The Culture of Sentiment,* edited by Shirley Samuels. New York: Oxford University Press, 1992. 172–90.

Keetley, Dawn. "Victim and Victimizer: Female Fiends and Unease over Marriage in Antebellum Sensational Fiction." *American Quarterly* 51, no. 2 (June 1999): 344–84.

Kellog, Edward. *Remarks upon usury and Its Effects: A National Bank a Remedy: in a Letter, &c.* New York: Harper and Brothers, 1841.

Kerber, Linda. *Federalists in Dissent: Imagery and Ideology in Jeffersonian America.* Ithaca, NY: Cornell University Press, 1970.

Kimmel, Michael. *Manhood in America: A Cultural History.* New York: Free Press, 1996.

Law, Thomas. *The Financiers* [sic] *A, B, C, Respecting Currency.* Washington City: E. De Krafft, 1919.

Lee, Mary E. "Aaron's Rod; or the Young Jewess." *Southern and Western Literary Messenger,* 12 (September 1846): 554–60.

Leggett, William. New York *Evening Post.*

Lemire, Elise. *"Miscegenation": Making Race in America.* Philadelphia: University of Pennsylvania Press, 2002.

Leverenz, David. *Manhood and the American Renaissance.* Ithaca, NY: Cornell University Press, 1989.

Levine, Lawrence. *Highbrow/Lowbrow: The Emergence of Cultural Hierarchy in America.* Cambridge, MA: Harvard University Press, 1989.

The Life of Ellen Jewett; Illustrative of Her Adventures with Very Important Incidents, from her Seduction to the Period of her Murder, Together with Various Extracts from Her Journal, Correspondence, and Poetical Effusions. New York: n.p., 1836.

Lippard, George. *The Quaker City; or, the Monks of Monk Hall. A Romance of Philadelphia Life, Mystery and Crime* [1845]. Edited by David Reynolds. Amherst: University of Massachusetts Press, 1995.

London Times. July 8, 1850.

Looby, Christopher. "George Thompson's 'Romance of the Real': Transgression and

Taboo in American Sensation Fiction." *American Literature,* 65 (December 1993): 651–72.

Lott, Eric. *Love and Theft: Blackface Minstrelsy and the American Working Class.* New York and London: Oxford University Press, 1993.

Maitland, James A. *The Lawyer's Story; or, the Orphan's Wrongs.* New York: H. Long, 1853.

Manchester Messenger. April 14, 1850.

Marx, Karl. *Capital: A Critique of Political Economy* [1867]. Volume 1. Translated by Ben Fowkes. Edited by Ernest Mandel. New York: Vintage Books, 1977.

———. *On the Jewish Question* [1843]. In *The Marx-Engels Reader,* edited by Robert C. Tucker. New York: Norton, 1978. 26–52.

Mather, Cotton. *Pietas in Patriam: The Life of His Excellency Sir William Phips, Knt. Late Governour of New-England* [1697]. In *Selections from Cotton Mather,* edited by Kenneth Murdock. New York: Hafner, 1960. 150–283.

McCarthy, Cormac. *No Country for Old Men.* New York: Vintage Books, 2005.

Melville, Herman. "Bartleby the Scrivener: A Story of Wall-Street" [1853]. In *Herman Melville: Selected Tales and Poems,* edited by Richard Chase. New York: Holt, Rinehart and Winston, Inc., 1950. 92–131.

———. *The Confidence-Man* [1857]. Edited by H. Bruce Franklin. Indianapolis and New York: Bobbs-Merrill Company, 1967.

Merish, Lori. *Sentimental Materialism: Gender, Commodity Culture, and Nineteenth-Century American Literature.* Durham, NC: Duke University Press, 2002.

Michaels, Walter Benn. *The Gold Standard and the Logic of Naturalism.* Berkeley: University of California Press, 1987.

Mihm, Steven. *A Nation of Counterfeiters: Capitalists, Con Men, and the Making of the United States.* Cambridge, MA: Harvard University Press, 2007.

Millner, Michael. "The Fear Passing the Love of Women: Sodomy and Male Sentimental Citizenship in the Antebellum City." *Arizona Quarterly* 58, no. 2 (Summer 2002): 19–52.

"Mina Lowe. The Pretty Jewess." *Brother Jonathan. A Weekly Compend of Belles Lettres and the Fine Arts* (November 5, 1842): 277–80.

Molin, Peter. "'Genteel Crime Fiction': The Case of Catherine Sedgwick's 'Wilton Harvey.'" Unpublished paper.

Moon, Michael. "'The Gentle Boy from the Dangerous Classes': Pederasty, Domesticity, and Capitalism in Horatio Alger." *Representations,* 19 (Summer 1987): 87–110.

Moretti, Franco. *Signs Taken for Wonders: Essays in the Sociology of Literary Forms.* Translated by Susan Fischer, David Forgacs, and David Miller. London: Verso Press, 1983.

Morrison, Toni. *Playing in the Dark: Whiteness and the Literary Imagination.* Cambridge, MA: Harvard University Press, 1990.

Nelson, Dana. *National Manhood: Capitalist Citizenship and the Imagined Fraternity of White Men.* Durham, NC: Duke University Press, 1998.

Newfield, Christopher. *The Emerson Effect: Individualism and Submission in America.* Chicago: University of Chicago Press, 1996.

———. "The Politics of Male Suffering: Masochism and Hegemony in the American Renaissance." *differences* 1, no. 3 (Fall 1989): 55–87.

Niles, Hezikiah. *Niles Weekly Register.* Multiple dates.

O'Malley, Michael. "Specie and Species: Race and the Money Question in Nineteenth-Century America." *American Historical Review,* 99 (April 1994): 369–95.

Paine, Thomas. "Dissertations on Government; the Affairs of the Bank; and Paper Money" [1786]. In volume 2 of *The Writings of Thomas Paine,* edited by Moncure Daniel Conway. New York: Burt Franklin, 1969. 132–87.

Palmer, Edward. *Usury, the Giant Sin of the Age; the Source of Poverty and Degradation.* New York: Perth Amboy, 1865.

Peacock, Thomas Love. *Paper Money Lyrics, and Other Poems* [1837]. In *Poems and Plays,* volume 7 of *The Works of Thomas Love Peacock,* edited by H. F. B. Brett-Smith and C. E. Jones. New York: AMS Press, Inc., 1967. 101–46.

Penuel, Suzanne. "Castrating the Creditor in *The Merchant of Venice.*" *Studies in English Literature* 44, no. 2 (2004): 255–75.

Plummer, Laura, and Nelson, Michael. "'Girls can take care of themselves': Gender and Storytelling in Washington Irving's 'The Legend of Sleepy Hollow.'" *Studies in Short Fiction* 30, no. 2 (1993): 175–84.

Pocock, J. G. A. *Virtue, Commerce, and History: Essays on Political Thought and History, Chiefly in the Eighteenth Century.* Cambridge: Cambridge University Press, 1985.

Poe, Edgar Allan. "The Gold-Bug" [1843]. In *The Fall of the House of Usher and Other Writings,* edited by David Galloway. New York: Penguin Books, 2003. 234–70.

———. "Ligeia" [1838]. In *The Fall of the House of Usher and Other Writings,* edited by David Galloway. New York: Penguin Books, 2003. 62–78.

Poore, Benjamin Perley. *The Mameluke; or, Sign of the Mystic Tie: A Tale of the Camp and Court of Bonaparte.* Boston: F. Gleason, 1852.

Raine, William. *The History of old Mother Goose, and the golden egg.* Baltimore: Wm. Raine, n.d. [1840–42?].

Reed, Naomi. "The Specter of Wall Street: 'Bartleby the Scrivener' and the Language of Commodities." *American Literature* 76, no. 2 (June 2004): 247–73.

Remini, Robert. *Andrew Jackson and the Bank War: A Study in the Growth of Presidential Power.* New York: Norton, 1967.

Reynolds, David. *Beneath the American Renaissance: The Subversive Imagination in the Age of Emerson and Melville.* Amherst: University of Massachusetts Press, 1988.

———. Introduction. *The Quaker City; or, the Monks of Monk Hall; A Romance of Philadelphia Life, Mystery, and Crime.* Amherst: University of Massachusetts Press, 1995. i–xvi.

Rezneck, Samuel. "The Depression of 1819–1822, A Social History." *The American Historical Review* 39, no. 1 (1933): 28–47.

Robinson, Peter. *Trial, Confession, and Execution of Peter Robinson for the Murder of Abraham Suydam, Esq., of New Brunswick, N.J.* New York: n.p., 1840.

Roediger, David. *The Wages of Whiteness: Race and the Making of the American Working Class.* London: Verso Press, 1991.

Rogin, Michael. *Black Face, White Noise: Jewish Immigrants in the Hollywood Melting Pot.* Berkeley: University of California Press, 1996.

Rotundo, E. Anthony. *American Manhood: Transformations in Masculinity from the Revolution to the Modern Era.* New York: Basic Books, 1993.

Rousseau, Peter L. "Jacksonian Monetary Policy, Specie Flows, and the Panic of 1837." *Journal of Economic History,* 62 (2002): 457–88.

Rubin-Dorsky, Jeffrey. *Adrift in the Old World: The Psychological Pilgrimage of Washington Irving.* Chicago: University of Chicago Press, 1986.

Ruffner, Henry. *Judith Bensaddi: A Tale, Second Edition, revised and enlarged by the author* [1839]. In *Judith Bensaddi: A Tale; and Seclusaval, or, The Sequel to the Tale of Judith Bensaddi,* edited by Michael Pemberton. Baton Rouge: Louisiana State University Press, 1984. 33–145.

——. *Seclusaval* [1843]. In *Judith Bensaddi: A Tale; and Seclusaval, or, The Sequel to the Tale of Judith Bensaddi,* edited by Michael Pemberton. Baton Rouge: Louisiana State University Press, 1984. 149–222.

Ryan, Mary P. *Cradle of the Middle Class: The Family in Oneida County, NY 1790–1865.* New York: Cambridge University Press, 1981.

——. *Women in Public: Between Banners and Ballots, 1825–1880.* Baltimore: Johns Hopkins University Press, 1990.

Sánchez-Eppler, Karen. "Then When We Clutch Hardest: On the Death of a Child and the Replication of an Image." In *Sentimental Men: Masculinity and the Politics of Affect in American Culture,* edited by Mary Chapman and Glenn Hendler. Berkeley: University of California Press, 1999. 64–85.

Sandage, Scott A. *Born Losers: A History of Failure in America.* Cambridge, MA: Harvard University Press, 2005.

Sanderson, Joseph. *The History of a Little Frenchman and his Bank Notes. "Rags, Rags, Rags!"* Philadelphia: E. Earle, 1815.

Saxton, Alexander. *The Rise and Fall of the White Republic.* London: Verso Press, 1990.

Schiller, Dan. *Objectivity and the News: The Public and the Rise of Commercial Journalism.* Philadelphia: University of Pennsylvania Press, 1981.

Schlesinger, Arthur M. Jr. *The Age of Jackson.* New York: Little, Brown and Company, 1945.

Schudson, Michael. "Was There Ever a Public Sphere? If So, When? Reflections on the American Case." In *Habermas and the Public Sphere,* edited by Craig Calhoun. Cambridge, MA: MIT Press, 1992. 109–42.

Sedgwick, Catherine. *The Poor Rich Man and the Rich Poor Man.* New York: Harper and Brothers, 1836.

——. "Wilton Harvey." *Godey's Lady's Book,* 23 (June–September 1842): 122–26; 215–19; 242–46; 326–31.

Sedgwick, Eve Kosofsky. *Between Men: English Literature and Male Homosocial Desire.* New York: Columbia University Press, 1985.

Sellers, Charles. *The Market Revolution: Jacksonian America, 1815–1846.* New York: Oxford University Press, 1991.

Shakespeare, William. *The Merchant of Venice* [1600]. In *William Shakespeare: The Complete Works,* edited by Alfred Harbage. New York: Viking Press, 1969. 215–42.

Shapiro, James. "The Jew's Daughter." Unpublished paper.

Shell, Marc. *Money, Language, and Thought: Literary and Philosophical Economies from the Medieval to the Modern Era.* Berkeley: University of California Press, 1982.

Sherman, Sandra. *Finance and Fictionality in the Early Eighteenth Century.* Cambridge: Cambridge University Press, 1996.

Silverman, Kenneth. *Edgar A. Poe: Mournful and Never-ending Remembrance.* New York: HarperCollins, 1991.

Simmel, Georg. "The Miser and the Spendthrift" [1907]. In *On Individuality and Social Forms,* edited by Donald N. Levine. Chicago: University of Chicago Press, 1971. 179–86.

A Sketch of the Life of Richard P. Robinson, the Alleged Murderer of Helen Jewett, Containing Copious Extracts from his Journal. New York: n.p., 1836.

Sketch of the Life of Miss Ellen Jewett. Boston: n.p., 1836.

Smith, Scott. *A Simple Plan.* New York: VIntage Books, 1993.

Smith-Rosenberg, Carroll. "Beauty, the Beast, and the Militant Woman: A Case Study in Sex Roles and Social Stress in Jacksonian America." In *Disorderly Conduct: Visions of Gender in Victorian America.* New York: Oxford University Press, 91–109.

———. "Domesticating Virtue: Coquettes and Revolutionaries in Young America." In *Literature and the Body: Essays on Persons and Populations,* edited by Elaine Scarry. Baltimore: Johns Hopkins University Press, 1986. 160–184.

———. "Sex as Symbol in Victorian Purity: An Ethnohistorical Analysis of Jacksonian America." In "Turning Points: Historical and Sociological Essays on the Family," edited by John Demos and Sara Spence Boocock. Supplement, *American Journal of Sociology,* 84 (1978): S212–47.

Specie humbug, or, The autobiography of Ferret Snapp Newcraft, Esq.: Being a full exposition and exemplification of "the credit system" [1837]. Philadelphia: First American Socialists Association, Office of the National Laborer, n.d. [1838?].

Spillers, Hortense. "Who Cuts the Border?" In *Comparative American Identities,* edited by Hortense Spillers. New York: Routledge, 1991. 1–25.

Stansell, Christine. *City of Women: Sex and Class in New York, 1789–1860.* Urbana: University of Illinois Press, 1982.

Stevens, John D. *Sensationalism in the New York Press.* New York: Columbia University Press, 1991.

Stowe, Harriet Beecher. *Uncle Tom's Cabin; or Life among the Lowly* [1852]. Edited by Ann Douglas. New York: Penguin Books, 1986.

Streeby, Shelley. *American Sensations: Class, Empire, and the Production of Popular Culture.* Berkeley: University of California Press, 2002.

———. "Haunted Houses: George Lippard, Nathaniel Hawthorne, and Middle-Class America." *Criticism: A Quarterly for Literature and the Arts,* 38 (Summer 1996): 443–72.

———. 'Opening up the Story Paper: George Lippard and the Construction of Class." *Boundary 2,* 24 (Spring 1997): 177–203.

The Surprising History of Jack and the Bean Stalk: Embellished with nine engravings. New York and Philadelphia: Turner and Fisher, [between 1842 and 1845].

Swan, James. *An Address to the President, Senate, and House of Representatives, of the United States, on the Means of Creating a National Paper by Loan Offices, which shall replace that of the discredited Banks, and supersede the use of Gold and Silver Coin.* Boston: Intelligencer Press, 1819.

Taylor, Vermilye. *The Banker; or, Things as they have been! A Farce, in Three Acts.* New York: n.p., 1819.

Tennenhouse, Leonard. "Libertine America." *differences* 11, no. 3 (1999/2000): 1–28.

The Thomas Street Tragedy: The Murder of Helen Jewett and Trial of Robinson. New York: n.p., 1836.

Thompson, George. *Venus in Boston; A Romance of City Life* [1849]. In *Venus in Boston and Other Tales of Nineteenth-Century Life,* edited by David Reynolds. Amherst: University of Massachusetts Press, 2002. 3–104.

Thompson, James. *Models of Value: Eighteenth-Century Political Economy and the Novel.* Durham, NC: Duke University Press, 1996.

Todd, John. "The Jew." In *Simple Sketches,* edited by J. Brace Jr. Northampton, MA: J. H. Butler, 1838. 63–68.

———. *The Student's Manual: Designed, by Specific Directions, to Aid in Forming and Strengthening the Intellectual and Moral Character and Habits of the Student.* Northampton, MA: J. H. Butler, 1835.

Townsend, Peter. *Evening Star.*

Traister, Bryce. "The Wandering Bachelor: Irving, Masculinity, and Authorship." *American Literature* 74, no. 1 (2002): 111–37.

The Trial of Richard P. Robinson.

Warner, Michael. "Irving's Posterity." *English Literary History* 67, no. 3 (Fall 2000): 773–99.

Watson, Harry L. *Liberty and Power: The Politics of Jacksonian America.* New York: Hill and Wang, 1990.

Webb, James Watson. *Courier and Enquirer.* Multiple dates.

Webster, John White. *The Extraordinary Confession of Dr. John White Webster, of the Murder of Dr. George Parkman, at the Medical College in North Grove Street, on the 23d of November, 1849.* Boston: Hotchkiss and Co., 1850.

Weyler, Karen. "A Speculating Spirit: Trade, Speculation, and Gambling in Early American Fiction." *Early American Literature* 31, no. 3 (1996): 207–42.

"The Wheel of Life." *The Southern Literary Messenger,* 11 (March–May 1845): 129–37; 213–18; 288–94.

Whiting, William. *The Age of Paper; or, the Bank Contest. A Poem: In Two Cantos.* Boston: J. N. Bang, 1838.

Wilentz, Sean. *Chants Democratic: New York City and the Rise of the American Working Class, 1788–1850.* New York: Oxford University Press, 1984.

Wilkes, George. *The Lives of Richard P. Robinson and Helen Jewett.* New York: n.p., 1849.

Williams, Raymond. *Marxism and Literature.* Oxford: Oxford University Press, 1977.

Winthrop, Theodore. *Cecil Dreeme.* New York: Dodd, Mead and Company, 1861.

Wise, Daniel. *The Young Man's Counsellor, or, Sketches and Illustrations of the Duties and Dangers of Young Men* [1850]. Boston: n.p., 1851.

Wood, Sarah. *Dorval; or The speculator. A novel, founded on recent facts.* Portsmouth, NH: Nutting and Whitlock, 1801.

Zimmerman, David. *Panic! Markets, Crises, and Crowds in American Fiction.* Chapel Hill: University of North Carolina Press, 2006.

Žižek, Slavoj. *Tarrying with the Negative: Kant, Hegel, and the Critique of Ideology.* Durham, NC: Duke University Press, 1993.

INDEX